H. Miriam Ross

ZAIRE
Midday in
Missions

ZAIRE
Midday in
Missions

Donald A. McGavran and Norman Riddle

Judson Press® Valley Forge

ZAIRE: MIDDAY IN MISSIONS

Library of Congress Cataloging in Publication Data

McGavran, Donald Anderson, 1897-
Zaire: midday in missions.

Bibliography: p. 249
1. Missions—Zaire. I. Riddle, Norman. II. Title.
BV3625.C6M34   266'.009675'1   79-1444
ISBN 0-8170-0835-7

DEDICATION

To the host of unnamed Zairian pastors and catechists who have labored faithfully alongside missionaries or more often alone to proclaim the Good News of Jesus Christ, often with little recognition and at great personal sacrifice, without whose personal commitment and devotion the Church of Jesus Christ could not have grown from zero to many millions in just one hundred years, we dedicate this book.

Without missionaries the Church would not have been established nor would it have grown; without Zairian leaders the great growth would not have been possible. Both statements are true and should be said.

"The course of the righteous
is like morning light,
growing brighter till it is broad day."
Proverbs 4:18, NEB

Foreword

Christian Mission or world evangelization faces tremendous opportunities and tremendous dangers. Persons discipling the nations face new open doors and new closed doors, new friends and new enemies in every land of Earth. This book about Christian Missions in Zaire, therefore, speaks to Christians on every continent who are obedient to the Great Commission.

While this book describes the major issues of Mission in one land, readers will recognize that these issues confront Missions in other lands also. Should the Church and Mission maintain a thoroughly Christian parochial school system? What is the relationship between development and Mission? What is the place of missionaries in the decades ahead? Do self-governing nations any longer need and want mission medicine? How can Missions nurture existing clusters of congregations and simultaneously press ahead vigorously with the enormous task of discipling the nations? As denominations rise in almost every nation, how can their achievements and growth be measured? In view of the three billion who have yet to believe, what should be the relationship of Churches and Missions? These and similar questions are asked in almost every nation.

The theory and theology of Mission set forth in *Zaire: Midday in Missions* is, we believe, applicable in most regions of planet Earth. As we discuss what Mission in Zaire *ought to be* and what its major opportunities and difficulties are, church members and missionaries in Korea, India, or it may be Brazil will say, "This theology illumines the basic issues in our lands, too. While the size of our congregations and denominations is different, the language is different, and the political and military situation is different, nevertheless, seeing a concrete case helps us think through what God wants his servants to do in the vineyards to which he has sent them."

A word is in order about the way in which this volume came to be. The International Church of Kinshasa, Zaire, under the leadership of its able pastor, Dr. John Melton, decided to convene a Conference/Retreat of missionaries and members of the International-al Church in July, 1977, and invited Donald McGavran to be one of the speakers. Dr. McGavran proposed that, to make his contribution of maximum value to the conference, he be flown to all the main mission centers in Zaire (Africa Inland, Alliance, Assemblies, Baptist, Disciples, Mennonite, Methodist, Presbyterian) to study the contemporary situation. With the very kind assistance of Missionary Aviation Fellowship and the cooperation of church leaders and missionaries in the various areas, this procedure was carried out.

Rev. Norman Riddle kindly accompanied Dr. McGavran and the two studied seven great areas. The opportunity thus offered—so much wider than that possible to any church person, mission executive, or missiologist who visits only one (his or her own) area— provided a comprehensive view of the *whole* country. The common problems seen were of such enormous significance that many at the conference urged that the present book be produced. Rev. Norman Riddle collaborated in gathering further data and came to the United States for two months in early 1978 to write half of the chapters.

The manuscript has been presented to representative Zairian leaders, missionaries of several denominations, and executives of several major boards to read and correct. Thus it goes to press well honed. It would be too much to hope that, in a land as many-faceted as Zaire, every facet has been precisely presented, but the convictions expressed about Church and Mission have had wide review and approval.

World evangelization owes a deep debt of gratitude to many, especially to the International Church of Kinshasa and to Missionary Aviation Fellowship. Without their substantial financial aid and constant encouragement, the book would never have been written. The Appendix tells the full story of the survey.

The tumultuous events occurring in Africa in 1977 and 1978 warn us that before the book is off press the scene may change in some regards. However, since Mission has always been carried on in a rapidly changing world, obedient servants of the gospel expect change and adjust their labors to meet it. They continue to preach the gospel and disciple the nations vigorously. That is what it means to carry on Missions at sunrise, midday, or eventide. Evangelize till the Lord comes!

June, 1978   *Donald McGavran and Norman Riddle*

School of Missions
Fuller Theological Seminary
Pasadena, California

Contents

TABLE OF MAPS

TABLE OF TABLES

TABLE OF GRAPHS

Glossary of Terms

In this book we have found that the use of a few special terms facilitates thinking. We trust that readers will find them helpful. For example, the five terms "Community," "Church," "church," "Mission," and "missionary society" enable exact thinking. The terms "Eurican" and "Latfricasia" eliminate the tedious repetition of "European and American" and of "Latin America, Africa, and Asia." Since we frequently have to speak about these combinations of continents, the contractions are convenient. Note also that names of places are sometimes spelled differently, Mongala and Mongeli, for example.

Church is the Church Universal or a denomination.
church refers to the congregation or is used as an adjective, as in church union or church administration.
Community is the denomination in Zaire with its missionary partners which is part of the National Church (Protestant)—the Church of Christ in Zaire.
community is the total number of communicants multiplied by three. (See chapter 5 for further details.)
Classification of Evangelism: E-0 evangelism is the renewing of Christians from one's own denomination and language; E-1

evangelism is the winning to Christ of people from the same tribe and language group but who are not Protestants; E-2 evangelism is the discipling of people of another language and tribe within one's own country. E-3 evangelism is the discipling of people of another tribe and culture outside the country, or from another completely different race and within the country.

Dark Areas: Sections of Zaire in which the gospel has not been believed, which are seriously underchurched.

Eurican: A contraction of European and American—also Eurica.

Four Stages in Mission: The Four Stages in Mission are: (1) exploratory, (2) the establishment of mission stations, (3) the proliferation of people movements to Christ, and (4) the completion of the discipling of the nation.

Latfricasia: A contraction of Latin America, Africa, and Asia—also *Latfricasian.*

Mission is the thrust of a group of sending churches from any part of the world who are proclaiming the gospel and spreading the faith. Mission impels sending churches to raise large sums of money, maintain groups of missionaries, make grants to young Churches, and assist them in many ways. It is a powerful influence in Zaire.

National leaders, National Church refers to those in Zaire. Missionaries are, of course, national leaders sent out by the Church of some nation, but as we use the term "national," we invariably mean Zairian. We use the word to avoid a tiresome repetition of the word "Zairian."

People Movements result from the joint decision of a number of individuals—whether five or five hundred—all from the same people, which enables them to become Christian without social dislocation, while remaining in full contact with their non-Christian relatives, thus enabling other groups of that people, after suitable instruction, to come to similar decisions and form Christian Churches made up exclusively of members of that people. Note that "people" here equals "tribe."

Theories of Church/Mission Relations are: (1) Friendly Dichotomy—a system of Church/Mission relationship in which the Mission retains a parallel existence to the autonomous Church it has brought into being. Friendly collaboration marks their relationship. (2) Friendly Fusion—

the Mission is fused with the autonomous Church but continues to be a responsible partner through the missionary staff and officers of the Mission Board. (3) Complete Fusion—Mission completely disappears. Little or no missionary presence is left. The autonomous Church is everything.

Glossary of Abbreviations

ABFMS —The American Baptist Foreign Mission Society

CBZO —Communauté Baptiste du Zaire Ouest (Community founded by ABFMS)

AIM —Africa Inland Mission (Interdenominational)

BMS —Baptist Missionary Society (British)

CIM —Congo Inland Mission (Mennonite Groups)

C&MA —Christian and Missionary Alliance

CPC —Congo Protestant Council (Formed by Protestant Missions working in Congo, in 1928)

CPZa —Communauté Presbyterienne du Zaire (Southern Presbyterian)

DCCM —Disciples of Christ Congo Mission

ECZ —Eglise du Christ au Zaire (Church of Christ in Zaire) (Evolved out of Congo Protestant Council—CPC)

ECM —Evangelical Covenant Mission

EFM —Evangelical Free Mission

GEM —Garanganze Evangelical Mission

LIM —Livingstone Inland Mission

MMCC —Methodist Mission of Central Congo

MMSC —Methodist Mission of Southern Congo

SMF —Svenska Mission Forbundit (Swedish Covenant Mission)

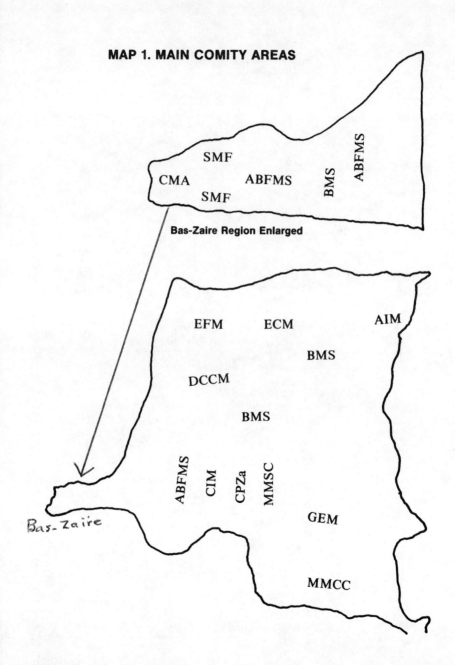

MAP 1. MAIN COMITY AREAS

SMF

CMA ABFMS SMF BMS ABFMS

Bas-Zaire Region Enlarged

EFM ECM AIM

BMS

DCCM

BMS

ABFMS CIM CPZa MMSC

GEM

Bas-Zaire

MMCC

MAP 2

REPUBLIC OF ZAIRE

Introduction

In the heart of Africa lies a huge country almost as big as the United States east of the Mississippi—Zaire. It is a great square about 900 miles by 900 miles in extent. For years Christians have devotedly carried on Mission in every part of Zaire. Fifty years ago, in 1925, there were 653 Protestant missionaries and twice that number of Roman Catholic missionaries at work.

Zaire has been most responsive to the gospel. Especially after World War II, tremendous church growth took place. Twenty-three of the 25.6 millions living in Zaire in 1977 claimed to be Christian. In few other nations has the response been as great. Zaire will be one of the substantially Christian nations of the twenty-first century.

Following Independence in 1960, Missions turned all authority over to Zairian Churches. Throughout the vast land Churches (denominations) are in charge of their own affairs. In a sovereign nation where the Church is under no Mission, what is the function of Christian Missions?

Mission Accomplished?

Can Eurican Churches and missionary societies write "Mission Accomplished" across their calendars and retire from the scene? From now on can the World Church say that Mission ought to be each denomination and each congregation in its own place reaching out in service and proclamation? If so, then sovereign denominations in Zaire need no further aid from abroad and no more missionaries. If so, then the presence of Western money and missionaries may prevent the rugged self-determination and heroic endeavor which Churches develop when thrown on their own. If so, Mission has ended.

The collapse of European empires has created a new world scene. In Asia, Africa, and Latin America, Christians are asking the same questions we have raised in regard to Zaire. Is our Mission accomplished? Is the great streaming out to the ends of the earth ended? Can Christians now live normal lives, serving and witnessing "at home," each in his or her own native place? Is this God's will for tomorrow?

The Thesis of This Book

Against these contemporary questions, repeated in many forms in many lands, the thesis of this book may now be stated. The collapse of Western empires and the rise of hundreds of self-governing young Churches, far from ending Christian Mission, usher in the time of its flowering. Particularly in Zaire, a hundred years of missionary labors have brought us to the midst of unparalleled harvest. Consolidating gains, bridging remaining gulfs, building Christ into the foundations of the social fabric of a hundred tribes, instituting a truly Christian system of education, discipling the cities, making the thorny thickets of tribalism bear the peaceful fruit of brotherhood, sending out thousands of Zairian missionaries to the three billion who have yet to believe—all this and much more remain to be done. The missionary movement works in midday, not sunset.

The Clock Cannot Be Turned Back

To be sure, there can be no return to the missionary task which existed in 1900. The unexplored rain forest, the trackless wilderness, the myriad tribes in constant warfare against each other, the animistic world view reigning supreme in all minds as the only possible explanation of the world, a powerful and advanced Europe busily seizing parts of the world as colonial possessions, tropical diseases posing substantial dangers to Europeans—all this has gone forever. Christian Mission then faced a solidly illiterate population. Today Zaire is dotted with schools everywhere. Every village of any size has its school. Towns have high schools. Three cities have universities.

There can be no return to demeaning views of African ability. In 1900 it was easy for a European civilization cresting in the power of industrialization, invention, science, military might, and complete command of the sea lanes to think meanly of nations and races where these technological advances were unknown. Then it was not believed that, given educational opportunity, all races and nations were about equally competent. Then the notion that European peoples were super-races was unchallenged. It was easy to hold that the less-developed nations did not have the ability required for modern life. There can be no return to these simplistic and untrue opinions, which moreover were not universally held. Missionaries, for example, fiercely championed the ability of their national colleagues.

The twentieth century ends with the conviction spreading that all races are equally competent. Given the same opportunities and the same knowledge of God, all can think equally accurately, work equally hard, and achieve equally formidable goals. Some peoples do temporarily forge ahead through the accident of mineral wealth, strategic location, or access to markets and power—witness the Arab renaissance fueled by oil, and the South African boom assisted by gold and diamonds. But, as the Bible affirms, God has made "of one blood all nations."

The only alternative to chaos is to work out a brotherhood of nations, each treated equally and afforded equal access to the good things of life. Each will direct its own affairs. None will be slave of others. The democratic process may be slower, but it is more just and in the long run more effective than any form of exploitation and tyranny.

The clock cannot be turned back. Mission must be carried on in this new world. When there was no congregation, the Mission alone determined how worship was to be carried on and what was to be taught in the schools. When the only money coming to the Church/Mission enterprise came from abroad, all decisions as to how the money was spent had to be made by the missionaries. In 1925, despite heroic efforts to educate an African ministry, the leaders of Protestant Churches in Belgian Congo were 653 missionaries and 5 ordained Africans. The small part Africans played in the direction of the upper echelons of ecclesiastical policy was necessary then. It has long since been outmoded.

In 1925 the educational efforts of the Protestant Missions were carried on without government aid. Education was considered the business of the Church, and what government aid was available was given to Roman Catholic institutions. Today the limitations which that imposed on educational policy and program have been outmoded. Government pours tremendous sums of money into education and expects to pour in more. The clock cannot be turned back. The educational program of the Churches and Missions must be geared to a nation determined to spend a large part of its national income on the education of its future citizens.

Nevertheless, many aspects of the congregations and the Missions of the first half of the twentieth century are *not* outmoded. In 1925 there were only 326 organized churches, almost entirely at the mission stations. There were also 2,744 other worshiping groups. At these outstations the *entire direction of congregations was in African hands.* This aspect of the 1925 scene has *not* been outmoded. It continues healthily today and will continue tomorrow.

Many New Tasks Face the Churches and Missions on Every Hand

Perhaps the most dramatic new task which faces Christians in Zaire today is the use of the air for travel and communication. As the tribal and regional clusters of congregations and denominations feel their way toward larger and larger unities, as regional policies are hammered out and national programs are framed, it is essential that the leaders be able to fly to meetings. The time saved is very important. Missionary Aviation Fellowship has suddenly appeared; God has created it to enable joint planning and joint action. In view of the deterioration of transport and the fact that oil and gasoline will become increasingly rare and costly, the maintenance of air communication is for Christians a matter of high priority. A proportion of the total Church income in Zaire and the Mission income from abroad ought to be devoted to this program for the foreseeable future. In Zaire the need will increase.

Again, the fact that educated Zairians now read the Bible in French, whereas at least twenty million can read it only in their own regional or trade languages, presents a new task to both Church and Mission. In which language should family devotions be carried on? If in French, then the older people hear it in a language in which, if they understand it at all, they are not fluent. If in tribal languages, then the educated youth tend to feel that the reading is unimportant, provincial, and passé. If in cities worship is conducted in the trade languages (Lingala, in many cases), considerable sections of the membership, who in their homes use a tribal language, are getting a rather thin, "least common denominator" worship experience. The task of making Scriptures, hymns, prayers, and sermons meaningful in a nation made up of many tribes, now in process of coalescing, is a new task. In the earlier decades of this century, the missionaries did not face this task since each group churched a specific segment of a tribe in a specific language.

Many more examples of the new tasks facing the Churches and Missions could be given. One more will suffice. All across Zaire we were told that animal husbandry is so new to Zairians that it does not prosper. The devoted service to animals, such that they will give milk, draw ploughs and carts, and provide fertilizer for fields, has to be learned. A whole new set of values, ways of life, roles and habits could be created. With sleeping sickness conquered and the tsetse fly no longer a menace, the huge amount of land in Zaire could be made to yield additional richness of life through the development of a tremendous cattle industry. On the material level, few advances would prosper the nation more. We saw one or two pioneer efforts in this direction, but for the most part Christian leaders have not seen the possibilities. Some readers may question whether this development is either possible or needed. Be that as it may, this is one way living conditions could be improved, which is one of the new tasks facing Churches and Missions on every hand.

To speak of "the Churches" in Zaire poses a problem. There are officially only three Churches—Roman Catholic, Protestant, and Kimbanguist. Until 1970 every Mission at work in Zaire was establishing a Church (denomination) which conformed to the pattern of its founders, so that before that year one correctly spoke of many Churches (denominations) in Zaire. After 1970, when Protestants formed the Church of Christ in Zaire, they declared the many Protestant Churches to be not Churches, but Communities (capital C). In fact, these Communities function today as though they were Churches and have practically complete autonomy. For example, if one refers to the Churches in Shaba Province today, possibly he would mean the three official ones listed above. Probably he would be referring to the Protestant Communities (such as the Brethren in Christ of Garanganze Church and the Methodist Church) as well as the Lubumbashi diocese of the Roman Catholic Church.

The picture is complex. Therefore, in this book we shall use the terms "Church," "Community," and "denomination" as synonymous. When describing clusters of congregations after 1970, we are likely to use the word "Community." When speaking of these clusters before 1970, we are likely to use the word "Church" or "denomination." When we indicate the Roman Catholic, the Protestant, and the Kimbanguist clusters, we shall use "Church." We trust that readers will realize that our purpose is to describe the Churches, Communities, and denominations (clusters of congregations as they exist) rather than to take sides in the debate as to whether or not the various denominations should have been merged into the one Protestant Church. We simply accept that as history and go on.

This book, written in 1978, sees many rapid changes occurring. Many factors will change perhaps before this book is printed. However, the main line of the picture will remain the same.

All that the Church Can Do, It Should Do

The thesis we are setting forth—that we stand at midday in Mission—strongly affirms that the Churches should do all they can do. The health and welfare of the Church demand this. Any arrangement by which Missions from outside Zaire take on themselves, or are given by the Churches of Zaire, responsibilities and burdens which the Churches there can carry defeats its own ends. The Church in Zaire is not weak. It has millions of members. It has prestige. No rival religions challenge it, persecute it, or arrest its development. It can do much. It can do much which it is currently not doing. The Golden Age of Missions does not mean and must not mean that the Church does less. Rather, it means that in cooperative brotherly relations with the Missions, Churches now stretch out to surpass their former achievements. They will give more, build better buildings, run better schools, worship God more devotedly, train more ministers and evangelists, send missionaries abroad, attack their social evils more resolutely, and church their cities more effectively. A healthy Church is a working Church which, under the direction of the Holy Spirit, is constantly stretching forward to new and greater achievements.

Many Urgent Tasks Remain for Eurican Missions to Do

When Zairian Churches have done all they can do, many urgent tasks will still cry aloud to be done. Into these, for the foreseeable future, Eurican Missions ought to pour substantial resources of men, women, and money. We trust that readers will not be confused by the fact that Missions in Zaire no longer have a separate legal existence. In the sixties the government forced the merger or fusion of all

<u>Missions with their Zairian Churches</u>. All that legally remained was the Community. As far as government is concerned, the Swedish Baptist Mission, the Africa Inland Mission, or the Presbyterian Mission no longer exist. There are no direct dealings between government and Missions.

While this is true, the Missions are all there, very much alive. They raise millions of dollars in Europe and America; recruit, train, and maintain large forces of missionaries in Zaire; make large grants to the Communities to carry on all kinds of work; and are very much a part of the picture. In this book, therefore, we continually speak of Mission and Missions. They are an essential part of the scene.

Within the nationwide mold of fusion there are several patterns of relationship between Missions and Communities. <u>No two Communities or Missions are exactly alike</u>. National <u>origins of missionaries, policies of their boards, convictions of church polity, attitudes and expectations of Zairian leaders</u>—all these <u>variables</u> go to make each Community and each Mission different from the others. We repeat, therefore, that Eurican Missions ought to continue to pour in substantial resources of men, women, and money. Justice demands this. The enormous inequity so clearly seen between the northern nations and the southern nations, between Eurican and Latfricasian nations, demands action. It is not right that 8 percent of the people of earth should use 40 percent of the resources. It is not pleasing to God that some nations should have an average income of $10,000 a year while others have $200. Affirmations like this pour from the lips of Christian leaders all over the world. Concerns such as these occupy the attention of many international gatherings. Much further inequity is within nations. In Mexico it is commonly said that the rich are getting richer and the poor are getting poorer. This is true in many other lands and is equally displeasing to God.

It is easy to say all this, but to change the situation is extremely difficult. It will not be achieved by tremendous sendings of grain, food, money, or other things from the developed to the developing nations. As we shall point out in chapter 1, Zaire is a potentially wealthy country with enormous resources of land, water, sunshine, favorable climate, and water power. Merely transferring ultimate power to the Zairians will not achieve the ends desired. Establishment of ways of life, standards of conduct, inner strengths, relation to God and to other persons, repentance for sin, striving for holiness, and the creation of family, tribal, and ecclesiastical systems which transmit the inner resources are essential if a new, just international order is to come into existence. The just order cannot be conferred on Zaire by outsiders who then retire from the scene. The new just order must be the fruit of joint labors of Christian brothers and sisters, each doing that which God ordains. The goal must not be the glorification of either Zairians or outsiders, but the actual measurable increase in faith in the triune God and in abundant life in this great nation. If that is achieved, it makes little difference who gets the glory. Justice demands that Eurican Missions pour in substantial resources of missionaries and money.

The Four Stages of Mission in Zaire

Realizing that Christian Mission exists in four stages will help us see the real situation in Zaire and other lands. These four stages are: exploration, occupation, people movements, and completion. Sometimes Stage One continues so long, and its leaders know their own situation so well and all other situations so little, that they think Christian Mission *is* Stage One. The same lack of vision may afflict church persons (nationals and missionaries) whose Mission enterprise is in Stage Three or Stage Two. Furthermore, in any one nation or region, it is quite possible for Mission in one district of the nation to be in Stage One and that in another district to be in Stage Four. Much of the confusion in mission thinking today arises from failure to distinguish the four stages of Mission and from advocating for the whole nation action and policies suitable to the particular stage of Mission required in a particular population.

Let us then consider the four stages of Mission and observe how Mission in Zaire is generally in the Fourth Stage. The First Stage of Mission, whether carried out by Europeans in Belgian Congo or by Koreans in the United States, is _exploration._ In Belgian Congo all Missions passed through this stage, some in the years 1882 to 1910, some in the years 1920 to 1940. Unoccupied fields were identified. Pioneer missionaries explored the land. In 1922 in the Ubangi region, the pioneer missionary cycled in from Uganda, using up four cycles in the process!

During this stage, missionary residences are built or rented, land is acquired, the language is learned, workers are recruited, preliminary and rather blundering proclamation is made, and humanitarian services are offered both to meet human need and as evidence of friendliness. Often much of the time is spent just keeping alive. It is common for years to pass before the first convert is won.

Stage Two may be called *occupation*. During this stage suitable centers are chosen; church, school, and hospital buildings are built. Congregations are established at these headquarters. All the territory which has been claimed for Christ is gradually occupied, whether this is one city or a whole province. Ongoing permanent works are started. Missionaries are recruited in the homeland and dedicate themselves for lifelong service. They come to the country; learn the language; get to know the people and their customs; plant schools, hospitals, leprosy homes, and agricultural demonstration centers. Outstations and outlying congregations are established. During this stage a much larger proportion of the missionary's time is devoted to effective evangelism and service. The new congregations forming under the wing of the Mission come to think of themselves as belonging to this or that Mission. The only Christian leaders they commonly see are those of their own branch of the Church.

Stage Three is that in which *people movements* from the tribes (castes or classes) occur. Movements develop in an uneven fashion. Around some stations most of a given people (tribe) move to Christian faith, and little churches and schools arise in many of the villages of that tribe. Around other stations the population is indifferent or resistant, or the mode of evangelization is ineffective, and few churches arise outside the congregation at each center. As Stage Three progressed in Zaire, most of the people in the neighborhood of the mission stations (Roman Catholic or Protestant) became Christian. Often the Christianization was tied to a mission school. The older people remained animist, but sent their boys and girls to school. There they studied the Bible regularly and engaged daily in Christian worship. After some years they decided to become Christians. They were baptized and formed the congregations. Some, going back to their families after school, reverted to animism, but in Zaire most of them stayed Christian. Not all were good Christians, but they were still Christians, not pagans.

In Stage Three we see the few mission station congregations of Stage Two becoming hundreds of congregations throughout the forest or across the hills. In Zaire people movements to Christ have brought very large numbers of tribespeople to Christ all across this land. During Stage Three, there is great development of the Church. National leaders multiply, are trained, and occupy all pulpits and administrative posts. Devolution of authority from Mission to

Church flourishes. Stage Three in Zaire has now ended, and Stage Four is what we see for most Missions and Churches.

Stage Four may be called *completing Christianization*. Zaire is now in this fourth stage. A great part of the population has become Christian. The following three tasks are urgent: (*a*) Converting each new generation, churching the cities, planting churches and schools in the isolated and remote sections of the land which have been bypassed, sending thousands of Zairian missionaries abroad to play their part in world evangelization, and developing strong self-supporting and self-governing congregations, conferences, unions, synods, and denominations. (*b*) Lifting the quality of physical, mental, moral, and spiritual life. A new thoroughly Zairian and thoroughly Christian culture must be created. The tribes who were in a state of endemic war against each other a hundred years ago, and have a high consciousness of being different peoples even now, must be welded into one people—the people of God. Social structures are to be Christianized and humanized. What this means under contemporary circumstances and in view of the present power of the Churches must be defined and described. (*c*) Forging effective Church-Mission relationships, such that a true partnership in obedience to God utilizes the full powers of each partner in the task of completing Christianization of this great land. The task is immense. The days are difficult. The resources of God, poured out through his Churches both in Zaire and abroad, are limitless. Stage Four will continue for the foreseeable future. In a country of the potential wealth of Zaire, we are confident God intends a quality of life significantly different from and higher than what we now see. Working toward this more Christian life, presenting the claims of Christ to every segment of every tribe, incorporating in faithful churches all those who believe, feeding them on the Word of God, and thrusting them out into the less-favored nations where Christ is not known is the task of the Church of Jesus Christ. Both the institutional form of Church, known as the denomination (or Community, in Zaire), and the dynamic form of Church, known as the missionary society, are essential parts of the Church. Both work in the high noon of Missions.

Plan of This Book

In Part 1 this book will lay out the *Zairian setting* of the Mission of the Church. We shall see the country and its peoples, the history of the Missions which have been working here for a hundred years, the Communities which have evolved from the Missions and the denominations, and tumultuous times through which the Christian enterprise has passed.

Part II describes in detail what Mission entails in Zaire today and tomorrow. It presents an accurate picture of the Christian population in all its complexity. It discusses the tremendous parochial school system now urgently demanded. The system must be large enough to educate six million children now and ten million in twenty years. It sets forth the four urgent evangelistic tasks which must be carried out. It indicates how the measurement and membership accounting of the great Zairian Church and all its branches may be carried out so the whole may prosper.

Part III deals with the great contemporary issues in Mission today. These are described partly in order that the true situation in Zaire may be seen, and also in order that through understanding the Zairian situation, Christian leaders in other lands may better understand the great movements of the Spirit which are taking place there. The model studied is Zaire, but the process of Mission is worldwide. It is at different stages in different lands, and we trust that our review of the great contemporary issues in Zaire will illuminate the same issues in many lands of earth. Zairian Mission is part of global Mission. We hope the book will commend itself to readers and they will find the exposition of vital interest to them and to the cause of Christ.

PART I
The Setting

1

The Land and the People

Zaire fills the center of Africa. It ranks second in size and third in population in African nations south of the Sahara. It is coveted by today's colonialists from Moscow and Peking because of its strategic location, size, and potential economic power.

Zaire has a wide variety of geographical features and ethnic groupings. Many volumes have been written on them. It is not our purpose, however, to write of scenery, geography, or anthropology. We are portraying the stupendous growth of the Churches in Zaire from nothing a hundred years ago to the giant Protestant, Catholic, and Independent Churches of today. Yet for full understanding, these must be seen in their setting, and to that we now turn.[1]

The Land

Zaire is four times the size of France and over eighty times the size of tiny Belgium, which was its ruler for many years. This size has implication for church growth as well as for efficient government.

The topographical features of the country are amazingly varied. Eternal snow blankets the towering Ruwenzori Range right on the equator. Elsewhere deep valleys cut the landscape; huge grassy plains extend as far as the eye can see; and a rich lush growth of varying kinds of grasses, bushes, and trees can be seen everywhere. Zaire has no deserts, such as the Sahara to the north and the Kalahari to the south. Huge rain forests are found chiefly astride the equator. The gloom beneath the trees is unending. From an airplane, glints of water appear between the foliage, indicating the presence of marshes.

Another phenomenon is the so-called gallery forests. Like corridors, these follow many rivers through grassy plains. The center of Zaire is a huge basin. The altitude drops from the rim to close to sea level at the center. Geologists think this was once covered by a huge inland sea.[2]

The huge river systems are worthy of note. These are partially shown on the map at the end of this chapter. One reason Zaire could be traversed easily was that once the rapids had been bypassed and Stanley Pool reached, hundreds and hundreds of miles of navigable rivers lay open before the explorers.

The central trunk of this huge river system, which ranks as one of the largest in the world, is the giant Zaire River. President Mobutu and some historians[3] think that the present name of Zaire, which the river, the country, and the currency bear, came from Diego Cao's corruption of "Maia Nzadi," the Kikongo term for "the river." At any rate, this tremendous river ranks right after the Nile in Africa in size and length. It is among the five largest rivers in the world. Tributaries flow from the north and the south, which means that in the lower stretches of the river there is an almost constant level of water the year round. The equator runs through the country to the north of the center. There are essentially two seasons: dry and rainy. Depending on the distance from the equator, these seasons vary in length. Directly on the equator are year-round rains with accompanying humidity and heat. The dry seasons at four degrees south of the equator are from mid-May until mid-September and from mid-December to mid-February. The growing season is extended greatly by planting some crops which do best in the dry season with irrigation and others which do best during the rains. Some crops can be grown and harvested twice in one year. The most fertile area is in the Kivu Province which has a temperate climate. Other areas grow crops well, also. With proper development, Zaire will one day export instead of import most of its food.

Zaire is greatly blessed with mineral and agricultural wealth. Among the major cash crops are cotton, corn, coffee, tea, palm oils and derivatives, fruits, and peanuts. Rice was formerly grown but now must be imported. Some potatoes are grown on the Bangu Plateau in Bas-Zaire and in the east. The years following Independence saw a sharp decline in agricultural products. The government hopes to reverse this trend. Zaire ranks as one of the foremost copper-producing countries in the world. Its economy is tied to copper, and the present economic slump is due in part to the depression of world copper prices. Gold, diamonds, and uranium are other sources of foreign currency. Bauxite has been found near the Inga Dam in Bas-Zaire. Low wages, plenty of power, and little transportation costs from mine to factory will, when properly utilized, give Zaire a commanding place in the aluminum industry.

An oil field has been developed off the coast near Moanda and Banana where several oil companies have drilled successfully. The government nationalized them but has reversed itself and returned control back to them. This oil field is a continuation of the one found off the Angolan enclave of Cabinda. In a short time the country expects to be self-supporting in oil.

Industrial development has taken a leap forward in recent years. One of the big pillars in the government's plans for the future is the huge Inga hydroelectric power dam. It is to be built in three phases and when finished will provide Central Africa with abundant power. One irony is that not enough funds have been allocated for step-down transformers, which are absolutely necessary for the domestic use of the power. The hugh towers and long power lines march past many settlements and towns without helping them. The present Inga project is only the first step to harness the mighty Zaire River, which drops six hundred feet in about 150 miles. Eventually more dams will be built generating more power.

A factory located in the Bas-Zaire Province manufactures many inexpensive and needed items. Also in Bas-Zaire at Matadi is a flour mill to process imported wheat. It has greatly helped to make flour readily available.

Two cement factories near Kimpese in Bas-Zaire ship hundreds of thousands of tons all over the country. The price of cement per bag has remained fairly stable in recent years, in spite of the spiraling costs of other locally produced products. In the same area is a sugarcane plantation and refinery which provides sugar for most of the country.

The main industry in the Bandundu Province is the production of palm oil for local use and export by Lever Brothers. A plant in Kinshasa makes soap and margarine. The palm nut kernels are shipped to Belgium where shampoos and other products requiring finer oils are made.

Factories in Kinshasa weave cloth. Others import cloth and dye it. The famous batik wax process is reproduced in one of these factories.

Both General Motors and Land Rover have assembly plants in Kinshasa. At the moment they are plagued by shortages of foreign currency which limit the materials they can import. This is also true of Goodyear Tire Company and other importers. Many auto dealers find themselves with huge amounts of zaires which they cannot convert into foreign currency in order to buy and import more cars. All this is the result of the recession that has hit the country. Nationalization of companies and stores was a setback for the country's economy. Therefore, the government returned business to foreign owners where possible. Some Zairian businessmen did not understand the need for laying aside money to replenish stocks. When the goods were gone, they closed their doors.

Other products manufactured in Kinshasa are furniture, shoes, chemicals, medicines, paper, and paint. This city uses much of the lumber shipped in from other parts of the country.

In spite of the recession brought on by depressed copper prices, erosion of foreign currency reserves, and mismanagement, the country has a tremendous potential economically. The American ambassador told a group of Americans in the early sixties that Zaire had the best opportunity of becoming the first Black African nation to be self-supporting.

The potential economic power of the Churches is also great. They have benefited from the growing economy. Though the recession has hurt them, the future potential is amazing to contemplate. It is only a fraction now of what it could be with proper education, motivation, and management. Profit-making projects must be carefully examined to see whether or not they will actually help the Churches or hinder them. Determined and constant stewardship education must be thoroughly planned and carried out by each denomination. There is yet too much "thinking poor" among Zairian Christians.

In the Ubangi-Mongala area we saw large plantations of coffee and cotton. These provide steady income for numerous Christians in the area and have contributed to the growth and maturity of the local congregations. The Vanga-Busala regions in Bandundu Province have been helped over the years by the presence of several palm oil companies which have provided steady employment for many members. In addition, the good roads they maintain aid missionaries and pastors in visiting all of the far-flung churches on a regular basis.

The People: A Brief Anthropological Summary

The population of Zaire is a mosaic composed of two major racial groupings: the Negroid race which has three subracial groupings, and over three hundred tribes, and the Pygmies. The cultural heritage of the many separate elements of this mosaic can be traced to widely different locations and ethnic origins.

Map 3, which follows this chapter, is taken from George Peter Murdock's *Africa: Its Peoples and Their Culture History.*[4] It is not complete but is the best authoritative portrayal available.[5] It shows where *major* tribes live and the approximate degree of evangelization of each tribe. In estimating the latter, we are indebted to David Barrett's "Frontier Situations for Evangelization in Africa."[6] The idea that people from varied ethnic origins could be "melted" into a common cultural mix has been prominent in North America for many years. Yet it is far from a reality everywhere, even there, and cannot be applied to Zaire. The giant city of Kinshasa (1.9 million in 1975) is a vivid mosaic with many tribal and regional residential patterns. This fact will be referred to often in this book since it is of vital importance for church-growth analysis.

Each of the races and subraces represented in Zaire has distinguishing features of language and culture. A general pattern is discernible throughout, though individual tribes may differ in some details from the majority. Thus, the Mongo and the Luba of the Bantu subrace practice a patrilineal pattern along with the Equatorial Bantu to the north in contrast to the uniformly matrilineal Central Bantu to the south.[7]

The Negroid Race

The majority of the tribes in Zaire belong to what anthropologists call the Negroid race. This race has three subdivisions.

The Bantu

The first and largest of the subdivisions of the Negroid race is the Bantu. In general, Bantu people are of medium height and have dark brown, rather than black, skin. They brought with them the knowledge of working iron, which gave them a definite superiority over the Pygmies with their stone-tipped weapons and tools.[8] According to Wiedner, Murdock, and others, the Bantu have been involved in mass migrations covering centuries and vast distances.

Before 300 B.C. the forebears of the Nigero-Congolese language group left the region around Lake Victoria and migrated slowly to the northwest across Africa to the coast. Part of them settled in the area of modern Nigeria. Others continued on to settle on the southern coast of the great bulge. Still others went southwest to what is known as the Cameroon Highlands to the south, southeast, and east to settle in the vast equatorial rain forests.[9] There followed a long wait because the Malaysian food plants which had enabled their ancestors to cross Africa and to settle the rain forests did not provide an adequate means of moving south across the savanna, dry forest, and upland grasslands.

The West African cereals, which would have provided the means for the southward expansion, had been lost in the earlier migrations. Murdock feels that the evidence points to the Cushite culture on the eastern periphery of the rain forests which flourished in the early centuries of the Christian era as the source of the knowledge which set them moving again. The use of African cereals in their Ethiopian forms could have been learned and passed from tribe to tribe across the tropical rain forests to the Atlantic coast. The southern expansion into the Congo Basin then began.[10]

The white sections of Map 3 show that most tribes have been heavily evangelized and are very responsive to the gospel. Seven major tribal groupings have been "evangelized over 50 percent" but are resistant. Two groups of tribes (Riga and Bira) are half evangelized, and one (Hunde) is only partially evangelized. We will be studying the results of this massive response to the gospel all through this book and especially in chapter 5: "Everyone Is a Christian." The tables and graphs will put into numerical form this startling and highly encouraging story.

The Nilotes

The Nilotic peoples of Zaire came originally from eastern Sudan and are distinctive enough to be classed as a definite subrace. They are tall, about five feet ten on the average (for adult males), have long limbs, extremely slender bodies, and narrow heads. Their color is dark brown.[11]

After developing the skill of surviving by nomadic cattle-raising as a primary source of food and other needs, with agriculture as an option where practical, they expanded swiftly southward.[12] This happened in the seventh, eighth, or ninth century after Christ.[13]

According to Murdock, the two main Nilotic tribes are found today within the borders of Zaire. The Alur tribe inhabits the Lake Albert region (now Lake Idi Amin) on the northeastern frontier which borders Uganda. In fact, the tribe straddles the border line. The larger portion of the 200,000 population of the tribe resides in Uganda with possibly two-fifths living in Zaire.

Near the eastern part of Zaire's northern border with Sudan, the Kakwa tribe is found. Other tribes of the Bari cluster may also be inside Zaire, but they are not on the map. In 1959 the Kakwa and the Fajulu were only about 90,000 people.[14] Both the Alur tribe and the Kakwa tribe are listed in the Frontier Survey as being highly evangelized and responsive to the gospel. This is quite a contrast to other Nilotic tribes, such as the Masai in Kenya and the Dinka in Sudan.[15] We wish it were possible to know the reasons for the difference, but it would require a separate study by those in close contact with the tribes in question.

The Sudanic People

The last of the subraces of Negroids represented in Zaire is the Sudanic. For brevity we are including in this group what anthropologists call the Central Sudanic and the Eastern Nigritic peoples. Deward[16] writes of Sudanic invasions into Zaire from the sixteenth century on. The conquerors formed sultanates in the Uele region, which is now northern Zaire. The most powerful of these were the Abandia, Avungura, and Mangbetu sultanates. These remained in power until Eastern Nigritic tribes began to move west and south. The Azande were a large nation which spearheaded the last Eastern Nigritic advance. Being more numerous and aggressive than the tribes of the Mangbetu sultanate, they broke it up in 1873.[17] They settled astride the frontier between what is now Sudan and Zaire with about two-thirds settling in northern Zaire. Farther west in the Ubangi-Mongala region (northwestern part of the Equatorial Province) appears an interesting pattern of settlement by other Eastern Nigritic tribes. The Ngbaka are in the center, and scattered all around are smaller tribes, some Eastern Nigritic, and a few Bantu. Some are shattered in pieces. It looks as if the Ngbakas came in like the Azande and took over a large territory, displacing other tribes in the process. Animosities and distrust exist even today between the Eastern Nigritic tribes, indicating that the Ngbaka were the villains in the scenario.

A supplementary explanation for this central location of the Ngbaka tribe which does not contradict the strong evidence for the early Sudanic invasions states that in 1920 the Belgian colonial government rounded up all the members of this tribe and placed them in one administrative region as part of a nationwide strategy.[18]

This intermingling of the tribes and races has great significance for church growth. We will explore this later as we further define the tribal mosaic and discuss the implications of this fact to the discipling of peoples and homogeneous groups. If this fundamental fact of the Zairian scene is fully grasped from the start, then the rest of the book will be more meaningful.

The Pygmies

The second race found in Zaire is the Pygmoid race. Pygmies were the original inhabitants along with the Bushmen, who have disappeared. Pygmies lived in the great equatorial rain forests until about two thousand years ago when Sudanese invaders began pushing them south. These were followed by other Sudanese tribes of Eastern Nigritic origin, and in the beginning of the Christian era until around A.D. 500 a horde of Bantu people from Nigeria and the Cameroon Highlands further displaced them and greatly limited their habitat.[19]

Pygmies live in rain forests and do not cultivate crops except under the influence of other races. They subsist mainly by hunting smaller animals, though even the hippopotamus and the elephant are not exempt from their arrows. Women do the gathering of wild fruits, roots, insects and larvae, lizards, and often shellfish. Fishing is mainly done by men. Almost nowhere today do Pygmies occupy independent tracts of land; rather they are attached, in small bands which vary in number from twenty to a hundred, to particular Bantu chiefs or headmen. Though reciprocal, the relationship is clearly dependent. In many areas Pygmies have disappeared through absorption or have become markedly acculturated. The Bantus trade agricultural produce and tools for game, forest products, and ivory.

There are two main groups of Pygmies in Zaire. First, the Central Twa live scattered among the Bantu tribes of the Mongo nation in the southeastern portion of the Equatorial Province. They are around 100,000 in number. The second group composed of the Mbuti, the Akka, and the Efe are located in the Ituri Forest (North East Zaire) and number about 32,000. A few strongly acculturated groups exist in the savanna country and along the Kwango, Kasai, and other southern tributaries of the Zaire River.

No record of the presumed former speech of the Pygmies exists today. Each group speaks the language of the tribe to which it is attached. Thus, those near Bantu tribes speak Bantu languages, those near Eastern Nigritic speak those languages, and those near Central Sudanic, those languages. We have, therefore, a distinct people which seems to have lost its own identity and have taken on that of its conquerors even to the extent of the language.

The problem of unsettled dwelling places, since forest Pygmies do not build sturdy houses and live in any one place very long, makes the discipling of this segment of the race very difficult. Evangelists who have attempted to win forest Pygmies and form congregations have found it an almost impossible task. Evangelists make regular visits to the group with which they have made contact, preaching and teaching and making some progress. Then suddenly one day they arrive to find the temporary village dismantled and all the inhabitants gone. They will not see this particular group again for a long time, or perhaps never. All trace of the gospel seems lost in them. We will pursue this later on in this chapter.

The survey on "Frontier Situations for Evangelization," referred to earlier, shows that the Central Twa Pygmies in the Equatorial Province are 60 percent animist, 10 percent Roman Catholic, and 30 percent Protestant. In sharp contrast, the Mbuti Pygmies are 90 percent animist, 7 percent Roman Catholic, and only 3 percent Protestant.[20] One ready explanation could be that the Twa group is intermingled with the Mongo people who have been highly evangelized and responsive to the gospel. They are also more stable in regard to habitat.

Inter- and Intra-Tribal Differences

Besides the differences which one finds between tribes even of the same racial or subracial classification, there are others just as sharp within single tribes, subtribes, clans, and lineages. These felt differences produce suspicion, friction, and animosity. In the early days it was often dangerous to travel more than a couple of miles from one's village because the neighbors down the road might kill or enslave him. They were of the same tribe but different in clan or lineage. Warfare was endemic.

Although after the coming of Belgian rule and of the message of peace and brotherhood brought by the Church open warfare ceased, these feelings of difference are still present.[21] The missionary from thousands of miles away and from a totally different culture is not regarded as more foreign than someone from another tribe. An illustration of this is the story of an Mbala pastor from the Vanga area (Bandundu Province) who went as a missionary to work with a neighboring tribe. These people are cousins to the Mbala, but he was regarded as a stranger the entire time he was with them. They resented his presence until he finally left. No Eurican missionary ever underwent this kind of treatment from them.

This feeling of being different is seen in the preparation of food. It is true that there are some variations of what is eaten in the Bas-Zaire by the Kongo, for instance, and by the Hungana or Mbala of Bandundu, but in general a large number of fruits and vegetables are common to all. The biggest differences seem to be in the preparation of foods: how much palm oil is used, how this one or that one prepares the manioc, how much pepper is put in—these are the crucial items. At the joint school of Kimpese (four cooperating Missions) where the students were mainly from the Kongo tribe, it was impossible for many years to have a central dining room. The reason was that no cook could be found who could please more than a few of the students. These seemingly superficial matters must be considered whenever the tribal mosaic is discussed.

Language is another barrier between races and tribes. The story of the Tower of Babel in Genesis illustrates the power of language to disrupt. Within the Bantu group of languages are quite definite clusters. Dr. Guthrie of London University, formerly a missionary with the British Baptists, came to the Vanga area (American Baptist) to study the Yanzi, Dinga, and Mputu dialects of the Yanzi language. He pointed out many striking differences between the Yanzi and Mbala languages. We then learned that the Yanzi did not come from the ancient kingdom of Kongo in Angola, but from the north across the Zaire River. In reality, the language difference was symbolic of a deep cultural rift between two large groupings of Central Bantu. The nearly three hundred languages in Zaire pose a problem for translation and printing of textbooks and Bibles, as well as for discipling the various tribes.

Four major trade languages cover most of Zaire. Lingala evolved from the Ngala tribal language. It is spoken throughout the Equatorial Province. It is found along both sides of the Zaire River from Kinshasa to Kisangani and is pushing Swahili back toward the east. Since it is the official language of the army and police, and since the president uses it as the second official language after French, it is gaining momentum and penetrating many urban centers of the country. In Kinshasa it is spoken by the vast majority of children of all ages and is the language of commerce.

Kituba, or Government Kikongo, evolved from the Kikongo of the Kongo tribe. It is mainly used in Bas-Zaire and Bandundu provinces. From being the main language of Kinshasa and other centers, it is descending to second rank after Lingala.

Tshiluba is a tribal language of the Luba tribe. It is spoken mostly in Western and Eastern Kasai provinces. However, Luba people are proud of it and speak it wherever they go. In the cities and centers of its domain, it does not yet feel the pressure of Lingala, but the time may come when it will.

The three preceding trade languages all belong to the Bantu cluster. The fourth, Swahili, is a mixture of Arabic and the East African Bantu language, Swahili.[22] It was created and spoken by the Arab slavers from early times. Today it is spoken throughout East Africa and along the eastern edge of the Upper Zaire, Kivu, and Shaba provinces of Zaire.

The Tribal Mosaic

We are now ready to consider the question: What is the tribal mosaic? It certainly is not a melting pot where everything becomes uniform in texture, color, and properties. Rather, it is a conglomeration of separate pieces. It is a bringing together of pieces of varying description, color, and shape. It is not, therefore, something which when applied to tribes or races means the complete opposite of unity. It merely recognizes unity in diversity as valid and desirable. It admirably fits a nation whose people have many ethnic origins. The U.S.A., like Zaire, is a mosaic. The Roman Catholic Church and the Church of Christ in Zaire (ECZ) are mosaics.

We have shown that all dark-skinned people are not alike any more than all light-skinned people are. This means that in terms of evangelism and church growth, account must be taken of the tribal mosaic. We mentioned the mosaic found in the Ubangi-Mongala area of northwestern Equatorial Province. One of the tribes studied, the Budja, was shown to be slow in accepting the gospel in significant numbers and depth. The answer as to why this was so came clear when we realized that pastors and evangelists from the Eastern Nigritic Ngbaka tribe who spoke Lingala, a trade language, were working among a Bantu tribe which had felt the shattering blows of the Ngbaka invasion centuries before. We counseled the leaders of the Evangelical Covenant Church to train and use Budja people as soon as possible.

Rev. Charles Harvey tells of a young Kongo pastor trained by the British Baptists and sent to the Pygmies in the rain forests of the north. He soon discovered that other Bantu tribespeople who came to minister to them had never eaten with them nor slept in their temporary villages. The Bantu regarded the little people as subhuman. This attitude was reflected in their inability to communicate the gospel effectively to the Pygmies. This young man resolved to live with them and identify with them as closely as possible. He began to have significant results in spite of the numerous differences which separated them.

We have attempted in a brief space to describe a tremendous and varied land and its people with markedly different customs, languages, and origins. We have not done this for the purpose of entertaining, but in order to help us understand what the Christian task in Zaire is today and will be for many decades.

MAP 3

LOCATION OF MAJOR TRIBES IN ZAIRE
AND
THEIR RESPONSE TO THE CHRISTIAN GOSPEL

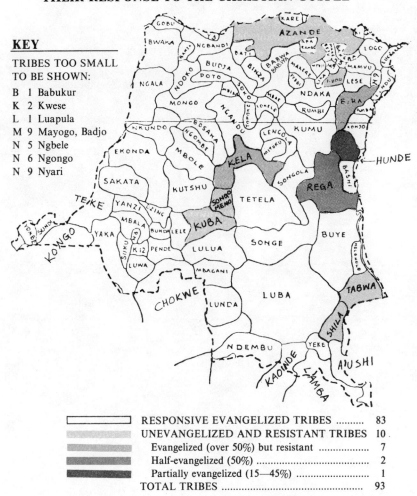

KEY

TRIBES TOO SMALL
TO BE SHOWN:

B	1	Babukur
K	2	Kwese
L	1	Luapula
M	9	Mayogo, Badjo
N	5	Ngbele
N	6	Ngongo
N	9	Nyari

RESPONSIVE EVANGELIZED TRIBES	83
UNEVANGELIZED AND RESISTANT TRIBES	10
Evangelized (over 50%) but resistant	7
Half-evangelized (50%)	2
Partially evangelized (15—45%)	1
TOTAL TRIBES	93

This map, adapted from Murdock's *Africa,* is reasonably accurate.[23] However, it does not agree with what we were told by nationals and missionaries at Gemena and Karawa concerning the present location of the Ngbaka tribe (see page 22).

2

A History of
Missions in Zaire

As the story of the discovery of Zaire (formerly Congo) unfolds, we shall see how exploration and pioneering for Missions were closely intertwined. Explorers opened up the country for missionaries, and missionaries often doubled as explorers—being the first Westerners to arrive in many places.

In this chapter we want to see briefly the beginnings of the country and the stages it passed through in order to understand the milieu in which the first missionaries worked. We shall glance at ancient kingdoms and at explorations related to Mission. We shall then look at the important work done by the Livingstone Inland, the British Baptist, and the Garanganze Evangelical Missions, and then present briefly the pioneer Missions in each province followed by the contribution of Belgian Protestants to the discipling of the nation. The founding and contribution of the Congo Protestant Council will be followed by a statistical presentation of growth through the years and a brief survey of the state of the Churches and Missions just prior to Independence. What happened after Independence is shown in chapter 3.

The acquisition of Congo by Leopold II, king of the Belgians, was not the result of conquest by arms or even the occupation of a territory because of superior arms. It was achieved as a result of Stanley's second expedition (1878–1879) during which he visited one hundred new tribes and made more than five hundred separate treaties with African chiefs.[1] One exception to this general policy, however, was the conquest of the Garanganze Kingdom by Congo Free State forces in 1891. (See page 55.)

Beginnings

Historians agree that Portuguese navigator Diego Cao discovered the mouth of the Congo River near the close of 1482, ten years before Columbus discovered the New World. He made several attempts to penetrate into the interior but was halted by the Crystal Mountains. At the point of his farthest penetration, he left on a rock not too far up river from Matadi an inscription which reads, "Here arrived the vessels of the squadron of King Dom John II of Portugal"; beside the inscription he wrote the date.[2]

The next chapter in the history of Missions involves the relation between several Belgian Calvinists and the Congo during the sixteenth and early seventeenth centuries. The first of the Belgian Calvinists was Adrian Saravia (1531-1613), who was trained at Oxford in England and who labored at Antwerp in the Low Countries. He collaborated in the translation into Flemish of the Belgian Confession of Faith, and was a member of the Translation Commission of the King James Bible. In an age when the leading Reformers were openly teaching that it was not our responsibility to find out whether or not the Great Commission had been fulfilled, Saravia devoted two chapters of a treatise on the ministries of the Church to the missionary question, clearly advocating the evangelization of the entire world until the gospel reached the uttermost parts of the earth.[3]

The promoters of several Holland-Belgian expeditions to India and America followed the injunctions of Adrian Saravia. The most noteworthy of these was Pierre Plancius who, after his escape from Brussels at the time of the Spanish conquest, fled to Amsterdam where he opened a school for the training of scientific navigation over long distances. He took special care to place pastors and missionaries on all fleets and thus became known as the father of Missions in India. Sometimes on the long journey to India the boats of the East India Company would stop in at the mouth of the Congo River. This introduced the Flemish commercial men to the new country.[4]

In 1619 Portuguese Bishop Manuel Baptista Soares sent a report to the pope indicating that he had run across some commercial centers run by Belgians. He affirmed that they were not confining themselves to business and trade but were also propagating pernicious doctrines by preaching and distributing books. He did his best to stop them, even going to the extent of asking help from the king of Kongo in Angola, but this was in vain, as the local people along with their chief refused to listen either to the king or the bishop and even roughed up the Catholics.[5] Whatever the effect of these efforts on the people at the time, no trace remained when the modern missionary effort began.

Livingstone and Stanley

David Livingstone arrived in Southern Africa in 1841 as a missionary. He was forced by the Boers, who sought pretexts to get rid of him, to travel to the North. His first encounter with slavery led him to open a route through Central Africa to the Atlantic Coast. This he accomplished in seven months traveling over 1,500 miles and arriving at Luanda in Angola. This expedition opened the way for further exploration and for Missions.[6] Subsequent expeditions revealed lakes and rivers of East Africa. By this time he was no longer working under the London Missionary Society, which thought that his dreams of exploring went beyond their mandate.[7] His one visit to what is now Zaire took place during the years 1869 through 1871 in the Maniema region of Kivu. He had decided to explore the Lualaba, thinking it was the source of the Nile, whereas in actuality it was the source of the Congo River. While living at Nyangwe he saw a terrible massacre perpetrated on the local population by Arab slavers. Disheartened, he returned to Ujiji.[8]

Henry Morton Stanley's first encounter with David Livingstone at Ujiji in 1871 inspired him to seek the backing of the *New York Herald* and *Daily Telegraph* for his first explorations. Subsequent voyages were financed by Leopold II himself who had dreamed dreams of empire in China, Brazil, and Congo since 1860. Stanley's memorable endeavors were remembered and honored in the naming of Stanley Pool and Mt. Stanley overlooking it. A bronze statue of Stanley has since been replaced by a series of bronze figures commemorating early Zairians.

Among many other important explorers was Alexander Delcommune. Sometime in 1873 he arrived at the mouth of the Congo River from Lisbon and planted the Belgian flag. His act caused repercussions in the chancelries of Europe but was never seriously challenged.

The boats and missionaries of the Livingstone Inland Mission and the British Baptist Mission Society also contributed greatly to the settling and opening up of the center of Congo, especially along the river, to the world and to Missions.

The Ancient Kingdoms

A historical resumé of major events in the history of the country will give background for our study of Protestant Missions. First, let us consider very briefly the kingdoms which existed centuries ago in Zaire. Some people have mistakenly concluded that, judging from the state of disorganization of coastal tribes in the nineteenth century, no political structure of any significance had ever existed. There have been, in fact, six significant political entities in the last four centuries.

The earliest of these was the Luba kingdom which was founded in the fourteenth century and lasted until the seventeenth century. The Yaka kingdom flourished on the East bank of the Kwango River in the sixteenth century and was so strong it launched an invasion of the Kongo Kingdom on the Atlantic Coast and except for the Portuguese would have demolished it. From the seventeenth to the nineteenth centuries the Lunda Empire flourished. It was the best organized, having provincial governors and a hierarchy of state officials down to local levels. We have already mentioned the Sudanese sultanates in chapter 1.[9]

The best known was the Kingdom of Kongo which Diego Cao and others found on the coast of Angola and Congo at the end of the fifteenth century. The Portuguese entered into a friendship pact and began trading and propagating the Catholic faith. The king's son was converted and sent to Lisbon for training and put the Catholic Church in power for many years. However, subsequent events destroyed the kingdom. In the sixteenth century the Yaka invasion shook the kingdom. Later, intrigues involving the Portuguese and the princes added to the decadence and disorganization. Toward the end the traders drove out the missionaries and began buying and selling slaves. When the Belgians arrived in the nineteenth century, there was not a trace left of this once influential kingdom, nor of the two and one-half centuries of Catholic evangelism and church planting.[10]

In the northern part of what is today the Western Kasai Province, the Kuba founded a kingdom in the seventeenth century. This kingdom was marked by its pride in its arts. It guarded and deliberately developed the artistic abilities of its subjects. Even today art objects from this area are highly prized. They form the majority of most museum collections.[11] This pride in its culture had an adverse effect on evangelization. The king refused to allow any mission stations to be built in his territory and even burned one the Presbyterians had succeeded in building. The old kingdom has been gone for decades, but there is still a king in power. Fortunately, he is strongly disposed toward the Catholics, having been trained by them; also, his mother is a Presbyterian. Using the station of Bulape as a springboard, a new thrust is being mounted by the Presbyterians which is meeting with very encouraging success.[12]

Belgium Acquires Congo as a Colony

The key personality in the events that led to the acquiring of the Congo by Belgium is King Leopold II. A Belgian professor in an orientation class Norman Riddle attended in Brussels described him as a Napoleon chained to a small, provincial country. He said that if Leopold had been king of a large and powerful country, he might have tried to conquer the world. Leopold II began his campaign to acquire the Congo by calling together a geographical conference in Brussels in September, 1876. As a result the African International Association was created with Leopold as its president. The steering committee met and adopted a flag with a gold star on a blue field in June, 1877. Five expeditions followed during the years 1877–1884.[13]

The joining of effort by Leopold II and Stanley in November, 1878, gave further impetus to events. They formed the Committee for the Study of the Upper Congo, which sponsored Stanley from that time on. The Conference of Berlin, held in 1885, legally recognized the Congo Free State and laid down rules for its relations with other colonial territories administered by the big powers.[14] This Act of Berlin, as it was called, was used by Belgium to give legal right to its presence in Congo to the end of the colony's existence.

The Congo Free State (l'Etat Independent du Congo) was under direct rule of Leopold II himself. At this time Belgium had not accepted any responsibility for it. This situation led to abuse as quotas for ivory and rubber passed down through the hierarchy of government were enforced at local levels by local methods. This policy came under violent attack from abroad due to a campaign spearheaded by an Englishman named Morel and strongly supported by missionaries and their Boards. A commission of inquiry was appointed by the king. Its report, submitted in June, 1906, brought about numerous reforms.[15]

On the positive side, we should mention the campaigns which ended the terror of Arab slavers once and for all in Congo. The army of the Congo Free State, composed of Belgians and Congolese, fought three campaigns in the eastern part of the country to evict the Arab slavers installed there. It then hurried north to Basoko on the Congo River where the Mahdist dervishes were encamped. They were defeated and chased all the way to Redjaf in the Sudan.[16]

Before his death Leopold II willed his sovereign rights over Congo to Belgium. Parliament debated the issue and then voted to accept the Congo as a colony on August 20, 1908.[17] Since that time much money and effort have been put into the country. The colony became prosperous and the education of the masses up through primary level was outstanding. However, the winds of change blew. In 1960 the people demanded independence. Belgium granted this on June 30, 1960, and the Belgian Congo became the Republic of Congo.

Pioneer Missions

The first Mission to begin actual work in the Congo was the Livingstone Inland Mission founded by Mr. and Mrs. H. Grattan Guinness, who had been inspired originally to think in terms of world mission by Hudson Taylor's work in China. They were challenged by the possibilities for evangelization in this vast land revealed by the daring voyage of Stanley down the Congo River. The great missionary explorer David Livingstone had inspired Stanley to call the Congo River the "Livingstone." This influenced the Guinnesses to adopt his name for their new society. The organization of the LIM, as we will refer to it now, took place rapidly in the spring of 1877.

In January of the following year (1878) two men, Henry Craven and Mr. Strom, a Danish sailor, set sail from Liverpool. A month later they arrived at Banana at the mouth of the Congo River. They went up the river to the first rapids, then, after a day's march around them, came to an imposing ridge where a village called Palabala was located. The chief, Kangampaka, received them well, and they decided to build a station there.

Strom returned to England not long afterwards, but help came that summer with the arrival of James Telford and Johnson. Telford became ill very shortly afterward and was the first Protestant missionary to give his life in Congo. At the beginning of 1879, other reinforcements came. Miss Bossy, Craven's fiancée, arrived accompanied by Charles Peterson. They were followed in turn by Henry Richards and a couple.

Strengthened by these reinforcements, the missionaries built a new station at Banza Manteke, eighty-five kilometers toward Stanley

Pool. A station was founded at Bemba at the end of 1880. Death and ill health reduced the staff of twenty to twelve, but in 1882 Richards and Clark once more set out for Stanley Pool. They reached it in March, 1883, after founding Mukimbungu and Lukunga along the way. They established a base on the Ngaliema Bay which today is the headquarters of the Community (CBZO) founded by the American Baptists, who inherited part of the LIM stations.

Further discouragements came when Bemba and Palabala were destroyed by flames and three missionaries died. The stations were rebuilt and other missionaries arrived on the field. Then came welcomed news. A well-to-do businessman, named Henry Reed of Tasmania, gave the money necessary to build a steamer which was dismantled and shipped to Congo in crates, then carried by porters over three hundred kilometers to Stanley Pool and reassembled there. The grateful Mission christened it *The Henry Reed.*

In 1883 the LIM, in accordance with its purpose of penetrating the interior of the country, founded Bolenge on the Congo River near what is now Mbandaka. Thus, after having recruited and sent twenty-five missionaries, founded seven mission stations, and penetrated the interior as far as Bolenge, the LIM Board took stock of the situation. It decided that the time had come to look for help from the American Baptist Foreign Mission Society and the Covenant Mission from Sweden (SMF). In 1884 the ABFMS took over the responsibility for six of the seven stations: Mukimvika (a new site for the Banana station across the Congo River), Palabala, Banza Manteke, Lukunga, Leopoldville, and Bolenge (first called Equatorville). Mukimbungu was given to the SMF, which had no work as yet in the Congo.[18]

The British Baptists Arrive

The thrilling story of the pioneering work of the British Baptist Missionary Society in Congo began in England, as did the story of the LIM. A rich businessman, Richard Arthington, who had already financed David Livingstone's first expedition under the London Missionary Society to Ujiji, felt that it was crucial to place a steamboat on the Congo at Stanley Pool above the rapids which had blocked previous expeditions. He wanted the gospel spread to the east by using the natural waterways and believed that it would lead to Lake Tanganyika. He, therefore, wrote to the BMS about this in May, 1877, and some days later offered fifty pounds to send a scout to find a site for the first station. Another businessman, Charles Wathan, donated five hundred pounds for the venture.

The BMS had been alerted to Africa as a strategic field by William Carey, who early in the century wrote from India, "I hope the Society will keep an eye fixed on Africa."[19] Accordingly, the BMS had founded a Mission in the Cameroons in 1844. It was here that the Society found its pioneers for the Congo venture.

Taking the call of Richard Arthington as from God, the BMS sent George Grenfell and Thomas Comber from the Cameroons to Congo in January, 1876. They went up the Congo River as far as Boma, where they were hindered from continuing by the rainy season. They wrote to Pedro V, King of Kongo, of their intention to settle in San Salvador and returned to the Cameroons to prepare for their expedition. On July 30 of the same year, they went directly to San Salvador in Angola and set up a base for their expedition to reach Stanley Pool. A year later W. H. Bentley, H. E. Crudginton, and J. S. Hartland arrived. These pioneers divided themselves into two teams and set out January, 1881. Comber and Hartland traveled by way of Makuta on the south bank of the Congo River but were abandoned by their porters and had to return to their base. Bentley and Crudginton, on the other hand, took the way by Vivi on the northern bank of the river and after twenty-one days arrived at Stanley Pool two years before the LIM expedition. They were met with hostility at both the Kintambo and Kinshasa villages but found a place to settle in spite of this. The station was later built at Kinshasa on the bank of the Congo. Along the way they had established overnight stations at Matadi, Manyanga, and Isangila. A small boat was donated by a Christian from Plymouth which enabled missionaries to avoid the hostile Sunde tribe by taking the river from Isangila to Manyanga. Six new missionaries were sent out by the Society to help run the stations.

At this crucial juncture Richard Arthington again came through. He offered a thousand pounds to build a steamer to ply the Congo from Stanley Pool into the interior. George Grenfell returned to London to supervise the building of it. It was christened *Peace* in accordance with the wishes of its donor, R. Arthington. George Grenfell returned to Kinshasa to wait for the crates containing the sections of the boat to come. At the end of the summer of 1883 all the crates had arrived. While waiting for the engineers to arrive, in a whale boat he made a trip upriver, lasting from January to April,

1884. On his return he learned of the great tragedy which had befallen the Mission. Seven people had died and two had had to return to England because of ill health. The two engineers who were to have assembled the *Peace* were among the dead. There was only one thing to do—assemble it himself. He set about it resolutely with the help of nine Congolese from the coast and a few local carpenters. His time spent earlier in supervising the original construction was a great help. Many times he sought guidance from the Lord at night and received it in the morning. Just two months later, on June 13, 1884, the *Peace* was launched. In early July, the first voyage was made with Sir Francis de Winton, chief administrator of the International African Association, on board. In two days the party reached the mouth of the Kwa River, which drains Kasai and Bandundu provinces through a series of tributaries. They then proceeded to Lukolela where a station was later established in 1885.

As we leave the story of the BMS temporarily, we find that it had three stations solidly established: Kinshasa, Wathan (1884, now called Gombe Lutete), and Lukolela. William Holman Bentley was well along with his Kikongo grammar and dictionary. We will recount further advances of this intrepid Society in connection with other provinces. The steamer *Peace* provided it with the means to travel beyond Stanleyville (Kisangani today), establishing mission stations along the way.[20]

The Garanganze Evangelical Mission

The third pioneering mission we will present is that of the Garanganze Evangelical Mission. Its name was taken from that of the territory in which it worked, which later became Katanga Province under the Belgians and is known today as Shaba. Fred Arnot arrived in Bukeya to begin work in 1886, five full years before the end of the independent Kingdom of Garanganze. From 1891 on, Garanganze was part of the Congo Free State. In a unique sense, then, this was indeed a pioneer endeavor.

In his childhood, Fred Arnot and his sister were friends of David Livingstone's daughter. Arnot was struck with the challenge to go to Africa and preach the gospel after hearing a letter from Livingstone read by his daughter. His dreams came to fruition in July, 1881, when he left for South Africa. Since he was a member of the Assemblies of the Brethren, he would not join a missionary society but left on his own, trusting only in God.

His plan was to follow the footsteps of David Livingstone, and in this he was successful right up to the banks of the Zambeze River. Here, however, his way was blocked for five months by the chief Liwanika. He was able to leave the village only because a Portuguese trader helped him. He was considering going to Angola with his benefactor when he met King Msiri's brother-in-law who read him a letter from the king asking white people to come to Garanganze. Arnot realized that the king was thinking of traders, but Arnot felt that the treasure he had to share was of far greater value than material goods; so he arranged with the brother-in-law for a guide. Before undertaking the expedition, he returned to his residence at Benguela on the Coast. After seven months of preparation, he set out for Bunkeya, Msiri's capital, with twenty-five porters. He arrived nearly eight months later in February, 1886, and pitched his tent on a hill facing the capital. Msiri received him with friendship and showed a sympathetic spirit during the years that followed. He never tried to hinder Arnot in his efforts to evangelize. In spite of this helpful attitude, Msiri did not accept the message of salvation for himself and seemed to regard Arnot and later reinforcements as his "white slaves." He sometimes treated them with disdain and rudeness. Observers wondered how they would stand this conduct and concluded that only a missionary could do it. This was a testimony to the unswerving purpose which the pioneers had, allowing nothing to turn them aside from proclaiming the Good News.

In December, 1887, two new missionaries arrived at Bunkeya: Charles Swan and W. L. Faulknor. Arnot, who was not in good health, took this opportunity to spend some time in Europe to recuperate. He also recruited twelve new missionaries, three of whom were women, and returned with them to Banguela in March, 1889. Swan wrote that it would not be wise to bring the women since Msiri had ideas about including them in his harem. Only three men were sent to Bunkeya, where they arrived in November of the same year after many difficulties. The death of Msiri at the hands of Captain Stairs' Congo Free State troops during an altercation, caused when the king refused to return from hiding to his capital, brought an end to the kingdom. It also ushered in the administration of the Congo Free State and closed the pioneering stage of the Mission.[21]

The Mission was very successful in later years. By Independence in 1960 it had founded twenty-six stations. This was the largest number of any Mission, four more than the Africa Inland Mission and six more than the BMS. In 1966 it had a Community of 45,000, making it one of the largest in the Shaba Province.

Further Missionary Expansion

We cannot continue to relate in detail the founding of all the Missions in Congo, as inspiring and arresting as that would be. The story of resolute purpose, unswerving faith in God who called them, unflinching surrender to all the hardships and sufferings, even unto death, which we have described for the three pioneers, is equally true of the others. We will mention, however, a few of the early Missions in each province, following the modern division of the country.

Map 2 on page 18 locates the provinces. The following descriptions will give further understanding of their tremendous effort to plant and nurture young Churches which today have become autonomous Communities within the Church of Christ. Tables showing sizes of the Communities are given in chapter 6. The map on the following page shows the number and distribution of Missions in 1960.

Beginning of Missions in Bas-Zaire

The Bas-Zaire Province lies roughly between Kinshasa and the Atlantic Coast. It is part of the former Leopoldville Province and comprised the Congo part of the ancient Kongo Kingdom already mentioned. Since this was the gateway through which so many missionaries passed, we have already told most of its story. We referred to the fact that the LIM ceded its work in this province to the ABFMS and the SMF. In later years the former turned Matadi over to the latter. Both have brought important Communities into being. The BMS also gave birth to an important Community. This brings us to the fourth Mission which began its work before 1890: the Christian and Missionary Alliance. Undaunted by the failure of its first endeavor in 1885 after only two weeks, the C&MA was successful in founding a station to the north of the Congo River below Matadi in 1888. Confining its efforts to the Mayombe region which borders on the coast, it has become an impressive Community. The Salvation Army, which completes the list of large Communities working in the province, began work in 1935.

This is the province where Simon Kimbangu labored for five months in 1921. The Kimbanguist Church, which was founded years later in his name (but not by him), was one of many groups which we

MAP 4

LOCATION OF PROTESTANT
MISSION STATIONS IN 1960

TABLE I

Protestant Missions and
Cooperating Institutions
with Abbreviations

ABFMS American Baptist Foreign Mission Society
ACM African Christian Mission
AEB African Evangelistic Band
AGM Assemblies of God Mission
AIM Africa Inland Mission
AMBM American Mennonite Brethren Mission
APCM American Presbyterian Congo Mission
BMM Baptist Mid Mission (heir to part of UTM stations, Kikwit and area)
BAMS Berean African Missionary Society
BMS Baptist Missionary Society (British)
CBFMS Conservative Baptist Foreign Mission Society
CBM Congo Balolo Mission
CEM Congo Evangelistic Mission
CGM Congo Gospel Mission (left after 1965. AMBM and BMM share stations)
CIM Congo Inland Mission
CMA Christian and Missionary Alliance
CMS Church Missionary Society (Anglican)
CPC Congo Protestant Council (Now ECZ—Church of Christ in Zaire)
CPM Congo Pygmy Mission
DCCM Disciples of Christ Congo Mission
  Deermore Mission in South Kwango (Independent Baptist)
EPI Pastors' & Teachers' Institute (now CECO at Kimpese and ISTK at Kinshasa)
ESAM Evangelization Society Africa Mission
FAGM Friends' Africa Gospel Mission
FWWM Fundamental World-Wide Mission
GEM Garanganze Evangelical Mission
HAM Heart of Africa Mission
ICC Congolese Christian Institute (Bolenge)

IM	Immanuel Mission
LECO	Evangelical Book Store in Kinshasa (now CEDI)
LM	Luanza Mission
MBC	Canadian Baptist Mission (Independent. Left before 1960.)
MBN	Norwegian Baptist Mission
MBRC	Canadian Regular Baptist Mission (left in 1960. Ceded two stations: Tono to ABFMS and Shakenge to CIM)
MEB	Evangelical Mission to the Bayaka (came late 1950s. Located south of Boko, ABFMS.)
MEKI	Emmanuel Mission to Kibali Ituri (came after 1952. Located in Oriental Province.)
MEU	Evangelical Ubangi Mission
MFP	Mission of Faithful Protestants of Lower Uele (came after 1960. Located in Oriental Province.)
MLM	Free Methodist Mission
MLN	Free Norwegian Mission
MLS	Free Swedish Mission
MMCC	Methodist Mission of Central Congo
MMSC	Methodist Mission of Southern Congo
NSM	Northern Sankuru Mission
SA	Salvation Army
SBM	Swedish Baptist Mission
SBMP	Belgian Protestant Mission Society
SDA	Congo Union of Seventh Day Adventists
SMF	Swedish Covenant (Sweden)
UFM	Unevangelized Fields Mission
UPMGI	Pentecostal Missionary Union for Great Britain and Ireland
UTM	Unevangelized Tribes Mission (left 1950; ceded stations to BMM and AMBM)
WGT	Worldwide Grace Testimony
WM	Westcott Mission

call Independent Churches. From the midst of a society which was under the pressures of acculturation since the Portuguese arrived at the end of the fifteenth century, many prophets appeared on the scene proclaiming messages from God and gathering groups of followers. Many have since disappeared, but a few are still in existence. This phenomenon has been ably chronicled and analyzed by missiologists.[22]

Bandundu Province

The Bandundu Province is the second part of the old Leopoldville Province and was developed on the whole much later than the Bas-Zaire. It is true that the BMS founded Bolobo (1888) and Tshumbiri (1889), but these were on the Congo River in the northwest on the border of the French Congo colony and did not penetrate much into the interior. The ABFMS missionaries based at Sona Bata (southwest from Kinshasa) began itinerating into the Bandundu for some years before the Vanga station was opened on the Kwilu River by Dr. Leslie in 1913. In chapter 3 we will pursue the fascinating story of its growth.

The next Mission to begin its work in Bandundu Province was the Swedish Baptist, which founded a station at Bendala in 1919 to the north of the ABFMS field. In 1920 the American Mennonite Brethren opened their Kikandji station and were followed in 1923 by another Mennonite Mission, the Congo Inland at Mukedi. We will speak more of this Mission since it began work in the Kasai Province nine years earlier.

Equatorial Province

As we saw in the section on pioneering Missions, the Livingstone Inland Mission was first in the Equatorial Province by virtue of the founding of Bolenge in 1883. A year later the ABFMS took it over but gave it to the DCCM in 1889 since it was far from its other stations and posed many problems relating to its care. The BMS was right behind the LIM with its station at Lukolele (1885), and by the end of 1890 it had established three others in the province.

The Disciples took over Bolenge and began an aggressive program of evangelism and church planting which has resulted in one of the largest Communities in the country. Tremendous reaping continued for some years. In 1969 the *Year Book of the Christian Churches* lists 229,568 baptized believers.

Only four years after the dissolution of the LIM, the Guinnesses formed a new missionary society: the Congo Balolo Mission. They had been disappointed that neither the ABFMS nor the SMF planned to penetrate farther into the interior along the Congo River. One of their former missionaries under the LIM, who was then working under the ABFMS, returned to England for furlough declaring that he felt called to go where no other witness to Christ had gone. He had surveyed a large territory comprised of the basins of the Lolonga, Lopori, Maringa-Juapa, and Busira rivers which he felt would be fruitful. A second indication that the time was right for a new venture in Congo came with the total support pledged to the Guinnesses by their oldest son. The furloughing missionary, John McKittrick, was released by the ABFMS to join the new society. During the year of the founding in 1889, two stations were opened— Lulonga and Ikau—and two more were begun within two more years.

We close our brief review of Missions in the Equatorial Province by noting the founding of the Evangelical Mission in the Ubangi. After his epic journey across North Central Africa by bicycle, Titus Johnson opened the Karawa station in 1923, which today has around forty resident missionaries.

Haut Zaire and Kivu Pioneers

East of the Equatorial Province, which in turn lies north of Bandundu, is the Province of Upper Zaire, formerly Oriental or Eastern Province. The BMS earns the right to be classed as the pioneer in this area due to its founding of Yakusu in 1885, Yalema in 1905, Bundu in 1906, and Yalikima in 1912. The large Africa Inland Mission arrived on the scene in 1912 and founded its first station, Kasengu. It has fathered one of the largest Communities in Zaire. The following year the Heart of Africa Mission began its work in the province at Nala. The Norwegian Baptists founded Monga in 1920 and were closely followed by the American-based Assemblies of God (1921). Finally, the Immanuel Mission opened Nyakunde in 1926.

Although the Church Missionary Society did not arrive at Mboga in Upper Zaire Province until 1925, it was actually founded much earlier by a Ugandan named Apolon Kivebulaya. Sometime after his appointment as catechist in 1895, he felt the call of God to go evangelize the Pygmies in Congo. He came to the Ituri forest and labored there amidst hardships and sometimes violent persecution for thirty years. The Anglican Church named him a canon, and a monument at Mboga was raised to his memory after his death. The Belgian Colonial Government asked the Church to send a missionary to carry on his work, and thus it was that this Mission came to work in Zaire.

South of Upper Zaire Province lies the Kivu. Here we find, thousands of kilometers from his home in Kinshasa, the intrepid missionary and explorer, George Grenfell. In May, 1903, he arrived at Nyangwe where David Livingstone had lived for a while. He pressed on to the Hind rapids where his health forced him to return home. In 1910 C. E. Pugh and Henri Lambotte came to Waika and left a Congolese teacher named Bolamba. The following year the Reverend Whitehead and his wife began to work there.

The 1920s saw several new Missions begin their labors. The Free Mission of Sweden opened Matshimbi in 1921, and the Central Conference of the Methodists began Tunda in 1922. That same year three Missions founded stations: the Evangelization Society of Africa, the Free Norwegian, and the United Pentecostal of Great Britain and Ireland. The Unevangelized Africa Mission founded Kitsombiro and Katwa in 1928. Of these the Free Swedish Mission has become the largest denomination, with a total community of around 90,000.

Shaba and Kasai Mission Beginnings

The gigantic Province of Shaba (formerly Katanga) lies to the south of Kivu. We have described the pioneering work of the Garanganze Mission earlier. Bishop John Springer and his wife, who were formerly associated with the Bishop Taylor Mission which ended in failure, explored Katanga and ran across the nephew of King Mwata-Yamvo of the Lunda. This contact opened the way for the founding of Kapanga and Kambove in 1913. In 1914 work was begun in Elizabethville, known today as Lubumbashi. In this striking way the Methodist Mission began its ministry.

The Congo Evangelistic Mission founded Mwanza in 1915 and Ngoimani in 1917. The Seventh Day Adventists were not far behind with their stations of Songa (1921) and Katanga (1925). Others came later, but we must limit ourselves to these.

To the west of Shaba lies what is now called Eastern Kasai. We will deal with both Eastern and Western together in this section since they were one province before independence. The pioneer Mission in this province was the American Presbyterian (Southern), whose first

two missionaries, Lapsley and Sheppard, founded Luebo in 1891. In
order to take care of some legal affairs, Samuel Lapsley had to travel
all the way to Boma near the coast, which was at that time the capital
of the Congo Free State. He was stricken with a fever and died less
than a year after his arrival in Congo. Since he was an American
Black and since the Mission had the policy of engaging numbers of
Black and White missionaries, his passing made a profound
impression in the States and stirred up many new recruits to carry on
the task.

The Wescott brothers were co-founders of their Mission and
began work in the province in 1897 by opening a station at Inkongo.
Later, in 1910, they began work at Bakwa Mbula. We mentioned the
Congo Inland Mission earlier in connection with the Bandundu
Province. It began work in the Kasai in 1912 by opening two stations:
Kalamba and Djoka Punda, later named Charlesville. The
Methodists began their Central Mission at Wembo Nyama in 1914.[23]

The Belgian Protestant Contribution

The Protestant community in Belgium is but a tiny portion of the
total population. When Spain conquered the part of the Lowlands
that is now Belgium, most Protestants either escaped to Holland,
were killed, or were imprisoned. For this reason there has not been a
large outpouring of missionaries or money for the discipling of Zaire,
as was the case for the Roman Catholics who were backed by the
government. Belgian Protestants have, however, done some
significant work in the country, and this we shall briefly examine.

Henri Lamotte was the first Belgian Christian to serve in Congo.
He was called to this task in 1908 during the debates concerning the
acquiring of Congo by Belgium as a colony. He was not ordained,
being a skilled mechanic and builder. He arrived in Congo the
following year and was stationed for his entire career in and around
the British Baptist station of Yakusu in the Eastern Province. He was
ordained by British Baptists during a furlough in 1917 and began
itinerating for evangelism. During the year 1911 he was guide for
Henri Anet, delegate of the newly formed Belgian Protestant Mission
Society in the Congo, to survey possibilities for a Mission. He was
also guide for the BMS missionary C. H. Pugh into Kivu to Waika
station. His service ended with his death in 1918.

The Salvation Army in Zaire was a Belgian Protestant
enterprise. Its first open-air service in the capital in October, 1934,

was led by a young Belgian adjutant, Henri Becquet. He and his wife
were the guiding lights of this new endeavor for many years. Other
Belgians came to help, among whom were the Motts, the Leseres, and
the Bodus. In later years the staff became more internationalized with
English, Dutch, and Swiss officers sharing in the task. The Salvation
Army today includes a community of 27,000 with work in Kinshasa
(two divisions), Bas-Zaire (three divisions), Kisangani (Stanleyville),
and Lubumbashi (Elizabethville).

Belgian Protestants pioneered in the chaplaincies of the army
and the metropolitan base at Kamina. The former was composed of
Congolese troops commanded by Belgian officers, and the latter were
all Belgians, units of the Belgian Army. Three pioneers of the Army
Chaplaincy were Josué Honoré, Paul Hamelrijck, and Marc Hunt.
The chaplaincy came under Congo Protestant Council auspices and,
since Independence, has been completely staffed by Zairians from the
chief chaplain down.

Roger and Eveline Duquesne were called to be missionaries in
Congo and worked with the MEU for two years at Tandale (1954–
1956). However, their support was raised by a newly formed Belgian
Committee on Missions in Pagan Lands. This group determined to
open a truly Belgian field, and in 1956 the Duquesnes began work in
an area to the north of the MEU called Bamboma territory which had
not yet been reached with the gospel. Some time after Independence
in 1960, the Duquesnes left. Their work is today absorbed into the
Evangelical Free Church Community.

A final effort by Belgian Protestants in Congo was begun by a
group of men in Katanga, of whom one was a missionary (Edmond
Clemann). Their purpose was to form a church in Katanga for Blacks
and Whites that was completely autonomous, with no ties with any
Mission or denomination based abroad. Even at the late date of 1954,
this was a bold concept. They further decided to work both in urban
centers and in all the tribes of the province, to establish adequate
Bible courses in all public schools, and to ally themselves with
Protestant Missions to maintain and propagate the Protestant
interpretation of the Christian faith. Two pioneers in this program
were Edouard Pichal and Henri de Worm. In 1955 the Belgian
Evangelical Protestant Church adopted the Elizabethville Church as
a synod. The new venture soon found itself with three worship
centers. At one services were held in French, at another services were
held in Tshiluba for the Presbyterians from Kasai whose families did

not understand French, and at the third center was a fast-growing Church which wanted to practice believer's baptism only. After 1960 all the Belgians left and the new community was on its own. Their General Secretary, Pastor Kayumbe, told us of remarkable growth after this event. In 1960 there were 500 members. By 1961 the number had doubled to 1,000; in 1965, 3,000 members, 1968, 5,000 in five churches. Today he counts 22,000 full members in 16 churches and in addition has taken in 10,000 members from the Wescott Community in Kasai. We report his community (three times communicants) in our tables as 90,000.[24]

The Role of the Congo Protestant Council

Beginning with the very early years, missionaries of different denominations have sensed the need for fellowship with one another. In 1884 Dr. A. Sims of the ABFMS voyaged with George Grenfell, BMS, on the *Peace.* But these opportunities of working together were not available to the majority due to vast distances and the growing number of missionaries. Consequently, in 1902 a General Conference of Missions working in Congo was called. This took place January 18-21 in Leopoldville and brought together thirty-four missionaries representing seven societies. Under the leadership of George Grenfell, who was chosen president of the conference, several pertinent issues were discussed. Among them were education, native evangelists, polygamy and the Church, uniformity in translations, relations with the government, etc.

Albert Stonelake of the BMS proposed to the General Conference that, as a follow-through on the recommendations of the World Conference of Missions in Edinburg (1910), a permanent committee be chosen. Many felt that not much of substance had been accomplished since the 1902 meetings because there was no continuing committee. Due to his untiring work, the committee was launched in 1911.

The Congo Protestant Council (CPC) came into being in 1928 following the Jerusalem World Conference on World Mission that same year. Rev. Emory Ross of the DCCM was selected as first general secretary. The Secretariat was built on ABFMS property where the LIM's steamer, *The Henry Reed,* had been based. Mr. Ross was succeeded by Rev. H. Wakelin Coxill in 1933.

Mr. Coxill's service was especially valuable in relating Protestant Missions to the colonial government during the years after

World War II. This was one of the major reasons for having a general secretary: the availability of a permanent, knowledgeable representative of the Protestant Missions to the government. From 1948 to the present, subsidies have been given to Protestant schools, which make this liaison with the government of even more importance to the Missions.

In 1960 the CPC voted to put the responsibility for running the Council in the hands of Congolese, with missionaries playing the role of technicians. At the General Assembly in February of that year, Rev. Joel Bulaya was elected President and Rev. Pierre Shaumba as General Secretary, a post he held until 1968 when he was succeeded by Dr. Bokeleale. The CPC rendered great service to Missions and missionaries by providing an annual opportunity to meet, discuss mutual problems, and pray together. Through the Brussels Bureau, missionaries staying in Belgium were provided with orientation and times of fellowship. The sense of working together, though scattered geographically, was enhanced by the publication of the monthly review, *Congo Mission News.*

Two other vital ministries brought into being by CPC were the Evangelical Printing House and Book Store (CEDI) and the Union Mission Guest House (CAP). The guesthouse was built in 1920 to provide reasonably priced lodging for the scores of missionaries who came through the capital on their way inland or who had to come there for a short period of time on business. Six Missions collaborated in this effort, which continues to operate today. The Evangelical Publishing House began operations in one of the UMH buildings in 1935. Eleven years later, forty Missions and two Bible Societies engaged George Carpenter, an American Baptist missionary, to build a large, two-story structure next door to the UMH on BMS ground. This institution has served most of the Protestant Communities by providing Christian literature and school supplies.[25]

We shall see in chapter 4 how the present Church of Christ in Zaire (ECZ) grew out of the vital roots of the CPC. The latter prepared the way by bringing missionaries, and later Congolese church leaders, together on a regular basis. It would be fair to say that had there been no CPC, the ECZ would have taken much longer to form.

Summary

A glance back across the many years of discipling the peoples reveals tremendous growth, not only in numbers, but in goals and maturity. Several of the pioneer Missions had as a primary goal the establishment of a chain of mission stations across the heart of Africa which would halt the southward advance of Islam. The military solution had been already implemented when, as we saw earlier, the Congo Free State army dealt decisive defeats to the Arabs and the dervishes. This, however, was not enough. A spiritual solution was demanded, and this gave birth to that outpouring of energy and wealth which succeeded in erecting a spiritual barrier to Islam in the form of many strong mission stations.

A second goal was to penetrate into the interior of the country using the rivers as highways, then leave them and labor in the vast areas in between. This was also achieved after some years. Then it was that the goal of discipling the entire country, of making it thoroughly Christian, came to the fore. Missionaries and nationals labored faithfully on, often little realizing that the encouraging results they were experiencing were only a small part of an accelerating series of movements which were bringing thousands into new life and incorporation by baptism into congregations. From this vantage point we can see that this was in actuality the beginning of what we describe in the Introduction as Stage Three of Missions. There is a wide variation in dates for this stage since no two regions of Zaire are exactly the same in point of development. As a matter of fact, we cannot fix the beginnings and endings of any of the four stages by means of dates. We do have evidence, however, from an examination of the statistics that a significant number of Missions entered Stage Three in the thirty years following World War I. Kenneth Scott Latourette was so struck by what he found that he did some calculating and declared that the communicant membership of Protestants was increasing by an average of 40 percent per year and the number of Roman Catholics by about 30 percent per year.[26]

Another significant statistic is the rapid increase of the number of Mission Societies working in the Congo. When Belgium took over Congo as a colony in 1908, thirty years after the founding of the first station at Palabala, there were only nine Missions established. Between 1912 and 1920 nine more entered the country. During the decade of the twenties, thirteen were added, making a total of thirty-one. The rate of increase slowed considerably after that, and thirty years later in 1960 only eleven more had begun work.[27] A close look reveals that the acceleration of the number of Mission Societies coincides with the beginnings of the People Movements of Stage Three during the thirty years after World War I. These early People Movements were the fruit of the pioneering Missions' work. As new Missions entered the country and began their ministry, they entered into Stages One and Two. Their Stage Three came at differing times, but, in general, much later. Thus we see a continuing dramatic harvest after World War II which in some ways surpassed the earlier one.

An example of this can be seen in the growth history of the CBZO Community (ABFMS). After laboring seven years without one convert, Henry Richards of Banza Manteke station (Bas-Zaire) was led to preach on giving to anyone who asked (August, 1886). His putting this into practice following the sermon, when villagers asked and got nearly everything he owned, opened the door for the Holy Spirit to work in their hearts. In a few weeks, over one thousand people broke with their ancient religion and declared themselves believers in Christ. Over five thousand were baptized in the following year or two. Sona Bata, founded in 1890 among a subtribe of the same Kongo people, took much longer to reach Stage Three. Between 1920 and 1930 the yearly average number of baptisms varied between two and three thousand. Vanga, founded in 1913 in the Bandundu Province among other tribes, did not crest in its growth until the years after 1946, though encouraging, steady growth had occurred before then.

A statistical table showing growth across the years from the beginnings in 1878 until 1959 will be presented next. These figures, however, are only symbols of an inner reality. When asked if the Church of Christ in Congo was mature enough to administer itself and go forward under African leadership, Rev. R. V. DeCarle Thompson, the General Secretary of the CPC, replied by asking if the Church in Paul's day was ready for its testings of false doctrines from within and persecution from without. In spite of deserters and apostates, the early Church did survive and grow, and because of this we have the gospel today. Likewise we can have hope for the young Church of Congo since it has the same founder and inspirer as the early Church—the Holy Spirit—who is in charge of all, and who uses feeble things to confound the mighty since God's foolishness is wiser than our wisdom and God's weakness is stronger than all of our power.[28]

H. Anet, to whom we referred earlier, had this to say about the state of the Church on the eve of World War II:

> We have the conviction that now Evangelical Christianity is planted in Congo with such strong and deep roots that nothing can uproot it, neither political upheavals, nor the absence more or less prolonged of missionaries, nor violent persecution. In many regions the indigenous evangelical Church has become a reality, with its weaknesses and its lacks, doubtless, but with its own life and power of propagation.[29]

The optimistic convictions of both men have been amply justified by subsequent events. That story will be told in the following chapter. We now present a table which recapitulates the figures covering the period 1878–1959. In order to preserve its authentic flavor, we take the liberty of leaving it in French just as found on page 348 of Braekman's valuable book which we have been citing liberally throughout this chapter.

TABLE II

STATISTIQUES COMPAREES.
1907 to 1959

Années	1907([1])	1936([2])	1950([3])	1959([4])
Sociétés missionnaires	9	38	44	45
Stations	29	177	271	345
Missionnaires	181	808	1.699	2.608
dont Médecins et Dentistes	5	49	56	78
et dont Infirmières	—	62	166	225
Navires missionnaires	6	—	—	—
Membres d'Eglise adultes	25.000	240.478	567.061	821.025
Catéchumènes	25.000	180.000	275.028	345.473
Population protestante	100.000	638.000	2.000.000	2.500.000
Pasteurs consacrés	—	8	315	645
Pasteurs non-consacrés	—	200	487	11.200
Catéchistes	600	14.398	19.005	20.128
(Ecoles de Pasteurs)	1	5	?	?
Ecoles primaires	?	9.239	11.534	11.179
éleves	20.488	307.844	387.598	469.667
Ecoles de moniteurs	1	6	?	34
Ecoles professionnelles	1	?	5	16
éleves	30	?	90	872
Ecoles spéciales	—	—	96	?
éleves	—	—	2.790	?
Ecoles secondaires	—	—	8	10
éleves	—	—	411	1.228
Hôpitaux et dispensaires	27	72	171	186
Auxiliaires médicaux	—	453	1.097	655
Ecoles médicales	—	17	29	36
éleves	—	220	432	586
(Lazarets maladies du sommeil)	—	9	—	—
Léproseries	—	17	35	?
Lépreux	—	1.178	6.598	14.882
Consultations	—	1.272.208	5.611.688	7.281.027
Lits dans les Hôpitaux	—	1.575	6.544	7.717
Consultations de nourrissons	—	5.978	19.681	72.980
Consultations pré-natales	—	—	66.951	74.712

([1]) J. RAMBAUD, *Au Congo pour Christ*, p. 131. H. ANET, *En Eclaireur*, p. 192.
([2]) A. R. STONELAKE, *Congo past and present*, p. 157, 166 et addenda.
([3]) G. W. CARPENTER, *Les Chemins du Seigneur au Congo*, p. 94-95.
([4]) *C.M.N.*, No 191, p. 9 et 15, juillet-octobre 1960.

3

Church Growth in the
Midst of Revolution

Introduction

The years of 1960 to the present have been marked by turmoil and change. From a peaceful colony having a population with varied ethnic origins and customs, loosely held together by a benign yet efficient colonial regime, Zaire has become a modern nation with a growing sense of unity and purpose; this transition has taken eighteen years. These years have provided pressures intense enough to shorten greatly the process of learning how to organize and administer an independent nation. One heartening fact has remained through the stormy years: the ability on the part of the country's leadership to learn from mistakes and to seek more practical methods and more suitable models. Learning from mistakes has prevented the experiments necessary for growth to political and social maturity from becoming hardened into permanent policy and thus bringing on complete collapse. This was seen clearly in the government's reversing the extreme decisions pertaining to its quest for authenticity.

In order to understand the context in which the Communities have grown in this period, we shall present the political currents and social factors at work in Zaire. These are related and we shall describe this difference. Next we shall present the religious background for this fascinating period. This includes the effects of the social and political factors on the Missions and Communities, and the effects of the National Evangelism Campaign. We shall describe the formation of the "Eglise du Christ du Zaire" (ECZ) out of the Congo Protestant

73

Council. Finally, we shall present the growth factors at work among the Communities and attempt to analyse them. We shall give the growth patterns of several Communities and tell what happened in others during this period. After reading the chapter, the reader will have a much fuller picture of what has happened in Zaire since Independence—both inside and outside of the Communities.

Independence and Its Aftermath
1960–1963

Although from the viewpoint of the Belgian colonial regime and observers from outside the colony the events leading up to Independence came rather swiftly and unexpectedly, in reality, the fires of desire for self-determination had been burning with growing intensity for over a year. Secret meetings had brought about the formation of the ABAKO party under the direction of the Congolese mayor of one of Leopoldville's communes, Joseph Kasavubu. In the Stanleyville area, Patrice Lumumba's "Mouvement National Congolais" came into being. The Belgians had no sooner taken inventory of their first fifty years of rule and begun to plan for the next fifty, than the winds of change blew from across the Congo River where the French Congo Colony was moving toward self-determination. The underground movements mentioned above, as well as dozens of others formed almost overnight, began clamoring for complete independence. After several rounds of negotiations in Brussels, the momentous decision was made to grant complete independence with no strings attached. The date chosen for this event was June 30, 1960.

Congo was less than a week old when the uprising of army troops of the "Force Publique" and their noncommissioned officers at Thysville in Bas-Congo erupted. What had been an orderly transfer of power to President Kasavubu and his prime minister, Patrice Lumumba, turned into chaos. Bands of military units roamed the Bas-Congo region, attacking Belgian government staff in particular, but also harassing commercial people and stations of the Catholic Church. One Protestant station was attacked and this caused the American Embassy to urge strongly the immediate evacuation of United States' citizens. Other expatriates left the country also, so that by the end of July only skeleton missionary staffs were left in the larger cities where their protection could be assured.

The United Nations was called in to help after initial skirmishes between Belgian and Congolese troops. In the midst of the turmoil (July 11), Moise Tshombe, governor of the mineral-rich Katanga Province, announced his secession from the Central Government. Soon afterward Lumumba was deposed and sent to Katanga as a prisoner where he was later killed under mysterious circumstances. The Russian Embassy staff was ushered unceremoniously out of the country by a junior army officer named Joseph Mobutu. Tons of propaganda were found and plans for a Communist takeover uncovered.

In October, 1961, the Central Government, backed by the U.N., launched a military campaign to retake Katanga and put an end to its secession. This bitter campaign lasted until the opening months of 1963. Many hundreds of the Katanga troops took refuge in Angola, which they used as a sanctuary until their attempt to retake the province (now called Shaba).

During all this confusion and bloodshed, Vice-Premier Gizenga set up his own regime at Stanleyville (now Kisangani) and allied himself with socialist states around the world, especially those in North America. However, this attempt at secession came to an end without military intervention.

The Rebellion
1963–1965

As the U.N. troops were preparing to leave the country, a new danger appeared. Pierre Mulele, one of the leaders along with Gizenga of the "Partie Solidaire Africaine," slipped into the country from a period of training for revolution in Peking during the summer of 1963. He brought money, arms, and supplies to organize a secret movement to train rebel fighting forces of teenage boys in the eastern portion of the Kwilu Province (now part of the Bandundu Province). Refer to the map on page 18. The timetable carefully planned for the rebellion called for a simultaneous uprising in both western and eastern sections of the country. However, before the eastern part could be put into effect, the government uncovered Mulele's preparations in the west so that he was forced to begin fighting before the planned date. It took the government forces until June, 1964, to put an end to his activities in the Kwilu Province. As a result of this part of the rebellion, missionaries and Congolese were killed and several mission stations, many government buildings, and palm oil mills were burned.

The eastern part of the rebellion was better organized. Its participants were more like soldiers than guerrillas, were better trained and equipped than Mulele's youths, and had direct supply lines from outside the country. They captured Stanleyville and penetrated west into the northern half of the Equator Province. At Wasolo, near the northern border of the Central African Republic, Dr. Paul Carlson was captured. In the east the rebels drove from the Oriental Province (now Haut Zaire) down across Kivu into northern Shaba. Many missionaries (Protestant and Catholic) and hundreds of Congolese were killed. The rebels were determined to rid the country of foreigners and any Africans who had worked with them. Even some hospitals were destroyed in this effort. Had the simultaneous uprising occurred, as originally planned, the results might have been disastrous.

President Kasavubu called Moise Tshombe to become Prime Minister of the country, and he quickly recruited mercenaries in Europe. These battle-hardened men stiffened the National Army and soon the tide turned. Even more dramatic was the release of most of the prisoners held in Stanleyville, by a daring drop of Belgian parachutists.

Just before the end of the rebellion, an event occurred which has had a tremendous influence on the course the country has taken. On November 24, 1965, General Joseph Mobutu quietly deposed President Kasavubu and assumed the function of president. The army was dissatisfied with the efforts of the government to lead the country; so it backed this bloodless coup. This regime has been in power since then.

A final aftermath of the rebellion was the revolt of the mercenaries at Stanleyville. After holding the city for some weeks, they went east to Bukavu, which they held until their supplies ran out. Then they slipped across the border into Ruanda. Expatriates from many countries felt the backlash from this as the government strongly reacted to this attempt by foreigners to control its sovereign territory.

Authenticity
1971–1975

Another important cluster of events was related to the president's drive for authenticity which he launched in October, 1971. During a trip by river boat up the Congo River into the interior, he had a mystical experience which caused him to identify more closely with his ancestors and to rethink the mode of life he and his people had adopted from Western sources in the light of traditional culture. As he later defined his philosophy, which he called "authenticity," he did not conceive of a wholesale return to all the old ways but rather attempted to find the enduring values of traditional society without at the same time renouncing all that the Belgians and the missionaries had brought. The movement he launched included the renouncing of foreign first names and the adoption of authentic ones. The official currency had already been changed from francs to zaires in 1967. Now the country and the Congo River were also named Zaire. More authentic clothing was created and Western dress was discouraged.

The ban on baptismal names among other things aroused the Bishops Council of the Roman Catholic Church to protest. However, the president held firm to his position since the causes of the conflict were deeper and of longer duration than the authenticity issue. Rome had considered Congo, while it was a colony of Belgium, a missionary field; and then when it gained Independence and Cardinal Mulula was appointed, Rome considered it an integral part of its jurisdiction. The president was in effect fighting for freedom from this tight yoke. Protestants and Kimbanguists felt the backlash from the struggle as restrictions were placed on public meetings and a general anti-Church climate prevailed throughout the government. Sunday worship was displaced by political rallies in many places. Religious broadcasting and publications were banned.

The president's trip to China and North Korea in 1973 gave added impetus to the movement. He brought back ideas which were modeled after the tight socialistic structure he found there. In December, 1974, many edicts were made by the executive committee of the one political party, "Mouvement Populaire de la Revolution." Local party leaders were sure that by January, 1975, they would hold the keys to the sanctuaries and that the Christian Church would, in effect, be closed down. Although the government backed off from this extreme position, it did carry out all previous decisions. The administration of the schools was taken out of the hands of the Communities, and school buildings, equipment, and funds were taken over by the government. All businesses were nationalized, and foreign-owned ones were given to Zairians to run. As part of the move toward secularization of the State, Christmas and Easter were removed from the list of national holidays.

Early in 1976 there began a gradual reversal of most of these edicts. The anti-Church climate faded, and government officials began to be cordial and finally openly supportive. Eventually the schools were returned to the administration of the Communities in September, 1977. As encouraging as this is, there still remain problems to be worked out by the Communities because of the quest for authenticity.

Some positive results which have come out of the movement toward authenticity are a greater unity of the many tribes by realizing a common culture with African roots and a new awareness of nationhood, new expressions of self-determination, and a freedom to accept insights from the West and from the gospel without destroying their own unique heritage. Those who thought authenticity meant a wholesale return to the paganism of the past have begun to realize their mistake and to take a more moderate position. There seems to be an understanding and even appreciation for the balance and steadfastness the Church has given the country through the seventeen years of turmoil. The vital role of the gospel in rallying the country in the aftermath of the rebellion has been realized in the wake of the experimentation and change brought on by the quest for authenticity. It is a fair evaluation that today in Zaire the doors of opportunity have never been wider for the discipling of the nation.

Recent Military Conflicts
1976–1977

A final cluster of events is grouped around the war in Angola and the invasion of Shaba. In 1976 the uneasy truce between the three factions of Angola erupted in open warfare. The Portuguese government kept hands off since they had granted independence earlier. Russia and Cuba intervened in a massive way on the side of Dr. Neto and his MPLA movement. Zaire threw its lot with Roberto Holden and his FNLA group which had allied itself with UNITAS, the third faction. At the end of several months of conflict, the MPLA gained the upper hand. The cost of this unsuccessful campaign was a further drain on Zaire's resources, already strained by the recession mentioned in chapter 1. The Zairian government finally bowed to the inevitable and recognized Neto's regime.

On March 8, 1977, units composed of former Katanga militia who had been living in Angola since the war of secession and who were trained there and equipped by Cubans sifted across the loosely guarded border of Shaba Province and quickly seized several key towns: Kapanga, Sandoa, and Dilolo. The United States and some African countries sent supplies to help Zaire. Morocco sent troops. At first the invaders played the role of fellow tribesmen who had come to release the population from the yoke of the Central Government. Later, as the tide of battle turned and the expected uprising by the population to aid the invaders did not take place, they began to take harsh reprisals. They forced thousands of Zairians to retreat with them across into Angola. It is now very difficult for them to return to Shaba due to the government's act of closing the border.

This conflict was renewed in mid-May of 1978 when four thousand ex-Katangan troops seized Kolwezi, the center of the copper-mining fields. Over 150 foreigners were killed before the Belgian paratroopers could recapture the town and release over 2,000 others who were mostly mining technicians and their families. It is clear that the rebels have not given up hope. Although they did not receive wide backing by the populace, and could not hold Kolwezi, they have seriously drained the financial resources of the Central Government by provoking military action and by stopping production in the mines. The rebels declare that they will return again and again until their objective is gained. It is clear that, as we write this in the summer of 1978, the struggle for the mineral wealth of Zaire is not yet resolved.

It has been impossible in this brief review to portray the total effects of these tumultuous events. Many Zairians and expatriates have been killed, imprisoned, or driven from their homes. It is indeed amazing that the country has not only survived this period but also is moving ahead with courage.

Social Factors

Two factors which we have labeled "social" have been at work in Zaire since Independence: massive refugee movements and migrations to cities and towns. The former is linked to the political events listed in the previous section. The latter has to do with the dynamics at work around the world called "urbanization" which has pulled millions from rural villages and countrysides into urban centers.

Refugee Movements

Beginning in 1961 thousands of Angolans fled across the border into the Bas-Zaire Province of Zaire. They were fleeing the conflict between armed rebels and the Portuguese troops. They came at night and during storms seeking to escape the planes and troops wanting to destroy them. Many were separated from husbands, wives, and children. They were absolutely destitute, having nothing but the meager clothes they were wearing. Many Christians succeeeded in salvaging a Bible or hymnbook and, if nothing else, their church membership card. The United Nations' Commission on Refugees estimated that by 1965 the total refugee population was nearly half a million. It began a massive program of aid, assisted by Church World Service of the Protestants and Caritas of the Catholics. Missionaries and their equipment were released by their Churches to join the fight against death by starvation. Once this threat diminished, plans went into action to help the newcomers find land, obtain seeds and tools, and put in crops. So well was the program funded and administered that by 1965 most of it was phased out.

In 1975 thousands moved back across the border into Angola with hope and joy seeking to reestablish themselves in their newly independent homeland. Many pastors and catechists were among them, and soon they had formed their people into active congregations. However, the raging conflict which erupted in 1976 caused thousands to return again into Zaire, along with many others who had stayed in Angola the first time. It is estimated that the total is much lower this time, reaching 30,000 near Kimpese and 10,000 near the Cabinda enclave.

During the decade of the sixties, civil war broke out in the Sudan, which lies north of Zaire. The Arab, Muslim North, was seeking to stamp out rebellion by the Christian and animist South. Thousands of southerners streamed into Zaire and were cared for by the U.N. and church-related agencies.

During the Mulelist rebellion, thousands of Zairians fled into Uganda, Ruanda, Burundi, and Tanzania. Probably most of these have come home. Other refugees are bands of rebels chased across the border into Tanzania where they mount forays into Zaire from time to time. These mini-invasions became particularly intense during the unrest experienced in 1975 due to the changes going on as part of the authenticity quest.

These movements have greatly contributed to the uneasiness and turmoil of the past eighteen years in a measure and in ways we have not yet realized. However, the results have not all been negative. Zairians were very generous in making land obtainable to refugees and in giving them clothing and other needed items. It made Zairians realize that they were not the poorest people on earth and gave them the satisfaction of helping others less fortunate than they. The hard-working Angolans made a real contribution to the agricultural production in the Bas-Zaire.

Migration to Urban Centers

The pull of Kinshasa and other cities and towns had begun in the forties. In 1940 Kinshasa had a population of about 45,000. Ten years later it counted 190,000, and by Independence in 1960, the number had more than doubled to 400,000. It was not until after 1960, however, that large numbers of people were drawn from other provinces. Before this time the bulk of the migrants came from the Bas-Zaire Province. In chapter 8 we describe this phenomenon in other urban centers around the country. Needless to say, these migrations have had a profound influence on church growth, which we shall relate in a later section.

The Religious Background
Effects on Missions

The events described in the previous sections resulted in changes in the work of the Missions working in the country. For instance, all of them felt to varying degrees the pressure to hasten the process of turning over responsibility to Zairian leaders. Those that were well along in this process felt less repercussions than those who were slower. Most of those in the latter group had entered the country at a much later date and had not had the time to train leaders adequately. Differing views of devolution also played a role in the variation in progress. For one and all, the events leading up to and following Independence were a sort of final date beyond which Missions dared not wait. Those that did found themselves in difficulty, and some of the conflicts which subsequently erupted stemmed from this slowness.

Some Missions were closed down after the evacuation of 1960. Their missionaries left the country, and their boards or supporting congregations decided not to send them back. Such was the case with the Canadian Regular Baptist Mission working to the south of American Baptists and west of the Mennonite Brethren. One of its two stations decided to rejoin its founding Mission, the ABFMS, and the other joined the Mennonite Brethren. This case was repeated more than once across the vast land. The rebellion caused other

Missions to stop their work in Zaire. An example of this was the Congo Gospel Mission working to the east of the American Baptist field of Busala. The Mennonite Brethren still try to help the stations left there but find it difficult due to reduced staff.

During the sixties, the fusion of Missions with their Churches made several of the Independent Missions very uneasy. The crowning blow came when the ECZ was formed. The Independent Missions had not joined the CPC because of their convictions against such organizations, and they felt the government requirement to join the ECZ went too far. These Missions ceased functioning and left the country. The Deermore Mission to the southeast of the American Baptist field is a case in point, as is the Baptist Mid Missions based in Kikwit.

Effects on the Communities

Although Missions left, to our knowledge no Community has ceased to exist as a result of the events already discussed. Although many Communities suffered heavy losses of top leadership and of many key buildings, the Communities have all survived. Internal conflict caused loss in evangelistic effort but, on the other hand, new and vigorous Communities were born out of some of these conflicts, and a few conflicts have been resolved.

The influx of Angolan refugees brought numerical, qualitative, and organizational growth. Membership was increased significantly in the Alliance, American and British Baptist Communities in the Bas-Zaire Province and in Kinshasa. Angolan pastors and catechists began to serve in villages and areas where no Zairians were available. Their dedication and spiritual fervor lifted these congregations to new heights of living and witness. Although their departure caused numerical losses, congregations they served maintained much of the qualitative and organizational growth. Zairian Christians were challenged to step in and replace the Angolans.

Mass migrations to urban centers caused redistribution of the Christian population. What rural areas lost in leadership and members was partly regained in the cities and towns. Rural congregations were often pushed to new efforts at finding pockets of bypassed animists and to do more among the nominals.

Some Communities abandoned by their missionaries have not grown well or have lost ground. Others have grown in numbers and have remained strong internally.

This period has been one of sifting. Many Communities lost members during and after Independence. To some Christians the newfound freedom meant freedom from all control or responsibility. Later on, the authenticity quest caused others to fall away. However, many of these have returned to their congregations, and those members that remained steadfast have been greatly strengthened. During the restrictions placed on worship in 1975, lukewarm members in Kinshasa suddenly became active. They wanted to be counted with the faithful no matter what the cost. This explains why churches were packed and attendance exceeded past records. As a whole, one would have to say that the Communities have emerged from this period in better shape than when they entered it. There are exceptions to this, to be sure. Some weaknesses that are not mentioned here had nothing to do with the series of events which we have chronicled.

The National Evangelism Campaign

In 1966 the General Assembly of CPC voted to inaugurate a national campaign of evangelism entitled "Christ for All." The delegates did not realize the full impact this campaign would have on the nation. Rev. Willys Braun had the vision for a campaign which would help unify the Churches, would galvanize their congregations into action to heal the wounds caused by the rebellion (1963-1965), and would rally Christians around the central purpose of winning people to Christ. The following year at Bukavu the General Assembly voted to open a Department of Evangelism and Life of the Church and to call Rev. M. Makanzu as full-time director. Thereafter he and the Reverend Braun collaborated in a gigantic effort which made a lasting impact on the Churches and the nation.

A national committee was formed and later on provincial ones were formed to set the major plans for the campaign and carry them back to provinces, regions, and congregations. Some provincial committees continued on after the end of the campaign in 1969. Norman Riddle was personally associated with the committees in Bas-Zaire and Bandundu provinces, which continued to focus the attention of the Churches in those provinces on the Great Commission task of discipling the tribes.

A veritable flurry of activity spread across the nation. Christians were summoned from the shock of the rebellion to renewal and purposeful service. Many rallies were planned and executed. A series of top evangelists were brought from abroad. Howard Jones and Ralph Bell led off with a rally in a smaller stadium in Kinshasa, followed by meetings in several key congregations. Timothy Dzao of the Spiritual Food Church of Hong Kong was the evangelist the next year in several successful rallies across the city. Barry Reed, a Baptist from New Zealand, ministered to the people, particularly pastors and leaders. Finally, Ford Philpott and his team came for a giant rally in the huge soccer stadium in the heart of the city where over 75,000 assembled and hundreds came forward at the invitation. This climaxed a series of five three-day rallies in key locations around the city. On a smaller scale, this was repeated across the nation. Howard Jones led a rally in Bukavu during the CPC General Assembly meetings there in 1967 and brought powerful devotions daily.

Needless to say, the Eurican missionary societies and the missionary forces, both by large grants of actual cash and by giving time without stint, were an essential part of this national movement. Without the cooperation between the Missions and the Churches, nothing would have been accomplished.

Rev. M. Makanzu made two tours of the eastern and northeastern sections of the country as part of this campaign. In both tours over 10,500 decisions were made, most of which were for receiving Christ as Savior and Lord. Government officials gave their support to these rallies, often requiring the attendance of prisoners and school children. The Word of God was blessed as it was preached with power. The spiritual healing of a nation was begun.

The example set by Rev. Willys Braun and Rev. M. Makanzu was followed by several Churches. In the western portion of Zaire the first Church to appoint a full-time evangelism director was the Missionary Alliance (CEAZ). Soon afterwards the American Baptist-related Church (CBZO) opened a full department of evangelism with a Zairian director and several subdepartments, each staffed by teams of a missionary and a Zairian.

As we have indicated, the total impact of the campaign cannot be calculated, but what is known makes us realize that this was a providential leading by the Holy Spirit. In chapter 4 we shall show how this campaign contributed to the formation of the ECZ.

These, then, are the elements which make up the religious background to Church growth in the period of 1960–1977. With these in mind we are now ready to examine the Church-growth patterns which emerge during this period.

Church Growth in Revolution

We continue our quest for information showing what happened to the Communities in Zaire during the span of years under study. Several case studies illustrate what was happening across the nation. We use the communicant figures rather than those indicating total communities because they are sharper and firmer. In order to arrive at the community totals, readers should simply multiply by three. Our sources are *World Christian Handbook for 1968,* our own survey, and Howard Crowl's thesis written in 1975. Further details are presented in chapter 6.

A Case Study of the Entire Period

We have chosen the Vanga-Busala field as an example of the dynamics in effect throughout these troubled years. Since Norman Riddle worked in this field from 1955 to 1964 and made many subsequent visits there for retreats and institutes in the years following, we believe we have a grasp of the work in sufficient detail to enable us to use it as a model for this period.

We shall study Vanga and Busala together because for many years they were under one administration, are neighbors, and are in a common cultural context. They also present some interesting variations. Vanga works mainly with the Mbala and the Hungana tribes. Busala works mainly with the Yanzi, the Mputu, and the Ndinga tribes—all three of which are subgroupings of the Yanzi tribe. Vanga and Busala became so large to administrate that they were divided in 1960 mostly along tribal lines as shown above.

We turn now to examine the growth picture of the Vanga and Busala areas revealed by the baptismal and membership figures. These fluctuate wildly; but remember, they are for churches in the midst of revolution. They show living churches, violently assaulted by rebellion, mass migration, change of government, evacuation of missionaries, and similar factors, surviving and growing. The Western statistician, living in a peaceful regimented society, may be skeptical of such figures. Any given one may truly be in error, but the general picture is both true and commendable.

Vanga

1961	1964	1965	1966	1967	1969	1971	1977
29,287	41,351	39,304	47,183	37,507	31,144	42,009	45,391

A large gain of 12,064 in three years was followed by a drop of 2,047 the next year. One year later the total jumped 7,779. This large gain was followed in one year by a drop of 9,576, followed in turn by another drop of 6,360 in two years. This trend was reversed by a jump in two years of just under 9,000. Six years later the total had climbed only 3,382. We do not have figures for those intervening years between 1971 and 1977. It is possible they would reveal more ups and downs.

Busala

1961	1962	1963	1964	1965	1966
17,949	14,031	17,949	14,969	18,000	16,820

1967	1968	1969	1970	1971	1977
13,700	13,991	11,542	12,913	12,439	14,000

These figures show an even greater fluctuation from year to year. Totals for 1961 are identical to those of 1963. Those of 1962 are very close to the ones for 1964. Busala reached its peak of 18,000 one year before Vanga reached its peak. Busala's largest drops came in the same years as those of Vanga (1966–1967 and 1967–1969). The upturns came at Busala during the same years as the upturns at Vanga (1969–1971 and 1971–1977). The last years are veiled from us due to lack of statistics.

For the 17-year period Vanga had a net gain of 16,104. This looks rather respectable on first glance. However, when we see that total baptisms for the period were 44,306, we realize the gain should have been at least twice that, if not more.

Busala had a net loss of 3,949 if the figure of 17,949 is accepted for 1961. The present administration states that they had only 13,000 in 1961, which would give them a net gain of 1,000. Leaving aside the fate of these 4,949 who were on the rolls at the time of separation, the fact is that 26,953 people were baptized by the Busala congregations during this period. Here again we have a massive loss of baptized believers. How are we to account for this in both the Vanga and the Busala fields? Without pretending to have all the answers to this mystery, we can give several factors which will illuminate at least some of the darkness and which also illustrate dynamics paralleling those taking place in other Communities.

One salient factor to be considered, first of all, is loss due to death of members. We are dealing with a period of eighteen years, which is about one-third of the average life span in Zaire. A sizable portion of the members in the Vanga-Busala churches in 1960 were elderly and quite a few sickly. It is reasonable to assume that about one-third of these would have died during this period.

We have previously mentioned as factors contributing to loss and gain defections experienced during Independence and after, as well as those resulting from the authenticity movement and the subsequent move back into the congregations. Losses due to mass migrations to urban centers is another growth factor present all around the nation. Kinshasa was not the only city pulling rural people to itself. All the provincial capitals, as well as other urban centers, have grown at a furious pace.

It is notable that sometime in the late sixties or early seventies the people movements of the area under discussion came to completion. The number of children baptized each year rose to over one-half of the total baptized by the congregations. As this occurred, the migrations to the cities picked up steam and further losses occurred. As fewer and fewer winnable adults were found, the age for baptism was lowered considerably. Before Independence most of the children baptized were ten or over. Afterward the average dropped to about seven. Since children require much more teaching after baptism than do adults, losses are bound to occur. Other losses occur when they move to further their education or look for work.

Some factors involve statistics. The job of gathering and evaluating statistics was given to Zairians who did not understand the importance of the task nor did they do it efficiently. They were often weighed down with many other tasks. As Churches became autonomous, they set up guidelines for representation to their general assemblies. Usually these were based on one delegate for a certain number of members after a basic minimum number for all stations and centers. The tendency was to count all available members in order to have the maximum number of delegates. Then, as the realization came home that *contributions* to the headquarters of the Church and to the CPC were based on membership, the elderly and youth who do not contribute much financially were left out of the counting. This practice was widespread across the nation.

It is encouraging to note that both Vanga and Busala show steady growth from 1971 to 1976. One contributing cause could be that more young people are staying in the areas served by these two stations and are returning there from other areas to live and work. The heavy movement of Angolan refugees into Bas-Zaire Province made membership figures rise in CBZO congregations of Sona Mpangu, Sona Bata, Kimbaka, and Songololo centers. Conversely, when the refugees returned to Angola in 1975, some experienced sharp losses. The Songololo center numbered slightly over 2,000 members. After the departure of the Angolans, it counted only about 850. The Makala congregation in Kinshasa experienced a drop as well.

Preoccupation with perfecting denominational structure was not a large factor at Vanga and Busala partly because they were not headquarters for the Community. However, across the nation slower growth than was possible for many Communities was partly caused by this natural tendency, especially during the early years of Independence.

Similar studies made all over Zaire would give greatly increased understanding to the church-growth picture. We trust that this brief study has helped give precision to the period under study.

Communities Affected Adversely by Major Upheavals or Change

Quite a number of Communities show a slowing of growth or actual losses during the periods of turmoil. The Community founded by the African Inland Mission (CECA) shows the following pattern. Communicant members increased only slightly from 26,306 in 1960 to 30,306 in 1966. Since that time it has grown greatly to an estimated 250,000 in 1976. The years 1960–1966 cover the period of Independence and the rebellion.

The Conservative Baptist Community (MBK) during the same years suffered not only from the rebellion but from a sharp internal division. The ironical twist is that the break-off group is officially recognized by the government whereas the original Community is not. In our reporting we give only the statistics from the original Community as those from the break-off group were not available.[1] In 1960, MBK recorded 19,402 members but in 1966 only 7,678. However, during the comparatively stable period since then they have grown to 16,901.

The Pentecostal Community based in Bukavu in Kivu Province suffered greatly from the rebellion. In 1960 it counted 45,000 members but in 1966 only 23,966.

The Evangelical Covenant Community (CEUM) was hit by the rebellion in its northern section. In 1959 it had 12,000 members. In 1961 it had gone to 13,900 members and was in a period of very slow growth. Four years later, 1965, it had increased only 100, making a total of 14,000. However, people movements evidently got under way, because subsequent growth was very good. The figures and years are: 1969—22,600; 1973—34,000; 1975—44,700. An increase of 10,700 in just two years amounts to an explosion which cannot be accounted for by a one-by-one approach. Only the multi-individual decision of villages, lineages, and clans to leave the old ways and follow Christ could make possible this kind of reaping.

The Alliance Community in Bas-Zaire was far from the rebellion but was affected by movements to the cities and by refugees. It also suffered a deep conflict during the fifties, which was eventually healed, and it regained most of its former strength in its Mayombe base, with an addition of about 1,600 in Kinshasa and other urban centers in Bas-Zaire. Its figures are: 1942—30,716; 1954—40,000; 1962—9,412; 1976—30,716.

Another Community in Bas-Zaire which reflects movements of population is that founded by the SMF, called "Communauté Evangelique de Zaire" (CEZ). In 1960 it numbered 27,954 and in 1966 only 22,487.

Many other similar cases could be presented showing a slowdown of growth or actual losses during this crucial period. Most Communities show gains thereafter, though not all. As was noted in the preceding section, Vanga and Busala also show steady gains since 1971.

Communities Which Registered Significant Gains

Some Communities grew even though they were affected by the turmoil which surrounded them. One example of this is the Protestant Community of Shaba. We gave details for this Community in chapter 2. The Belgian missionaries left as a result of the upheavals accompanying Independence. Beginning with 500 members in 1960, the Community grew to 3,000 in 1965, 5,000 in 1968, and 22,000 in 1976. They not only survived the difficulties of Independence but also the war to end secession and the recent invasion from Angola. More than merely surviving, this Community grew at a rapid rate.

The American Mennonite Brethren were directly affected by the Mulelist segment of the rebellion in Kwilu Province south of Kikwit. Some stations were attacked, pastors killed or wounded, and general disruption shown. They counted 5,399 members in 1960 and 8,875 in 1966. This means that from its founding in 1920, it grew very slowly; yet in only six years which were marked by great upheaval, it increased over 3,400. In 1976 it numbered 17,000—nearly doubling in ten years.

The Southern Presbyterian Community (CPZa), working in West and East Kasai and based in Kananga, is an example of a Community which was fairly isolated from most of the turmoil. However, it has felt the pull to the cities as well as early fighting between the Lulua and the Luba. In 1960 it registered 69,509 members. Six years later it counted 144,000. The figures for 1977 were not available, but their headquarters accounted for 90,000 in 1976. Our impression was that this total did not represent loss so much as confusion in gathering statistics.

The Disciples of Christ Community (CDCZ), based at Mbandaka and covering a large area of Equator Province, is another example of great gain. It was also isolated from most of the currents mentioned, but some migration to Kinshasa and to Mbandaka has taken place. Between 1958 and 1968, 137,000 believers were baptized and added to the Church rolls. Of these, 10,000 were baptized in one six-month period. Here again, however, Community records for 1976 show an estimate of only 92,000 members.

Summary

At the close of Rev. M. Makanzu's report on the state of the Protestant Churches in Congo in 1968, given to the West African Congress on Evangelism at Ibadan, Nigeria, a delegate leaped to his feet with tears streaming down his cheeks. "We are amazed," he shouted, "to hear that the Church in Congo is still alive after all the trouble we have read about in the papers. We were sure that its life was choked out." A spontaneous response of praise followed as other delegates echoed his sentiments by thanking God for this mighty sign to the world and the Church of His keeping power.

Church growth occurred in the midst of the revolution and after the revolution. When the nation was shaken, the Church often appeared the most stable rock in sight. Even when terrible events caused losses, these were recouped in later years. Both national leaders and missionaries played important roles in this story of church growth in Zaire. The last eighteen years bode well for the next twenty.

4

"L'Eglise du Christ au Zaire"

Introduction

The Church of Christ in Zaire (ECZ or "Eglise du Christ au Zaire") is a very important factor in the church-growth picture in Zaire today and for the future. Zaire presents us with several "givens"; the ECZ is one of these. Whereas in other countries Missions and Churches decide whether or not their polity, theological stance, or some other considerations will permit them to form Councils or Federated Churches, in Zaire these questions have largely been settled. It is not possible for Missions working with Communities in Zaire to think and plan as though the ECZ did not exist.

Whatever the events which led to its formation and whatever the reasons for its founding (and these we will deal with later on in the chapter), the future of the ECZ is assured by the impelling fact that since the early seventies no Community has been able legally to exist apart from the umbrella of the ECZ, the Roman Catholic Church, or the Kimbanguist Church. There are exceptions to this law, but they must be regarded as exceptions. The thirty new Communities accepted into the ECZ in 1977 are examples of those which could not function outside a legal umbrella. This presents us with a unique situation in overseas Mission and merits our attention.

We shall describe how the ECZ grew out of the Congo Protestant Council. We shall then explain its shape—giving its description, size, and structure. Next we shall present its goals and its ministries—both actual and planned; and finally, we shall discuss its external and internal relations.

In order to write this chapter, we draw on Norman Riddle's years of experience working within the context of the CPC and ECZ. We use statements made by ECZ leaders in public addresses, private conversations, and in official publications—especially brochures by Rev. M. Makanzu and his co-workers in the Department of Evangelism and Life of the Church.

The Founding of ECZ
Its Roots

The ECZ did not appear abruptly on the Zairian scene in 1970 with no antecedents whatsoever. It was not a sudden inspiration of Zairians reacting to the era of Missions and unthinkingly throwing off "yokes imposed by missionaries." The Congo Protestant Council, its predecessor, originally conceived of and formed by missionaries, had accepted Zairian delegates in the fifties and had been totally autonomous and staffed by Zairians since 1960. The present General Secretary of the ECZ, Dr. I. Bokeleale, had already been General Secretary of the CPC since 1968. The present Director of the Department of Evangelism and Life of the Church, Rev. M. Makanzu, had been named co-founder of the Department in 1967 with Rev. Willys Braun. Organizationally, therefore, the ECZ evolved in 1970 from CPC with no break whatsoever in the functions of the staff, though a new constitution was written later.

A fine pattern of unity and cooperation between Missions and Churches in Zaire had been established through the years by CPC. This was the major reason for its founding, as we saw in chapter 2. Regional meetings in each province were encouraged. As a result, the Churches [1] working in Kinshasa met to discuss forming one Federated Church. This idea was finally abandoned, but the present Pastors' Council of Kinshasa was begun in its place as being more realistic in view of the stage of development at the time. Churches working in Bas-Zaire Province met often to discuss many issues of common concern in an effort to arrive at more uniformity of practice and agreement of thought. An initial gathering at Vanga in Bandundu was warmly received by the Churches which could attend, and other such meetings were scheduled. Unfortunately, distance prevented some Churches from sending observers, and the events preceding Independence prevented further action. As a result, many Churches began printing a common membership card with the title "Church of Christ in Congo" at the top and the name of the denomination underneath. Members of one Church could join a congregation in another locality on the strength of that card. No further requirements were added where the Churches involved practiced the same mode of baptism. The ECZ did not break with this practice.

The finest example of cooperation within the CPC was the "Christ for All" campaign which was accepted at the General Assembly of the CPC in 1966 and launched later that year. It was this campaign which highlighted the need for a department of evangelism staffed by Zairians. Never before had the Churches and Missions been challenged to such a nationwide task. It caught the imagination of a shattered constituency reeling under the blows of the rebellion (1963–1965) and gave inspiration and orientation to the Churches and Missions. Barriers of misunderstanding fell as men and women from various denominations and provinces worked together on the national and regional committees. This important task paved the way for the formation of ECZ in 1970. It was a living demonstration of the benefits of working together for a united purpose.

Reasons for Its Founding

As we shall see, one of the major goals of the ECZ is unity. As a result of years of hearing the gospel, of experiencing the unifying love of Christ, and of participating in the growing visible unity expressed by the CPC, Zairian Christians were able to transfer their strong feelings of solidarity within the tribe, clan, lineage, and family to the larger entity—the family of God, the Church of Jesus Christ. This was in turn strengthened by the government's increasingly determined effort to weld a unified nation out of the over three hundred tribes which live in Zaire. These factors taken together help explain why the delegates to the final General Assembly of the CPC voted for a United Church structure.

This cultural orientation to unity influenced what Zairians saw in Scripture. The New Testament model of the Early Church was more fully understood by them as a close unity than by those of us from Western fractured society. Its very name, the "Church of Jesus Christ," indicates to them the imperative of closer and more visible unity. In addition, they had not experienced the historical causes of denominational divisions, and they could not accept these as normative for themselves. Though they recognized differences in polity and doctrine, still these did not form for them the often insuperable barriers to unity that they often do for Western Christians.

Another factor pressuring for closer unity was the desire for a more centralized administration. This was especially true of the leaders of the CPC just prior to 1970. They felt that centralization allowed greater implementation of directives and guidelines proposed by the Secretariat and voted on by the General Assembly. As a matter of fact, the CPC had been increasingly operating as a United Church rather than a Council all during the decade of the sixties. Thus, the ecclesiastical development with which the delegates were familiar strongly influenced them to accept the United Church concept.

A final strong impulse toward closer structure was the fact that Missions and Churches had of necessity been fused during the sixties. Whereas a few Missions from the beginning chose the path of merging with their newly formed Churches, the majority opted for a policy which they had followed around the world—a dichotomy in which Mission and Church became separated yet equal. The Mission retained its legal standing with the government and applied for legal standing for its Church. However, the government steadfastly refused to grant legal standing for the Churches, insisting instead that the Missions cede their legal standing to their Churches and cease to exist. By the end of the sixties this process was nearly completed. In the minds of many Zairians, the merging of the many Churches of the Council into a United Church of Christ was a logical outcome of the fusion of Mission and Church.

In our view, the formation of a Council or a United Church is a good thing. Whereas we advocate strongly in this book the discipling of homogeneous units of whatever composition out to their limits, we do not thereby advocate anarchy at the regional or national level. The unity of the Body is clearly shown here and that unity is the more real as the Churches composing the Council or United Church are strong. The Churches experience true unity insomuch as the local and regional congregations and associations so often tribal in nature are truly discipled. Only vital, healthy Communities working voluntarily together within the framework of a Council or a United Church can produce the evangelistic thrust needed to complete Stage Four of Mission in Zaire. There is, therefore, no contradiction between the idea of energetically multiplying congregations among tribal groupings and the gathering of Churches formed by them into a

National Council or United Church or in some countries a Federation of Churches for the purpose of fellowship and of undertaking together the larger tasks of discipling the nation and sending missionaries abroad. We clearly recognize the difficulties faced in forming the ECZ from the CPC. Power has become more centralized and Communities have reported abuses of it. We do not condone misuse of power when it, in fact, occurs, but, on the other hand, we do not feel that the ECZ should be dismantled—even if this were possible. Rather we favor, as do most of the Communities involved, a clear analysis of the problems encountered on the part of Communities and a concerted effort to modify structures where necessary.

The Shape of the ECZ
Description

The ECZ is a United Church, but not a monolithic Church. A true monolithic Church has never existed except in people's imagination. The early Church was never a monolithic Church, nor is the Roman Catholic Church today. The ECZ is, therefore, a federation of eighty-three Communities. Many of these have denominational connections through Missions to overseas Churches. The names of the Missions which existed before 1970 reflect the wide variety of polity and theology which go to make up the Church of Christ in Zaire.

Each Community is autonomous, having its own legal standing with the government, its own elected leadership, its own constitution, polity, doctrines, and programs. The Secretariat of the ECZ does not attempt to meddle in the internal affairs of the Communities, with one noticeable exception. It reserves the right to intervene in the case of conflict within a Community or between Communities whether invited in as a mediator or not. To our knowledge, all reported misuses of power by the ECZ have been concerned with the application of this principle.

In view of the great stress placed by President Mobutu on peace and harmony in the country in the wake of many tribal disputes and conflicts between political parties, why the ECZ is very uneasy when conflicts erupt between its members is understandable. It feels directly responsible for maintaining harmony at any cost in order to prevent direct governmental intervention. In fact, the CPC and the ECZ reported the settling of sixty-six conflicts within or between member Communities since 1960. Some of these were of such magnitude that the army and the police were called in to support various factions, creating tremendous tensions in the country. This in no way excuses misuse of authority, but it does give the context in which the ECZ is operating.

We are aware that government regulation of religion has historically been the cause of persecutions and oppressions beyond number. The separation of Church and State should be complete. Yet the Church has to operate under many regimes: totalitarian, Communist, anti-Christian, anti-Protestant, as well as just and fair governments which protect equally all the religions and leave all internal matters to the Churches themselves. Consequently, we take the position that Churches and Missions in Zaire should heartily support the government, while constantly working toward an abundant measure of religious freedom.

Although the ECZ is completely autonomous and is staffed largely by Zairians, it has always sought missionary and Eurican Christians to work within its framework, as did its predecessor, CPC. These do not assume the responsibilities of directing departments but, rather, take supporting roles where their special skills can be utilized for the advance of the gospel and growth of the Church. There are at present nine Christians from Europe and America working at the ECZ Secretariat.

Size

In 1975 the ECZ counted a total Protestant community of five and one-half million. It recognized 11,220 local congregations, 2,538 ordained pastors, and 7,784 pastors with at least a Bible School training. It reported 1,117 missionaries working with the Communities. This is under half of the pre-Independence total, which estimated 2,600 missionaries, but is still a significant number.

Structure

According to leaders of the ECZ, the basic unit of the Church of Christ is the local congregation. Accordingly, much emphasis has been placed in the last year on developing local congregations. If they are strong, Communities and the ECZ are strong; if weak, then Communities and the ECZ are weak. An evil government could close down the ECZ and the Community headquarters fairly easily. It would, however, have a much harder time with the thousands of local congregations, which are often divided again into smaller units, such as prayer groups, home Bible study groups, and other subdivisions. Local congregations form Communities which in turn compose the ECZ. The Secretariat of the ECZ provides for a General Secretary who presides over three departments. The accounting and finance operations do not form a separate department but are the direct responsibility of the General Secretary. The three departments are Evangelism and Life of the Church, Diaconate, and Christian Education. This latter department replaced the supervision of general education when the government took over responsibility for schools. With return of the administration of schools two years later, the Education Department was reconstituted and the Department of Christian Education merged with Evangelism. The National Executive Committee, composed of presidents of eight synods, meets between sessions of the General Assembly or National Synod and deals with matters which the National Synod has delegated to it or which cannot wait until the next session of the National Synod.

Ministries of the ECZ
Goals

Goals of any organization reveal what it would like its ministries to be. Progress toward achieving these goals is never uniform, often varying widely with each goal. Some are achieved more readily than others which take far more effort and time to fulfill. Such is the case concerning the goals set by the ECZ. These should be understood as ideals toward which it and the Communities are striving.

The first goal proposed is to disciple every tribe (ethnos) in Zaire (Matthew 28:19). Rev. M. Makanzu takes this very seriously in his ministry. The second major goal is unity between Zairian Christians, between Zairian and missionary workers, and between the Communities of the ECZ. A third major goal is to seek a Zairian expression of the Christian faith under the leadership of the Holy Spirit and acceptance of the Bible's authority. This is not syncretism but a Zairian approach to worship and to patterns of living that are authentically scriptural and Zairian. The quest for authenticity covers forms of worship, theological vocabulary, methods of evangelizing Bantu peoples, ceremonies of dedication of babies, marriages, baptism, and the Lord's Supper. Music and the use of instruments are other ways of authentic Zairian expression. Western forms of worship are studied and appreciated, but not copied.

The goal for authenticity is summed up by the ECZ slogan: "Return to the Bible for an authentic Christianity." It gives a positive Christian content to the national push for authenticity.

The ECZ regards the spiritual deepening of Christian youth in secondary schools, universities, and theological schools and seminaries as a very important goal. Along with this is the desire to find ways of reaching the intellectuals of the country with the gospel and to discover valid contributions to the nation in the economic, social, intellectual, and moral areas of life.

The area of stewardship is of vital importance to the true maturity of the Church of Jesus Christ, according to the ECZ. Therefore, it has placed high value on teaching the members their responsibility and the privilege of supporting the Church with their money, time, and skills. A thorough program needs to be implemented and passed on to the Communities.

Ministries

The Department of Christian Education in its short life of two years has sought to provide materials and training for the leaders of the Communities in this field of service. It has collected many samples of Sunday school courses of study from other areas of Africa, as well as those printed in Zairian languages. It attempts to educate the Communities to understand the importance of Christian Education planning, programs, and training.

The Department of the Diaconate has as its goal the providing of expert advice on service and self-support projects which the Communities want to launch. For example, a Community needs a gas pump at one of its stations or centers. The Department will study the proposal with the leaders of the Community and will give all the requirements necessary for the installation and sound operation of the pump. The Department helps the Community sort out its goals for each project and sometimes advises against certain projects as not being feasible.

The Department of the Diaconate also seeks to educate the Communities on ways of serving people in the name of Christ. We feel that this area could be strengthened to advantage since the main interest of the Communities at present seems to be how to create financial resources apart from the offerings of their members.

The Department of Evangelism and Life of the Church has many ministries. The Division of Evangelism leads campaigns in the city of

Kinshasa as well as in other cities where it is invited. At the time of this writing a national campaign is in process of being launched. Through the Pastors' Council of Kinshasa it leads in a continuous tent ministry. Child evangelism, retreats for pastors of the city, distribution of materials for evangelism, counseling, visitation, formation of prayer groups, and the creation of model congregations in areas where Communities are not working are other kinds of ministry. Of particular note are the seminars for evangelists. One such seminar was held in October, 1976, at the Nganda Retreat Center for coordinators of evangelism from Communities throughout the country.

The Division of Evangelism would like to create other ministries. Some of these are: an evangelism choir for Kinshasa and one for the nation; teams of traveling evangelists for boats, trains, and airlines; lay evangelism teams; teams to evangelize factories; and the development of audiovisual aids. If funds and full-time leaders were available, much more could be done. True maturity will be shown by the ECZ when it allocates money from its own funds to carry out these worthy ministries.

The Division of the Life of the Church carries on several important ministries. It maintains a service for the reconciliation of conflicts and provides counseling for local congregations of the city. Refresher courses and in-service training are offered to the pastors of Kinshasa. Information about the ECZ and materials orienting the Communities in ministry are prepared and distributed. A theological commission studies various key issues for which the Communities need solutions. Publication of theological and general Christian literature is another ministry of this Division. Finally, chaplains are provided through the Kinshasa Synod for hospitals and prisons, the university campus, and the army.

The Division looks forward in anticipation to creating other ministries it regards as necessary for the full-orbed development of the Communities and their congregations. Some of these are: preparing and distributing cassettes containing sermons, lectures, translation of existing books, lessons, and other materials in local languages; development of authentic hymns and church music; pioneering in small discussion groups; and the revision of existing translations of the Bible. Whereas the Bible Society gives direction and counsel in the translation and revision of the Bible, it puts the responsibility for the recruiting of translation teams and for doing the work on the Communities. Since all major languages are used by more than one Community, the ECZ sees the guiding of this work as one of its ministries.

Of special interest to us is the proposal to send out missionaries. This is the only program which would practice E-2 evangelism, that is, the discipling of people of another language and tribe within the country, or E-3, the discipling of another tribe and culture outside the country. An example of E-2 evangelism is a person from the Luba tribe going to the Azande in the north, learning their language, proclaiming the gospel, and multiplying churches. An example of E-3 evangelism is a person from the Mbala tribe going to disciple the Pygmies or a Zairian going to another African country, Asia, England, or any other country in the world. This emphasis is greatly needed not only within the ECZ Secretariat but also in the programs of all the Communities. Present programs of evangelism of the ECZ are almost entirely in E-0 and E-1 categories. E-0 renews Christians from one's own Community, tribe, and language. E-1 happens when people from the same tribe and language group, but not Protestants, are evangelized. Evangelistic rallies in cities, though they seek to disciple people of various tribes are examples of E-0 and E-1. They are carried out in a trade language and on neutral ground—the city. But were Mayombe evangelists in Kinshasa to learn Lonkundu and multiply congregations there which worship in that language, they would be carrying on E-2 evangelism.

Zairian Christians supported by their Communities should consider the possibility of serving as missionaries in Europe and America. There are millions of undiscipled people in both places who need the gospel. Zairian missionaries would not go primarily to serve Euricans, but to preach, teach, evangelize, and disciple them. Zairian Baptist pastors who spent a year in the United States communicated the gospel effectively in private conversations and in public meetings. The field to be considered by the ECZ and its Communities when thinking of where to send Zairian missionaries is the entire world, just as it is for Churches in any land.

A section dealing with communications, news, and information is directly attached to the General Secretary. The government has granted permission for the Roman Catholics, Protestants, and Kimbanguists to broadcast programs over the radio and TV. A full-time pastor will no doubt be appointed to take charge of these programs so that they can be made meaningful and effective.

External Relations

In its dealings with the Zairian government, the ECZ seeks to cooperate as much as possible with its programs of social uplift and economic development. On the other hand, it has been able to speak in a strongly prophetic fashion to the government when led to do so. Knowing just when and how to protest takes great skill since the line dividing prudent silence or protest in private to the government and a strong public protest is very fine. The ECZ has not been able to please all of its constituency all the time by its relations with the government. It is in a difficult position between a strong, nationalistic government and Communities who wish to be faithful to their consciences.

In order to preserve its internal unity, the ECZ voted to follow the example set by the CPC in not aligning with either the World Council of Churches or the Evangelical World Alliance. Individual Communities are free to choose with which body to affiliate. This policy has kept Zaire Communities from division along lines which separate denominations in other countries. Thus the ECZ makes it possible for all the Communities to be unified in many national programs, such as the "Christ for All" evangelism campaign.

Internal Relations

No human organization is free of fault: the ECZ is no exception. Individual Communities often differ widely from its official stance. Some are members only because they see no possible alternative. They participate hardly at all in programs emanating from the ECZ Secretariat. The ECZ needs to be specially concerned about these dissenting Communities. Rather than just defend or explain its own point of view, it should seek to understand the truth imbedded in what they are saying. Other Communities are active in ECZ affairs while still recognizing its faults and failures. They believe that it has a valid role to play in leadership and fellowship and that it can be corrected from within. They choose which programs they wish to support, leaving the others aside. Both of these approaches are possible within the structure of the ECZ.

Summary

Understanding the role of the ECZ gives the reader a better picture of the state of the Church in Zaire. In no other nation have the denominations been so unified. Granted the pressures from without and tensions within, a new thing has been done in the work of the kingdom. We pray that its potential for good might be developed to the full as it learns from past failures and grows into Christ who is head of the whole Church, which is his Body.

The generous sharing of financial resources and of dedicated Christians with the ECZ and its Communities by the overseas Churches, which has marked the planting and nurture of Christianity in this country from the beginning until now, will continue. Genuine autonomy carries with it the privilege of accepting help offered in Christian love and concern and is certainly not diminished by such acceptance. The realization of this fact has allowed the ECZ to take a strong stand against moratorium as moving in a contrary direction to the spirit of love and mutuality experienced in the gospel.

The Missions and Communities working together within the framework of the ECZ have found that much more can be done in this spirit of cooperation than separately. The African manner of seeking a true consensus, rather than forcing the will of a majority on a helpless minority, has proven its worth and will prove it again in coming years.

PART II
Today and Tomorrow

5

"Everybody Is
a Christian"

During the four years, 1966–1969, Norman Riddle called on thousands of families in Kinshasa and asked them to what religion they belonged. Almost everyone claimed to be Roman Catholic or Protestant. A few claimed to be Kimbanguist. It would be easy to conclude that in Kinshasa today "everyone is a Christian"; but what would that mean? And would it hold for all Zaire?

Validation of Statistics

In this chapter we attempt to give an accurate statistical picture of the religious affiliations of the 25.6 million persons living in Zaire in 1976 ("1976 World Population Data Sheet").

Four Qualifications

Our conclusions as to the number of Christians in Zaire were formed and must be read with four qualifications in mind. First, since Independence, 1960, the nation has been through many upheavals. Keeping accurate records of members and churches has been greatly hindered. Often pastors and their fellow Christians were hiding in the forest. In 1964–1965 rebels burned many records. Systems of transportation broke down. It is surprising that we found as many educated estimates and solid facts as we did. That there were any at all speaks well for the strength of Churches and Missions during a very trying period.

Second, during the same period, Missions were transferring leadership to Churches. Record keeping at the district level was new to most pastors. The purpose for keeping accurate membership records was often misunderstood. Other things seemed more important to the ongoing of the Church. Naturally, the accuracy of the records suffered.

Third, in times of turmoil, annual reports often do not reach headquarters. When congregations, associations, or synods failed to send in figures at the appointed time, the person at headquarters in charge of gathering statistics had to repeat the figures given for the preceding year. As we perused denominational tables, we found that this had happened quite often. However, these annual variations do not invalidate the general trend. Statistical errors of one year are corrected in later years. The general trend is substantially reliable.

Unevenness in the time of writing down the figures is the fourth factor we had to take into account as we constructed the following tables and graphs. As we toured Zaire, we obtained statistics of one group of denominations for 1975–1976. For others we had to rely on 1974–1975 figures. For still others, all we could get were the figures in the *1968 World Christian Handbook*. Often these were really the figures for 1966 or even earlier. Reasonable 1976 figures had to be deduced from the earlier ones.

Sources Used

We relied on United Nations' or Zairian government figures for the population of regions and the country as a whole. Here also we had to be on guard. Often the comparison had to be made between government figures for an earlier date and church statistics for a later one. In the Roman Catholic year book, *Annuaire de l'Eglise Catholique au Zaire, 1974–1975,* the population figures are from the 1970 census, whereas church figures are for the years cited. The opposite also has been found. Church figures from an earlier year have to be compared with later government figures. There has been a further hindrance in forming an accurate picture of the proportion of the population which at various times has been Christian. Until statistics are refined and corrected, they often present an erroneous picture. Much of our work, therefore, was in checking and cross-checking figures until the truth emerged. The goal was a true, reasonable picture of the whole Zairian nation.

Procedures Followed

That this has never been attempted before in the way in which we have gone about it, and that each denomination is usually content to compile its own figures and to stop there, has made compiling the national figures both difficult and fascinating. For each region we would have liked to present Roman Catholic figures alongside Protestant ones, but this was impossible. Catholic ecclesiastical provinces and dioceses do not coincide either with governmental administrative divisions or with the Protestant jurisdictions. For example, British Baptists are spread through parts of three ecclesiastical provinces and several dioceses. Other Protestant denominations also are working in these same regions. Therefore, a one-to-one comparison is not possible. However, since the size of the Roman Catholic and Protestant Communities is a matter of some interest, we have made great efforts to discover what the ratio of one to the other is. In some regions where the facts could be ascertained, we found that Roman Catholics outnumber Protestants four to one. In others, Protestants form a majority of the population. For the country as a whole, we estimate that there are 2.4 Catholics for every Protestant. Consequently, it would be well to assume that in most areas if there are 100,000 Protestants, there will be 240,000 Roman Catholics.

The percentage of Roman Catholics to the total population of Zaire is of interest also. The official Catholic year book for 1974/75 gave a total of 9,900,000 Catholics. If the total population at that time is taken to be 24,000,000 (it was 24.5 million in 1975, according to the "World Population Data Sheet") then Roman Catholics composed 41.2 percent of the total population. We used this guide to arrive at their present total strength based on latest population figures, 25.6 million. The Catholic Diocesan Authorities for 1966 counted Catholics as 39.9 percent of the total. A comparison of the two percentage figures indicates growth in the Catholic Church's percentage of the total population.

As we traced the figures given us by the authorities and by leaders of the Communities we visited, and as we refined them in the direction of realism and accuracy, following the guidelines suggested by the previous paragraphs, we arrived at figures and proportions which we believe are substantially correct. We have done everything possible to give these conclusions a factual base.

We present our conclusions in the tables and graphs at the end of this chapter. When we first began to glimpse the totals, we felt our numbers were too large. We did not expect so many Christians. But the facts demanded the figures we present. Church persons (nationals and missionaries) working continually to help their people become real Christians of necessity hold up a high standard. We ourselves do the same. We have talked to village people who, without knowing much about what it meant, asked for baptism or spoke favorably of the Christian religion. We are not among those who are easily deceived by such light assertions into thinking that such persons are fully discipled Christians. And yet, the Christian Community (defined as those who, vaguely perhaps, think of themselves as Christians) is very much larger than those who are practicing Christians.

On the other hand, it may be felt that our figures are too small, too conservative. The growth of the Church ought to keep pace with the skyrocketing general population. Certainly great growth of the population is taking place. According to the "1976 World Population Data Sheet," the population is doubling every twenty-five years. Consequently, Churches may expect that the number of those who call themselves Christians will automatically double every twenty-five years. The difficulty here is that we Protestants believe that only those are *really* Christians who, generation by generation, consciously accept Jesus Christ as Lord and Savior and the Bible as their sole rule of faith and practice. We Protestants do not believe that anyone is a "born Christian." Nevertheless, those who are born into Protestant families certainly think of themselves as Protestants; and they are doubling every twenty-five years. Our numbers may be too small. Like all Protestants, the 1977 Survey Team was inclined to count as Christians only practicing Christians. However, we tried to resist the inclination. We deliberately tried to count as Christians all those who were, or at one time had been, bona fide Christians and their minor unbaptized children and dependents. However, we did keep to the reality of what was reported to us from the various sources, even though we now believe them to be generally too conservative.

Explanation of Figures on Community

A more precise word as to the communicant and community figures will further help our understanding. In our tables we list communicants—full members or baptized believers in good standing. We also list community. Communicant numbers are the principle figures kept by many Missions and Churches. They are hard figures, carefully weighed and recorded. When through the decades, Missions and Churches reported Christian *community,* however, their soft figures varied enormously. Sometimes they reported as Christian community exactly the same number as baptized believers. Sometimes community was reported as *six times greater.* Roman Catholics report only total community, never communicants.

As one compares Christians with the total population of the country, one must not list communicants (adults) only. To do that would be to compare incomparables. It is strictly impermissible to compare selected adults (communicants) with the total population consisting of everybody—good and bad, young and old, infants and adults. In an effort to treat all Communities equally and to give the true picture, we have, therefore, assumed that the total Christian community *of any denomination* was three times the size of its body of communicants. In Table I, we have, therefore, multiplied all communicant figures given us by three. Then in order to be entirely open, we have added after our figures in parenthesis the *community* figure reported by some of the Communities. For Roman Catholics we divided their figures—which always show total Christian community—by three to obtain the number of their communicants. Christian Community, in our definition, includes the following six kinds of people, in addition to practicing Christians in good standing:

a. the unbaptized children of practicing Christians,
b. those who were once practicing Christians but are not now,
c. the minor unbaptized children of *b,*
d. those who live in largely Christian villages, are related to Christians, and attend worship on occasion,
e. those under discipline and out of the church (and their minor children),
f. those Christians who have moved to the city and have not joined churches there (and their minor children).

When Christian community is defined in this way, we are confident that today in Africa in general and in Zaire in particular, it does number three times the communicants. Several reasons require our using the figure three. Of these, the first is the enormous number of children. De St. Moulin states that there were 10,671,000 adults and 10,966,002 children in 1970.[1] Though he does not give the age at which persons are counted adults, we presume he has eighteen in mind.

Another reason for multiplying by three is that, due to the upheavals experienced since 1960, the population is scattered. Migration to the cities has displaced thousands. A large majority of those moving to the cities are not on any church rolls. In many cases they are baptized believers. They and their children ought to be counted as part of the Protestant community.

Still another reason is that many thousands of church members were displaced during the rebellions of 1963–1965. Some were killed. Others died of starvation. Many did not return to their home villages. However, today, only twelve years later, most of the displaced regard themselves as Christians. Thousands of others count themselves as Christians even though they cannot be baptized because of a polygamous marriage or for other reasons. They worship and give their gifts but cannot get on the church rolls. Often the number of people attending worship services exceeds the number of baptized believers. In view of all these considerations, we felt it reasonable to multiply the number of communicants by three.

The Size of the Protestant Community

While Protestant denominations have been moving forward each in its own area, no one has produced a really authoritative total figure for all Protestants. In 1976 the ECZ did make an estimate of five and one-half million Protestants. It may be that its figure is more correct than ours. However, we arrived at our figure after the most careful examination of each claim, and extensive cross-checking. We have decided that 4,474,137 is in the near neighborhood of what really exists—give or take a half million. Table III (following) gives details.

In Table III we have grouped the denominations according to the year their statistics were obtained. This will help in understanding the status of the statistics of each denomination. Readers who possess later figures will forgive us for using the earlier ones. They were all we could get.

Recent Additions to ECZ from the Independents

In September, 1977, ECZ admitted into full membership thirty Communities. A few of these had split off from existing Communities. In order to bring harmony into the nationwide picture, especially since the government is very anxious for harmony in all sectors of society, ECZ voted them in as members. A few others are duplicates

TABLE III

DENOMINATIONS IN THE PROTESTANT FOLD

Group One
Denominations whose community figures for 1976 were obtained by interview:

Name	Community Total
1. Christian and Missionary Alliance	100,000
2. British Baptist (Haut, Moyen, Bas-Fleuve)	150,000
3. American Baptist (CBZO)	340,000
4. Southern Presbyterian (CPZa Kasai)	200,000
5. Mennonite (CMZ, old CIM)	100,000
6. Methodist (Shaba and East Kasai Conferences)	210,000
7. Protestant Church of Shaba (Old Eprokat)	90,000
8. Africa Inland Mission (CEGA)	750,000
9. Evangelical Free, Mission Covenant, Ubangi Mongala (MEU)	175,000
10. Disciples of Christ (CDCZ)*	600,000
11. American Mennonite Brethren (CFMZ)	51,000
12. Salvation Army	27,000
13. Seventh Day Adventists (CEASJ)	150,000
14. Assembly of God—U.S.A. (CADZ)	80,000
Group Total	3,023,000

* In the *1969 Year Book and Directory of the Christian Church (Disciples of Christ)* on page 127, it is reported that the membership in the Christian Churches in the Democratic Republic of the Congo (Zaire) was 229,856 baptized believers in good standing in the churches of that body. Because of the turmoil in that province and the complete withdrawal of missionaries from all the stations except Mbandaka, and in view of the fact that when we visited Mbandaka we were told that the membership of that Community was only 91,000 (the 1956 figure given out by the UCMS in Indianapolis was 96,000), we have listed the Disciples Community at only 600,000 rather than 689,568.

Group Two
Denominations whose community figures were obtained from Howard Crowl's Research.[2]

Name	Community Total	Their Estimate
1. Free Norwegian Church (CELZ)	20,100	(16,070)
2. Free Swedish Church (Pentecostal, CEP)	89,331	(139,624)

3. Baptist Church of Kivu (MBK)
   (Conservative Baptist—U.S.A.)   50,700   (73,624)
4. African Christian Church (CECA)   30,000
                           Group Total   190,131

Group Three

Denominations whose figures (in parentheses) we took from the *1968 World Christian Handbook*, pp. 64, 65. To get community figures comparable to those of Groups One and Two, we took the communicant figures from the *Handbook* and multiplied by three.

Name	Our Community	WCH Community Total
1. Assembly of God—G.B. (CADEZA)	40,368	(30,000)
2. Anglican Church in Zaire (CAZ)	100,353	(23,000)
3. Swedish Baptist—Maindombe (CBB)	58,506	(45,000)
4. Evangelical Church of Bulonga (CAEEL)	100,000	(69,000)
5. Evangelical Church of Manianga-Matadi (CEZ)	67,461	(49,922)
6. Evangelical Church of Bas-Uele (CBBU)	48,000	(30,000)
7. Evangelical Church of Upper Zaire (CEHZ)	39,000	(25,000)
8. Free Methodist Church of East Congo (CLMZ)	29,094	(18,600)
9. Pentecostal Church of Zaire (Shaba, CEPS)	140,163	(65,000)
10. Evangelization Society of Africa	21,378	(17,000)
11. Brethren in Christ Garanganze (CFCG)	45,000	
12. Heart of Africa Church (CECCA)	19,500	(22,000)
13. Evangelical Church of Maniema (CLMK)	68,322	(65,000)
14. Presbyterian (Southern) of Kinshasa (CPK)	15,000	
15. Evangelical Berean Church (CEBZ)	15,000	
16. Other smaller denominations	53,574	(31,000)

17. The list is not complete. Three Communities did not report; seven are not listed. We propose taking the figure of 4,000 as the average for community for these ten small denominations.

These multiplied by 10 become	40,000	
1968 Group Total	900,719	
Plus 40 percent Growth in Ten Years	360,287*	
Probable 1976 Group Total	1,261,006	
Grand Total Protestant Community	4,474,137	

(*)The total of 900,719 is in reality the 1966 figure printed in the *1968 World Christian Handbook*. What is the 1976 total? The general population in those years increased by 40 percent. The Church has increased proportionately. We, therefore, add 40 percent of 900,719, or 360,287, to indicate the true 1976 figure.

of member Communities, but are unknown to the latter. For instance, one is a second, newly admitted Seventh Day Adventist Community of which the original SDA denomination knows nothing. Most of the thirty are prophetic-type Churches which for one reason or another want to get under the umbrella of the ECZ. It might be helpful to point out again that the Zairian government recognizes only Roman Catholic, Protestant (ECZ), and Kimbanguist Churches. Only these can operate schools, own property, hold worship services, and in general operate as Churches. A strict application of this law has not been made in regard to worship and church buildings, but in regard to operating schools, it has held firm. Many Protestant leaders in Kinshasa think this is the reason these small Churches wanted to join the ECZ. The Kimbanguist Church[3] had already refused them. The government has made special concession to Jews, Muslims and Greek Orthodox who are allowed to worship and own buildings in Zaire.

We have no firm data on the size of these new Communities. Estimates range from "small" to "large." The ECZ will begin to make inquiry in the near future no doubt.

The Independent Churches

Dr. David Barrett wrote, "In 1958 [The Kimbanguist Church] claimed 196,998 members, though observers estimated 60,000."[4] In 1968 a Catholic estimate gave the Kimbanguists, together with all other independent Churches, only 1.1 percent of the population (186,000) but admitted that this was probably low. Dr. Barrett estimated that in 1966 the Kimbanguists alone numbered 200,000 members and over one-half million community.[5] Today the Kimbanguist Church claims two million! We feel justified, therefore, in calculating communicants in the Independent Churches in 1975–1976 as 250,000. This gives them a total community of 750,000. They may be larger.

Many small denominations, most of which number members in the hundreds only, remain outside the three official Churches. However, when classed according to religious type, they belong with the Kimbanguists under the category of Independent Churches. They possess the same antipathy to close ties to Western Missions. We, therefore, include them in the Independent Churches' total of 750,000.

The Population of Zaire by Religious Groupings

In light of the foregoing material, we propose that the clearest picture of the religious situations in Zaire today can be obtained by dividing the population into the following six categories: Roman Catholic, Protestant, Independent Churches, Marginal Christians, Practicing Animists, and Muslims. Let us look at the first three.

Name	Communicants	Community
Roman Catholic	3,515,734	10,547,200
Protestant	1,491,379	4,474,137
Independent	250,000	750,000
Total Churched Christian Community		15,771,337

This is 61.6 percent of the total population.

We divide the remaining segment of the population of Zaire into three portions: Marginal Christians, Practicing Animists, and Muslims.

"Marginal Christians" well describes the nature of the first group. It is composed of people who are not counted by Roman Catholics or Protestants as part of their Churches. Independents, on the other hand, may well get their large figures (Kimbanguists—two million in 1976) by including many Marginal Christians, since these by their own confession are neither Animists nor Muslims. Marginals announce themselves as "Christians." Most do not attend worship services. They are on the margin of the Christian community, often appearing to be Animists. However, because of their own choice they should not be classed as Animists, but as Christians—Marginal Christians.

David Barrett describes this phenomenon in Kenya. He calls this group the "nominal fringe":

... the nominal fringe in Kenya—the 1.26 million nominal Catholics and 200,000 "nominal" Anglicans and Protestants—cannot properly be described as nominal at all: They are intending Christians who have already made some sort of break with pagan society, who have already decided "Ni Mkristo," and who have already begun the long process of moving into the churches. The fact that it may take them up to ten years before baptism is probably less their fault than that of the churches, whose ponderous machinery of initiation cannot let in fast enough those who ask for instruction and baptism.[6]

We cannot draw exact parallels between the situation in Kenya and in Zaire. For one thing, the size of the two Christian communities is substantially different (six million in Kenya and sixteen million in Zaire). In Kenya whole tribes, such as the Turkana and Maasai, have strenuously resisted the gospel. In Zaire there are no such tribes. Even the Azande are 50 percent evangelized. Nevertheless, like Kenya, Zaire has millions who have little relationship to the Churches and yet think of themselves as Christians. They cannot, therefore, be catagorized as Practicing Animists: we call them Marginal Christians.

The next segment of the population we are classifying according to religious belief is the Practicing Animists. We calculate that there are 2.5 million of these people. They are found chiefly in rural areas far from mission stations. Some live in cities and practice their faith secretly. They are not reproducing themselves, though their beliefs form part of the substructure of the mind of very large numbers of citizens—including those who are counted as members of the Church.

In 1972 Dr. Barrett estimated that there were 2,164,000 of them. Practicing Animists for the most part live in what we call the "Dark Areas" where the discipling process is not yet completed. An illustration of such an area is that of Kindi-Mosambo, adjacent to the Boko field of the American Baptists (CBZO). In 1969 a team of two missionaries, the local pastor, and two top leaders from Kinshasa—the General Secretary and the Supervising Pastor for the city churches—made an exploratory trip into the area. They found a complete absence of chapels and of any knowledge of Christian worship, much less any practice of it. The entire population of those villages knew nothing of Christian hymns or prayer. They were, in fact, Practicing Animists. And yet, in spite of this, they manifested a hunger and willingness to hear and to learn. In three years, 3,500 have become baptized members of the Church.

The last segment of the population we are classifying according to religious beliefs is the Muslim. Barrett and others in "Frontier Situations for Evangelization" estimate them at 1.7 percent of the population in 1972.[7] If this proportion has been maintained, they now number 435,000. They live mostly along the eastern edges of the nation.

In tabular form we can see these last three segments of the population:

Name	Communicants	Community
Marginal Christians	nil	6,893,337
Practicing Animists	nil	2,500,000
Muslims	nil	435,000

The Population of Zaire by Religious Affiliation

We are now ready to examine the population of Zaire as a whole. The following graphs depict the situation.

First, we look at Graph 1, "Comparison of Christians to Non-Christians." When we count Marginal Christians in with Christians, an amazing picture leaps out at us. Zaire appears 88.5 percent Christian. We must caution readers to understand the graph. They must remember that if we count Marginals as Christians (Dr. Barrett calls them "intending Christians," which we think is a little strong), the contrast of the present situation with that which obtained a hundred years ago is striking. Zaire has become a Christian country. When we realize the very large number of Americans, Englishmen, and Swedes who are very slightly connected with any Church, and the other large numbers of these populations who specifically disavow any Christian faith at all, and when we recall that these three nations are often called Christian countries, it does not seem extreme to say that Zaire is now a Christian country.

Second, we look at Graph 2, "The Population of Zaire by Religious Groupings." At a glance we can see the proportion of the total population which falls in each of the six categories. Readers should remember that it would be quite possible for honest persons to arrive at slightly different proportions. However, slightly different proportions would not materially affect the overall impressions which Graph 2 conveys. *Something of this magnitude,* we believe, truly represents the religious situation in this great nation in the heart of Africa. We trust that Christians will give it prayerful consideration.

How Christian Is Each Tribe and Each Homogeneous Unit?

The field totals for each denomination for Zaire as a whole tell us something, but they are very thin figures. No one faces the task of Christianizing Zaire as a whole. The task of each denomination and congregation is Christianizing particular units—this section of the

GRAPH 1

COMPARISON OF CHRISTIANS TO NON-CHRISTIANS

REPUBLIC OF ZAIRE
(1975–76)

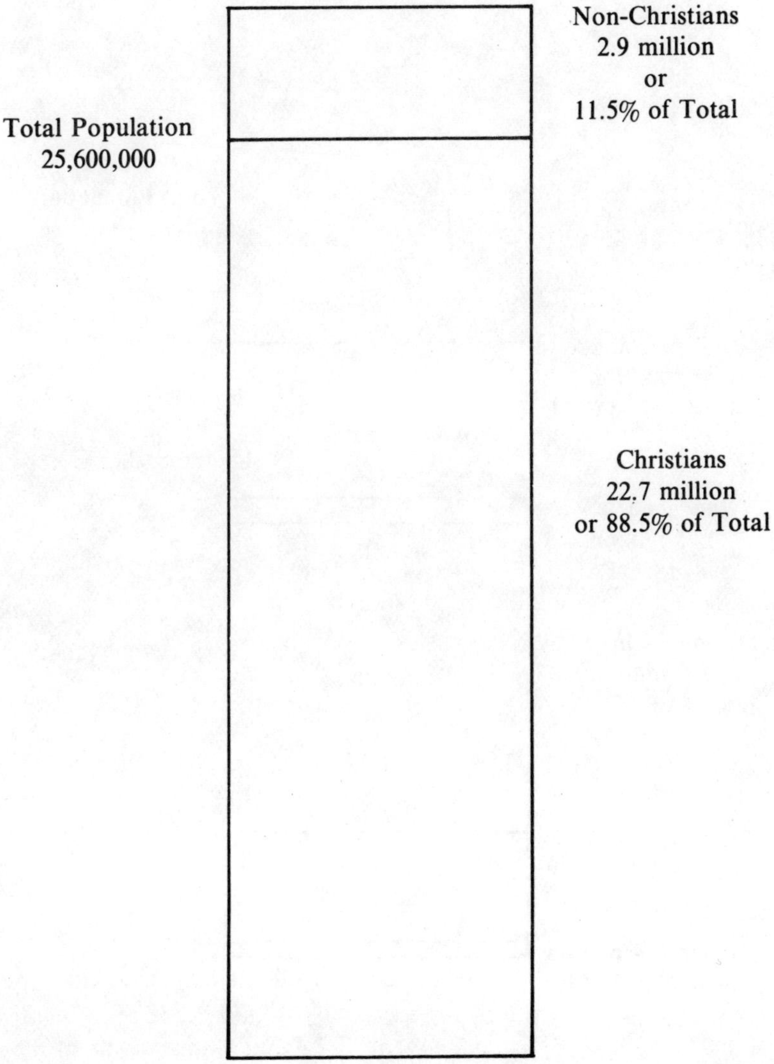

Total Population
25,600,000

Non-Christians
2.9 million
or
11.5% of Total

Christians
22.7 million
or 88.5% of Total

GRAPH 2

THE POPULATION OF ZAIRE BY RELIGIOUS GROUPINGS

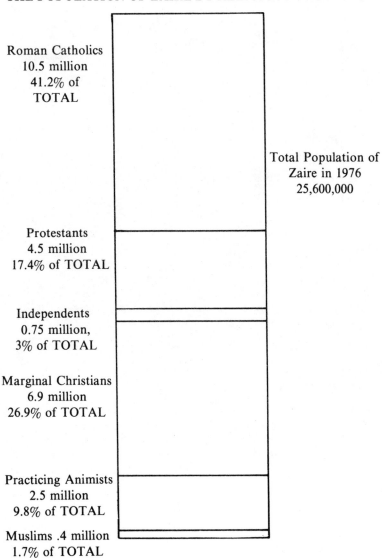

Roman Catholics
10.5 million
41.2% of
TOTAL

Total Population of
Zaire in 1976
25,600,000

Protestants
4.5 million
17.4% of TOTAL

Independents
0.75 million,
3% of TOTAL

Marginal Christians
6.9 million
26.9% of TOTAL

Practicing Animists
2.5 million
9.8% of TOTAL

Muslims .4 million
1.7% of TOTAL

Mayombe tribe, that cluster of villages of the Azande, this Mongo ward of Kinshasa or Lubumbashi, or other specific pieces of the tribal mosaic. So we go on to ask, *How Christian is each tribe and each homogeneous unit?* Zaire has more than three hundred tribes and thousands of homogeneous units.

CBZO leaders need to know, for instance, not merely that they have a total community of 340,000. That for them is almost an irresponsible figure. They need to know every tribe and subtribe (homogeneous units) in their field, the area occupied by each, and the degree to which each is Christian. This very valuable information will enable them to plan their program for the next half century to the best advantage. In imagination one can see hanging on the wall of the CBZO headquarters office, where the General Secretary for the whole Community works, a large map portraying in different colors the fifteen or more tribes and subtribes in which CBZO labors. Every homogeneous unit would have a graph of growth from 1950 to the current year, showing the number of communicants in each year. Every homogeneous unit would also have a bar graph showing the total population, and what part of it was Baptist, Roman Catholic, Kimbanguist, or Practicing Animist. At a glance, the General Secretary could see the exact task remaining to be done.

The degree to which each is Christian will *begin* to be known when the number of Baptists and other Communities, their rates of growth, and the size of the remaining pagan reservoirs are perceived. But Christianization is a much richer reality than physical size. How many congregations are there? How many schools? How self-supporting is the entire enterprise? How deep is the consciousness of being Spirit-filled Christians? What proportion of the adults read, love, and obey the Bible? How many homes have regular family devotions? How adequate is the training of village pastors? Is public worship regularly attended? How many missionaries does this section of the Church send out per ten thousand members? All of these are measurable entities and ought to be measured for each homogeneous unit and tribe in all of Zaire.

A noticeable factor affecting Christianization is the variation within a given segment of society. Near the old mission stations and in centers of population, Christianization tends to be advanced. The best-trained pastors live there. The mission hospital is there. The secondary school is there. The highly educated staff comes from that area and has relatives and land in nearby villages. Maximum impact of the Christian faith has occurred there. But across the river, back in the swamps, fifty miles down the road, that same tribe is much less Christian. The villages "back there" generally have less able leaders, school tends to be sketchy, and the proportion of Marginal Christians rises. Animistic practices continue or creep back into segments which were at one time reasonably Christian.

All this means that the degree to which each homogeneous unit is Christian must be understood, not only tribe by tribe, but area by area. The Dark Areas, to which we call attention in this volume, are extreme instances of populations which have yet to be Christianized.

Sometimes populations have become Christian in areas where only one denomination has worked. There has been no cross-fertilization from other denominations, no competition, no example of better and more devoted Christian life. If such isolated populations are neglected, the standard of Christian faith tends to be low. At one of our regional conferences where Zairian and missionary leaders gathered to lay before us the facts concerning their Community, we were told that where Protestants and Roman Catholics have worked in the same territory and the Roman Catholics have been stimulated by the Protestants, there Animistic survivals are rare. But where the Roman Catholic villages have been far from Protestant labors, so much Animism has come over into the Catholic community that it is hard to call it really Christian. We surmise that the same thing could be said for blocks of Protestant congregations which have not been cross-fertilized and have been neglected. Each piece of the vast mosaic which is Zaire constitutes a special project in Christianization. Christianization proceeds at a different pace in each; and to guide the whole enterprise correctly, the state of Christianization in each piece needs constantly to be measured and known.

Everyone Is a Christian . . . and Population Densities

As we view the population densities on the following map (reproduced by kind permission from *Atlas des Collectivités du Zaire*), we realize immediately that where the people are, there the strength of the Missions and the Churches has been concentrated. Where population is light, there Christianization tends to be slight. Observe the light density for the country as a whole. Zaire is 895,000 square miles in extent, which means that in 1976 each square mile had an average of twenty-nine people living on it; but in fact, nine-tenths of the square miles have far fewer living on them. For a nation in which there are no deserts and no snow-covered tundras, this scanty population is remarkable.

Note that if densities of twenty persons per square kilometer and above were all to be represented by solid black and densities of nineteen and below by solid white, Zaire would be a vast expanse of white with only a few small black areas!!

Observe further that while a few Communities operate in the black areas, most operate in white. Consequently the common problem of most Missions and Communities is how to supervise and connect congregations, conferences, synods, mission stations, and church headquarters which are relatively far apart. Most interior communication in 1920 was by river steamer. As roads were developed, river communication declined somewhat in importance. As roads have deteriorated in the last twenty years, river communication is coming back into more importance.

The degree to which "everyone is a Christian" and the tasks of further Christianization must be seen against the physical problems of reaching isolated areas. A significant part of the task faced by Missions and Communities is keeping in operation a system of communication which enables them to function. If the oil fields in the Atlantic off the western tip of Zaire do in fact develop, if the roads of Zaire are built back up, and if the ferries across the rivers are maintained in effective operation, motor transport is clearly one way of tying the far-flung parts of each Community together. (Air travel will grow increasingly expensive and be reserved for the top echelons of the Church and Mission.) If motor transport does not improve rapidly, then some kind of decentralization will be desirable which establishes centers, all parts of which can be reached by a long day's walk. Extensive use of bicycles (and oxen, and possibly horses or donkeys as animal husbandry develops) would seem to be indicated.

In view of the extremely light population and the extensive swamps, grassy savannas, and jungles between villages, the task of keeping everyone Christian must be carried out in other ways than those used in densely populated Europe and America.

MAP 5

DENSITY OF THE POPULATION OF ZAIRE: 1970

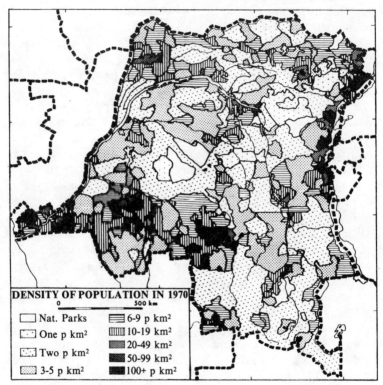

DENSITY OF POPULATION IN 1970

0   500 km

☐ Nat. Parks   6-9 p km²
☐ One p km²   10-19 km²
                          20-49 km²
☐ Two p km²   50-99 km²
☐ 3-5 p km²   100+ p km²

Atlas des Collectivités du Zaire (front cover)

6

A Thoroughly Christian
Parochial School System

The Church faced a tremendous opportunity and challenge in September, 1977, as the schools formerly administered by the Churches (which were then and are now about 95 percent of all schools) came back into its hands. The size of the challenge lies in two factors.

The first factor is the tremendous number of children. Children fourteen years of age and younger make up 44 percent of the total population of 25,600,000. In 1976 Zaire had 11,220,000 children. More than half of these—about six million—were six to fourteen, that is, of school age. The school system in Zaire must provide eight years of schooling for six million children, train and employ teachers sufficient for such a task (say 200,000 teachers), and maintain school buildings enough to house the six million. If, remembering the sparse population of so much of Zaire, we assume an average enrollment per school of three hundred, twenty thousand school buildings are required. Every pupil needs books, paper, pencils, and slates. Without a corps of some thousands of inspectors and supervisors, quality declines.

In the past, Missions and Churches have supplied top level supervision with their missionaries, experienced pastors, and Zairian directors. The Roman Catholics may currently be able to provide this, for they have maintained large numbers of Brothers, Sisters, and priests from overseas. So will those Protestant Missions which have maintained their missionary force.

The second factor which makes the educational challenge

unique and tremendous is the fact that Churches are now responsible for practically the entire enterprise. If schools are run, the Churches will run them. If the Churches and Missions provide poor education, that is what the children will get.

Something else must be said. If a given Church and Mission does not run its schools properly, does not build buildings which are needed, does not train sufficient teachers, does not supervise with enough diligence, does not give solid education which allows graduates to do well in higher schools, does not provide the needed books, government will hand those schools over to neighboring denominations which, with the aid of their assisting Missions, will do the job. This is not being said. We heard this in none of our conferences, but if some Community steadily fails at educating the children in its villages, government is not likely to wink at the failure.

It is unrealistic to suppose that some genial arrangement will be worked out between the Communities so that the educational load will be carried by the Methodists, let us say, in Presbyterian villages where the Presbyterians are steadily failing to provide schools, *and the rising generation will continue to be Presbyterians.* Those who provide the schools and pay for them will claim the people as their own. A Community too weak or indifferent to educate its own youth will forfeit its right to the allegiance of the next generation.

Not only does the Overseas Church, therefore, face unparalleled opportunity in Zaire, but each individual Mission and Church, each Community, faces both a tremendous opportunity and a considerable danger.

Children Should Grow Up Christian

The six million children in Zaire should grow up Christians. The issue of religious liberty—as between Hindus, Marxists, Buddhists, Jews, and Christians—is almost nonexistent in Zaire. Most of the six million school age children already consider themselves Christians. So do their parents. Most parents want the child instructed in the Christian faith. The public wants children to grow up Christian. This is a most unusual situation. It is not found in most nations. It *is* found in Zaire, and Churches and Missions there should rise to the challenge.

The numerous school plants greatly assist the successful accomplishment of this purpose. Most schools rose on church grounds. The main church building was used for school purposes and still is today. On land immediately adjacent to the church and owned by it are the classrooms and administrative offices of the school establishment.

Indeed, it may be said that the Church is the school. In the early days, but for the devoted services of educational missionaries, the teachers they trained, the buildings they built, the books they produced, and the funds they brought in from outside, there would have been no school system. When later, government began giving grants for buildings and paying the salaries of the teachers, had it not been for the missionaries and supervising pastors, the tremendous educational system would never have prospered. During the fifty years between 1910 and 1960 a remarkable training program was maintained. First, teachers were developed, then headmasters and headmistresses, and then supervisors of districts. Finally, African clergy became top authorities in the parochial school system. With the revolution and self-government, missionary supervisors were replaced by Zairian supervisors. All of these latter, of course, were on salaries paid by government.

When in the 1940s teachers' salaries began to be paid by government, headmasters, supervisors, and teachers alike tended to say, "We are now no longer church employees." The whole system became somewhat secularized. With the government takeover in 1975, it became thoroughly secularized. A "Thoroughly Christian Parochial School System"—which is the theme of this chapter— cannot be established with a staff which thinks of itself as separate from the Church. The self-image must be that of a truly churchly system. This is not in any sense to impugn the conviction of ordinary Christians. It does, however, record our experience that when parochial schools are managed outside of and apart from the Church, they become increasingly secular. This might be expected. No group of men and women in any land has a greater understanding of the Christian faith, a greater commitment to it, and a greater passion to see it incarnated in the lives of others than the ordained ministers of the Church. If control is vested in any other group, Christian quality declines. We believe that authentic parochial school education must be part of the parish and ultimately under the control of the Church.

Government Pays the Bills

In September, 1977, government handed the school system back to the Churches with the understanding that government was to pay the salaries and other expenses of the schools, while the Church was to provide the direction and control of the whole process. The national leaders of the Churches, both Protestant and Catholic, insisted that before they took the schools back, they must have the right to get rid of teachers who were not agreeable to their church rules. This was written into the contract. The Roman Catholic schools served notice to some good Protestant teachers that their services would no longer be required. Protestant schools notified teachers whose moral life was a scandal that their services would be terminated.

Instruction in the Evangelical or Catholic faith can be given on the school premises and during school hours. If they demand it, Roman Catholic pupils will be excused from attending Protestant instruction and Protestants from attending Roman Catholic instruction. It has been widely charged that in the old days Protestants who attended Catholic schools were not given graduation certificates until they had been baptized in the Roman Catholic Church. This violation of freedom of conscience has now been prohibited by law and, in the post-Vatican II climate, may not be an issue in the future.

The Missionary Educationist

The missionary educationist has been a prominent and essential part of the parochial school system—both Roman Catholic and Protestant. Brothers and Sisters, single women missionaries, and missionary principals, in very considerable numbers, have created the vast system of education now in operation.

As young Churches rose all around the world, they absorbed the time and energies of well over half of all missionaries. The educational work of most Missions consumed the largest part of the budget. Missionaries who went on to master's and doctor's degrees were for the most part those in educational work. Principals of high schools and colleges were prominent figures and had a great deal of influence in both Mission and Church.

Without the missionary educationists, women as well as men, the parochial school system in most countries could neither have been born nor prospered. This is particularly true in Zaire where there was no competing governmental system of public schools. In 1977, some of our informants were inclined to think that the prominent part which education had played had led some Churches to depend quite largely on the school for converts. The normal way in which people became Christians was to go to school. If one did not go to school, he or she did not become a Christian. The Church was chiefly the school at worship. All this was an oversimplification, but uncomfortably close to the truth.

After 1960 the role of the *missionary* educationist decreased in importance. This seemed natural for Zairians who were giving full time to teaching, had had special training in education, and as headmasters had administered schools for years to become principals and administrators. The process occurred all over the world and was entirely normal.

What was not fully realized, however, as a Zairian principal said to us in one of our conferences, was that the missionary educationists were not only unusually dedicated persons and much more tied to the Church than most teachers, but they were also *free* labor. Missionary educationists cost the parochial school system nothing. Their salaries were provided by funds from overseas. When missionary educationists stepped out of the picture, the school system lost a valuable resource. For instance, when the eight missionary educationists in the DCCM were sent back to the United States as no longer needed, that parochial school system lost its free labor. The Zairian principal had to be paid for by Zairian money.

As the tremendous burden of the parochial school system comes back on the Churches of Zaire (doubly difficult because of the losses suffered during the years of government management), missionary educationists are going to be needed, but they will not be easily supplied. French-speaking Eurican educationists, without missionary passion and purpose, do not queue up for the privilege of living and working in Zaire. Missionary educationists when enlisted have yet to learn the language. Men and women who do not know the language are seriously handicapped. Unless they anticipate working in Zaire for ten or fifteen years or more, they do not take the people on their hearts. Missions which have kept their educational missionaries are in a favorable position.

Other Missions are in a difficult position. Just how they will make up for the lack of teachers is not clear. Possibly the Communities in Zaire, recognizing the need, can call for their former educational missionaries to come back—as the government is calling back some of the business heads. We do not know how it will be done but are of the opinion that it should be done. Unless it is done, we anticipate that Communities which can run parochial schools will take over schools (and the congregations in the area) from Communities which cannot.

To be sure, all Communities will be able to run parochial schools in and near the centers where their congregations are strong and their educated leaders are numerous. The crunch will not come there. It will come in the outlying districts. It will come in villages where new buildings need to be erected, new school staffs trained, and a viable apparatus developed; *there* the educational missionaries who bring their own salaries, spiritual resources, overseas contacts, and an ardent Christian faith will, we believe, be a most valuable part of the parochial school system. They will help the system become and remain thoroughly Christian.

Basic Goals of a Thoroughly Christian Parochial School System

What makes an educational system thoroughly Christian? To begin with, it gives good secular education. We assume that a parochial school system, particularly when it is the only system in an entire nation, will provide good instruction in the traditional subjects—reading, writing, arithmetic, geography, science, languages, social studies, history, and the like. This aspect of education will not be slighted. But competent teaching in these subjects, while a part of the whole, does not make an educational system *Christian.* That comes from recognizing five great goals and working systematically toward them.

First, a Christian educational system imparts adequate biblical instruction. Its graduates have learned God's Word. They are accustomed to reading and applying it to their corporate and individual lives. The Bible is a vast treasure of knowledge. When taught daily year after year, it enriches the life of the student.

Second, a Christian educational system sets before the students Christian models in the lives of the teachers and provides Christian experiences in which teachers and pupils together play and plan, work and worship. The Christian impact of the school will rise no higher than the life of the teachers. Consequently, it is of the highest importance that the teachers be not nominal, but ardent Christians, leading dedicated lives and praying God to enable them to pass on their Christian convictions to their students. This goal is emphasized by Zairian leaders who during the last years have seen the ill effects of

agnostics or immoral persons teaching the secular subjects.
Third, a Christian educational system provides a curriculum and
a pedagogy designed to produce men and women who are loyal to the
Church, love the Church, serve the Church, and rear children who are
earnest Christians. The Christian faith is not something which
operates outside of and independent of the Church. The Church is the
Body of Christ and there is no valid Spirit-filled Christianity outside
it. Respect for the Church, and for its ministers, pastors, leaders, and
holy days, flows naturally from a Christian educational system.

Fourth, a Christian educational system leads boys and girls to
personal conversion and incorporation in the Church. Conversion
does not come automatically through studying the Scriptures and
taking religious classes. Students must be evangelized, led to repent
of their sins, and become conscious, deliberate followers of the Lord.
An undue dependence on the schools as if mere passage through them
automatically makes students Christians must be avoided. Place
must be made in the system for encouraging conscious decisions to
follow Christ. Sometimes this may be done by weeks of evangelism
and revival, such as that led by Rev. M. Makanzu at Sona Bata and
Rev. V. Mavungu at Vanga. Sometimes a full-time teacher/chaplain
who is part of the teaching force will establish such contacts with the
students that conversions will occur every week all year long. The
work of Dr. Masamba Mampolo at Kimpese High School is a case in
point. Sometimes liaison of school with church will be the means
used. Whatever the means, conversion and incorporation in the
church should result.

Fifth, a Christian educational system maintains a close and
affectionate linkage with the Church. It is ultimately controlled by
the Church. Its final authority is the minister who stands at the head
of the Church. For some Communities this person will be the Bishop.
For others he will be the Moderator or the General Secretary. It may
be too much to hope that the local pastor will be the final authority in
local schools (the headmaster of the school often has more education
and a larger salary) and yet that should be the goal. We are talking
about a parochial school system. The head of the parish must be the
head of the parish school.

The Curriculum of a Thoroughly Christian School System

If the Communities in Zaire now merely take over the system

and the curriculum which the government had and maintain *it*, they will fail in attaining the values which a Christian school system ought to exhibit. The blocks of knowledge imparted in a Christian school differ from those imparted in a secular school.

In a Christian school even the secular subjects will be taught somewhat differently. Arithmetic and French in a Christian school carry overweights of meaning quite different from those carried in secular schools. But here we wish to emphasize the parts of the curriculum which have a distinctively moral and religious character.

First comes systematic knowledge of the Bible. The riches of the Bible can be made available to millions of potential Zairian citizens, but this will not come by haphazard study of biblical stories and books. Impregnating the mind of the future citizens of this State with the great stories of the Bible, both Old and New Testaments, is how the process starts. Young children who grow up on the eternal truths about God and humankind which God has revealed in his Word are the most valuable assets any nation can have. In story form, drama, movement, suspense, climax, they learn value systems, attitudes, and life-styles which are in line with God's unswerving purpose. Later on in other classes, they will study the Bible as a whole, learn its structure, become skilled in its use, enjoy its history, and accept it as their own personal rule of faith and practice. They will memorize various forms of catechetical instruction. Systematic study of the Holy Scripture graded to their age and intellectual ability is the foundation of all Christian education.

Second, a thoroughly Christian parochial school system will develop a biblical curriculum in accord with the culture, genius, and special needs of Africans in general and Zairians in particular. We were delighted with the authentic African quality of much of the church and school life. The authenticity we are commending does not, of course, consist of worshiping evil spirits and taking plural wives, but rather of African music, dancing, and joy in worship. The culture of Africa is rich and must be preserved. In many ways it is in close harmony with that of the peoples of ancient Israel. The reality of the spirit world and the divine order, so natural a part of both Old and New Testaments, is a present reality to Africans. It must be preserved and enhanced by their biblical studies. Biblical knowledge should be applied to contemporary Zairian needs. The points at which a culture ought to be purified and beautified by the Bible must be addressed. In India, for example, a biblical curriculum ought to speak clearly about idolatry. In America, biblical teaching on the sin of racial prejudice ought to be emphasized. So, in Zaire, those biblical teachings should be emphasized which are particularly needed by Christians living there today.

To create a biblical curriculum for all twelve grades which fits the culture and speaks to the ethical and spiritual needs of these peoples at this time is a very large undertaking. Fortunately, Christians in East Africa have been at work on this project, and most of their curriculum offerings can be used in Zaire substantially as they stand. While some further adjustment to Zaire ought to be done, the chief and very big task is translating the East Africa curricular materials into French and the other major languages and printing millions of books.

As we contemplate contemporary ethical and spiritual needs in this mighty nation, we think immediately about the place of women and the dignity of labor for men. In old Zaire, men did the fighting and women did the cultivation. Men in Zaire traditionally scorn field labor. The Bible can speak powerfully to this situation, and any real progress in Zaire depends on reversing the male attitude toward farm work. The same is true of animal husbandry. The biblical records portray the loving care which men took of their flocks and herds. A Zairian curriculum will lay heavy stress on respect to elders and reverence (but not worship) of ancestors. It will teach and illustrate from Scripture the power which Christ abundantly has over evil spirits. It will stress the important part repentance and righteousness play in access to God's presence.

Industrialization and urbanization rush on in Zaire. The development of hydroelectric power will cause them to increase still more. Only the strong medicine of biblical faith will keep these two potent modernizations from damaging these fine peoples. As tribal bonds weaken, society becomes more and more fragmented, and the temptations of a money economy proliferate; much teaching of honesty in modern life and much opportunity to be honest in the affairs of school life will be required.

A special word must be said about the delicate balance between tribal and national loyalties. Tribalism appeared to the Belgians as the great enemy. They did everything they could to break it down. The present government, too, intent on building a great nation, is constantly warring against "tribalism." It wants to replace tribal loyalties with a supreme loyalty to the nation. Nevertheless, what individuals know is that their chief resource in time of trouble is the family and the tribe. Their heart language is their tribal tongue. In cities, they live in tribal neighborhoods. In the country, they occupy villages and lands where only their people have lived for generations. They are acutely aware that their neighbors have for hundreds of years been their deadly enemies. Loyalty to family, clan, and tribe is fundamentally a good thing. Paul could say proudly, "I am a Hebrew born of Hebrews, of the tribe of Benjamin." He could also say that all this he counted of little value compared with the excellence of knowing the Lord Jesus Christ. This simultaneous valuing of one's cultural heritage and yet counting it as transient compared with the Christian faith is that which a thoroughly Christian education ought to develop.

Third, a Christian school system develops beautiful, meaningful worship liturgy and music. The Christian school creates a purified environment in which the youth of the community spend the better part of each day. In these godly surroundings, worship plays a large part. The Christian school by its style of life proclaims clearly, "We are God's people and count the joyful adoration of God a precious part of our lives. We praise him. We listen to him. We unite in petition to him. We delight in opening ourselves to the sunshine of his Presence."

Perhaps better than most nations, Zaire has developed an educational system where the church building is close to the school and is often used as a classroom. Gathering in God's house to bow before him is natural and expected.

The wonderful gift of song, which God has given to Zairians with lavish hand, is a rich resource. In no nation of which we know is spontaneous part singing so commonly employed in the worship of the Church. At a baptismal service at Molembe, near Vanga, six choral groups from various churches stepped forward to praise God in song as the two hundred new believers were baptized in the river. The youth sing extraordinarily well—without organ or piano. On all festive occasions and in worship services, one or more choirs will break out in well-disciplined song containing dramatic harmony, splendid rhythm, clearly Christian words and sentiments, and impressive unity.

The best choir at Molembe was led by a layman—not a teacher or catechist. The style of singing—the full-throated volume, the varied rhetoric, the biblical sentiments, the rhythmic swaying and spontaneous gestures—were all intensely African, but not old pagan African which had little of the beauty of this, no harmony, and not much discipline. In churches all across Zaire such singing is commonplace. Special numbers are variations of antiphonal congregational singing complete with rattles and dancing.

The parochial school system, with aid from missionary societies in Europe and America, could readily establish a School of African Sacred Music. It could discover the best in each of several different forms of song and reward and publicize the best choirs, composers, and poets. Every Mission cooperating with the National School of Sacred Music in Kinshasa or some other center could appoint a missionary whose sole task would be the development of sacred music. He or she would encourage in all the schools and congregations of the tribes of that particular area beautiful, meaningful Christian music. With tape recorders, amplifiers, and machines to cut platters, the best could be heard in all schools. Latent talent could be developed. Tribal competitions and celebrations would help the entire Church to rejoice and praise God, using more fully the great gifts he has given to these peoples.

During the coming decades, the Missions and Communities in Zaire might very well cut and polish the diamond of music until it becomes the brightest jewel in the crown of the King. Were a very good choir, trained to sing in English, to tour America, it would receive a tumultuous welcome and greatly bless Christians there.

A thoroughly Christian parochial school system must have inspectors and supervisors of the *program of Christian education.* Inspection paid for by government is now confined to the secular subjects. If an equally prestigious and powerful system of inspection is not instituted for the religious and moral part of the program, pupils and teachers will conclude that the really important thing in the schools is the secular education. Actually the reverse is true. *The religious and moral aspects of education are and must be made to appear the most valued parts of the whole.* The only way to achieve this, we believe, is to create an inspection and supervisory system for the distinctively Christian parts of the program. Let a competent, impartial educator from outside the local school *grade each teacher and each school.* Let schools and teachers of high quality in the religious program be rewarded and acclaimed by the Church and school. Let administration know where excellent moral and religious instruction is being given and where it is not.

Christian parochial schools can maintain freedom of conscience and at the same time impart moral and Christian teaching of a high order. Promotion must not be made dependent on competence in biblical knowledge, participation in worship, or conversion. The school must not be an instrument in the hands of the Church to pressure members of one denomination to join some other. On the other hand, as so often happens in the United States, schools must not advocate and teach agnosticism and secularism. We believe the Protestant Communities can agree on a biblical curriculum which all will use. Were Roman Catholics to join in establishing a basic curriculum which included what both they and Evangelicals want, great good would result. Furthermore, worship can be made so interesting, agreeable, and beautiful that boys and girls will participate in it freely and joyfully. Teachers, also, should realize that their participation in worship and in teaching the Bible will form part of their permanent record. A thoroughly Christian parochial school system must have teachers who are themselves earnest Christians. Those who are not should shift out into commerce, industry, or cultivation of the fields.

The Role of the Missionary Society

The desirability of a thoroughly Christian parochial school system should be clearly understood by the missionary societies. Funds for refurbishing the school systems and making them Christian should receive high priority. An opportunity like this is not likely to be handed to missionary societies again in the near future.

Great danger exists that the schools, even in church hands, will remain chiefly secular. If that happens, not only will the great good of a thoroughly Christian school system be missed, but also the secular school will drain the Church of its financial resources, its time and attention, and its personnel. Secular teachers will appear more important than pastors, and the Christian enterprise will be dealt a serious blow. The danger must be avoided. *Missionary societies must encourage the Communities to make the parochial system deeply, creatively, and innovatively Christian.* Missionary societies must provide the funds and personnel which such a major move requires. The simplistic theory which holds that modern Mission consists chiefly in throwing young Churches on their own and making them function without missionary aid must be recognized as bankrupt. In this chapter we have set forth what a thoroughly Christian parochial school system should entail. We now point out that the only way the tasks we have set forth will be accomplished will be *by substantial and continued assistance from missionary societies abroad.* Dreams that the day of Mission is over and missionary societies can cease recruiting and sending missionaries and raising substantial funds to make their work possible must be recognized as fanciful and unrealistic. In regard to Christian education in Zaire, "Midday in Missions" means renewing our determination to be partners in obedience to God for the foreseeable future.

Zairians, too, are called on to put forth heroic efforts. Unless they do all they can, their overseas partners will sadly conclude that they must withdraw, that African denominations will sit on their hands as long as missionaries are there to provide leadership and money. Churches must do much more than they have done. Although parents have been paying fees so their children can go to school, it may be that they will have to pay more. We do not know. We urge that concerned missionary societies carry out careful surveys to find out what part of the total cost of education parents are now bearing, and determine whether, as part of the justice which northern countries seek to do to the less-developed lands, the missionary societies might not do more. Be that as it may, we are certain that the education of the children of Zaire—a potentially wealthy country with abundant land and water—*is the responsibility of the Zairians.* Their Christian friends from overseas will help, provided the Churches in Zaire give generously and systematically.

Conclusion

A thoroughly Christian parochial school system is a high goal for the Church in any nation to set for itself. It is not easily attained anywhere. This chapter explores what Christian education means in Zaire in the last two decades of the twentieth century. We believe the goal is attainable but are sure that both denominations and Missions will have to devote substantial thought, prayer, and resources to it. The danger of a largely secular system coming back and, even while being controlled by the Church, remaining secular is real. We trust our review of the situation will help missionary societies, Missions, and Communities see the dimensions and rise to the challenges.

7

Four Urgent
Evangelistic Tasks

Despite the fact that 62 percent of the population can be counted as church-connected Christians and another 27 percent as marginal Christians (not yet church-connected), four substantial tasks of evangelism remain to be done. Were the Communities now to rest on their laurels and cease to emphasize evangelism, they would suffer a disastrous defeat. The fragile nature of the great advance God has granted his people must constantly be kept in mind. Unless further evangelism brings millions to active, responsible discipleship, the present favorable situation could easily be reversed.

Many communicants are illiterate or semi-literate. It is easy for whole clusters of congregations out some distance from the centers to lapse back into nominalism. The animistic mind-set of the common people, the almost universal belief in witches, the chaotic changes involved in urbanization, the secular materialism of modern life, and many other factors militate against the Christian faith. As we wrote chapter 6, portraying the sixteen million who are now church-connected Christians, we trembled lest the unwary conclude that now Mission is complete. The truth is that unless continuous and arduous evangelism is carried on, the remaining twenty years of the twentieth century will see not further advance but major decline in Christian strength in Zaire. "Evangelize or perish" should be the motto which every Community and Mission inscribes on its heart.

This chapter, therefore, describes the four great campaigns of evangelism which Missions and Churches must carry on.

I. The Discipling of Each New Generation

Zaire possesses a most valuable Christian resource in the extensive parochial school system. It is excellent preparation for the personal conversion so necessary for genuine Christian life.

The whole school system, which is such a formative influence on the youth of the nation, is a churchly institution. Control of the system gives the Communities priceless opportunities to rear the coming generation in the Christian faith. All children are given daily instruction in the Bible. Daily worship of God in the church becomes a cherished experience. Christian teachers who lead exemplary lives provide good examples and become figures to respect and emulate. Sports are seen as part of the church program. In short, the whole youth community is closely tied to the Church. During their formative years, most of the six million school-age children in Zaire have the privilege of study in Christian schools. One has only to think of the situation in Russia and China where the school system is closely tied to atheistic and secular philosophies and power structures to realize the enormous advantage Zaire possesses in its far-flung parochial school system.

While all these good influences prepare the way for boys and girls to become Christian, unless they culminate in conversion, the greatest good may be lost. Every boy and girl ought to have the privilege of personal commitment to Christ, personal conversion. This deliberate turning away from sin and self, this conscious yielding to the Lord, this individual resolve to enthrone Jesus Christ as Lord and to believe on him as Savior is the heart of the discipling of each new generation. Unless this takes place, the good teaching, good example, and churchly connections fail to produce their intended fruit.

We have placed the discipling of each new generation in this chapter on evangelism rather than in the previous chapter on the parochial school because persons are not saved by being enrolled in Christian schools, no matter how good the schools are. They are saved by belief in Jesus Christ and incorporation in his Body, the Church. In the ultimate analysis, therefore, the Communities of Zaire must carry out the first great campaign of evangelism. They must make sure their children become responsible practicing Christians through the influences of home, church, and school. The Communities which control the schools must make sure that the latter prepare the children for conversion, and that becoming a Christian does not appear to the children as an inevitable automatic process which occurs after one has spent a few years in school. It would be tragic for them to think that conversion involves no personal struggle, no repentance, no inner cleaving to Jesus Christ, and no resolve to follow him whether peers and parents do or not. The Communities must make sure that only youth who have enthroned Christ and who intend to obey the dictates of the Spirit in their own hearts become members of the Church. Conversion, confirmation, and believer's baptism must not mean automatic promotion to the next class.

Each school will have some children each year who reach the age of discretion and who wish to become responsible Christians. All the schools taken together deliver into the hands of the Church about one million young people every year. Year after year, wave after wave of youth thus march up to the gates of salvation. Who evangelizes them? What provision does the Church make?

Sometimes it is the dedicated teachers in their free time. Many teachers are elders and deacons. A normal part of their duties, and a significant part of their privilege, is to gather young people, whom they know well, into baptismal or confirmation classes and help them make the most important decision of their lives. Sometimes the pastor of the local church, who also knows the children and their parents well, provides the teaching, the counsel, the prayers, and the guidance needed during these crucial weeks or months in the lives of the youth.

Sometimes chaplain-teachers have this responsibility assigned to them. This is possible in upper level schools which have the funds to employ such persons. Ordinary village primary schools or ordinary city schools attached to some congregation could not employ a chaplain-teacher.

Annual periods of revival and evangelism are acceptable means for bringing youth, as well as adults, to surrender to Christ or to receive him and confess him before others. In well-churched communities near Church headquarters or stations, for such annual periods for the deepening of spiritual life they can easily secure the services of noted preachers. Neglected and isolated villages far off the beaten path cannot; the church at the center will have to make provision for the special meetings. This takes time, thought, money, and prayer. Unless it is done, a generation of "Christian" youth which has never consciously accepted Christ and is therefore not saved grows up. All the moral advance which God intends his Church should pioneer then suffers because those who look like Christians and count themselves such have not made the culminating decision to obey the Lord.

Post-Conversion Christian Experience

Conversion is normally followed by deepening Christian experience. Not only will the upper classes in the school provide Christian youth with factual information geared to Zairian needs and the crises of the day, but also the Church should lead youth studying in the upper classes to higher reaches of dedication. The girl of twelve, who quite sincerely took Jesus Christ as Lord and Savior, needs to understand what being a Christian woman, wife, and mother means when she reaches the age of eighteen and faces courtship, marriage, and the temptations so common in all walks of life. She ought to take the further step in discipleship which that entails. Young men also, as they come to understand the changes needed in the social structure of Zaire, ought to see them as those which the Master demands his true followers to bring about.

Evangelism which disciples each new generation will call not only for the initial dedication to Christ, but also for many subsequent dedications as Christ points to individual and social advances which his followers and his Churches should make. Labor/capital relationships, the responsibilities of Christian citizens, social structures which assure fair treatment of minorities, regulations of drugs and drink, limitations on power, the inner discipline essential if corruption, theft, and extortion are eliminated—all are areas in which evangelism can call for decision. All are included in what the discipling of each new generation entails.

The Annual Youth Audit

The Communities ought to conduct an annual audit of their youth. How many of the million who reached the age of discretion each year have been incorporated into the Church? How many remain to be? What sections of the youth have been reached and what have been neglected by the congregations? How deep an experience is incorporation into the Body of Christ? Is the Church in grave danger of allowing incorporation to become an automatic by-product of the Christian school, and thus to minimize conversion?

The Churches might delegate this annual audit of youth to teachers who, in their after school hours, could easily amass the information needed. Or it might be done by the pastors. Whoever does it, it should be done.

II. Evangelizing the Nominals and Marginals

The second great campaign of evangelism which should form a permanent part of the normal life of Communities and Missions in Zaire is that addressed to the nominals and marginals. By nominals we mean those who have at some time been baptized and incorporated into the Church but who have become careless Christians. They worship on festival days or special occasions. When the supervising minister rolls up in his truck, the Mission executive from abroad makes an occasional visit, the school graduation ceremony occurs, or the governmental head comes to address the populace, careless Christians are in the church. Otherwise they stay at home and sit around with others drinking palm wine. Some nominals have fallen into sin—theft, adultery, or drunkenness—and have been put under discipline by the congregation.

The number of nominals varies from time to time and from denomination to denomination. More nominals appear among the men than the women. If systematic and ardent evangelism of these millions is not carried out, the Church soon becomes a small band of earnest Christians existing in villages full of nominals. The nominals set the pace, and the entire life of the people suffers.

Nominality is characteristic of Churches everywhere—regardless of denomination. Protestants have their nominals and Roman Catholics have theirs. But while the situation is common, it should not be tolerated as unavoidable and natural. Nominals are a standing challenge to each Community to work for their conversion and return to the fold. Revival of existing Christians is part of the solution. Programs planned to reach the nominals and bring multitudes of them into a living relationship to the Savior is the other part. To be avoided at all costs is the belief of the State Churches that the Christian population (everyone is a Christian in those lands: everyone is baptized in infancy) will be largely nominal. Ardent Christians are quite the exception. It is commonly thought that the parish priest can do nothing about changing the situation. The Free Churches, on the contrary, hold that the nominals constitute a body of winnable men and women. Ardent Christians should be constantly laboring, praying, and working to bring nominals into the fellowship of Christ and unite them with others who know themselves to be his and who intend to live consecrated lives. We hope that the Communities in Zaire will pattern themselves on the Free Churches. The marginals also will be evangelized in this second campaign. Marginal Christians are unbaptized persons who consider themselves in some vague way Christians. Maybe they were away when their class in school was baptized, and so they have never been incorporated. Maybe they had a second wife and so could not be baptized. Maybe their village lay across a difficult swamp and has been bypassed. The only time they see a pastor or an evangelist is once a year. Perhaps they are so neglected that whether they should be classified as practicing animists or as marginal Christians is an open question.

In cities very large numbers of people call themselves Protestants or Roman Catholics because they went to a school twenty or thirty years ago, but they never attend the nearby church, which is made up of the people of another tribe. The Community they knew back in the interior has no congregation within two miles of them, and maybe none in the city. If pressed, they claim to belong to a congregation in a village back in Equatorial Province or Shaba.

Who Will Evangelize Nominals and Marginals?

Marginal and nominal people are out of the habit of going to church—if indeed they ever had the habit. Consequently the normal services of the Church, the caring for the members, and the calling on the sick do not influence them at all. If they are to be helped, then special programs must be prepared to reach them.

Evangelism campaigns in villages or sections of the towns, where there are many nominals or marginals, are one way to reach this goal. The kind of campaign will depend on whether the group being evangelized lives in a village with relatives and friends all of the same tribe, all forming one social unit, or whether it lives in a city and has no congregation of its own sort of people who worship in its own tribal language within walking distance. In a village where there is already a church, nominals are added to it as soon as they confess Christ. In cities where there is no church of their kind of people within walking distance, a new congregation, replete with its own deacons and elders, should be established.

As the schools are reinforced and play a more significant part in the life of the Church, they ought to help congregations find and incorporate the nominals and marginals in their districts. Schools far away from the center will have a large field and those near the centers a small field.

They can use and to some extent are using what Christians in the Philippines and other parts of the world, including North America, are finding effective. Evangelistic home Bible studies reach out into the community and enroll non-Christians who want to study the Bible. As Christians and non-Christians study the Word together, particularly those parts dealing with repentance and conversion, men and women are converted. In the study group they find community. The Bible speaks to them. They begin attending worship with their newfound friends and are baptized into the Church.

Fervent faith on the part of Christians and conviction that those who do not follow Jesus Christ are lost combine to produce lay Christians who do good, do find the lost (nominals and marginals), and do bring them back to the Father's house.

The Measure of Discipling

Only God knows the heart. Who is truly Christian and who is not can never be completely known by pastors, missionaries, or other Christians. Nevertheless, there is a close correlation between what people do and what they believe. Consequently, when we measure and record attendance, giving to the church, conducting family devotions, going out to spread the Good News to others, praying to God, and being filled with the fruits of the Spirit, we can form a rough idea of how Christian a community or an individual is. Conversely, works of the flesh (Galatians 5:19), when manifested, can be measured. They bear eloquent testimony to the need for conversion.

III. Churching the Cities

Congregations must be multiplied in all the great cities. Take Kinshasa, for example. All the members of all the Protestant Communities in Kinshasa taken together number less than 100,000 and all the congregations number less than 200. This is pitiful in view of the 2,000,000 citizens, and of the 600,000 who call themselves Protestants. To church these latter only will require at least 2,400 congregations in 1980 and 5,000 congregations by the year 1998. If the 2,000,000 Zairians in Kinshasa who call themselves Christians but are not church-connected are not to become secular materialists, at least 8,000 congregations (Protestant and Roman Catholic) are

needed *now*. Hundreds of congregations are needed in Kisangani,
Mbandaka, Kananga, Boma, Matadi, and other burgeoning cities.
The following table summarizes the fantastic growth that has
taken place not only in Kinshasa but also in all cities and towns. From

TABLE IV

PRINCIPAL CITIES IN ZAIRE WITH POPULATION
FIGURES FOR 1970 and 1975

	1970*	1975**
KINSHASA	1,300,000	1,944,236
Bas-Zaire Province		
Matadi	110,436	139,084
Boma	61,054	93,933
Mbanza Ngungu	55,838	71,046
Bandundu Province		
Bandundu City	40,000	94,110
Kikwit	111,960	127,606
West Kasai Province		
Kananga	300,000	474,657
East Kasai Province		
Mbudji-Mayi	256,154	283,219
Shaba Province		
Lubumbashi	318,000	551,975
Kolwezi	83,418	143,287
Likusi	200,000	280,000
Kivu Province		
Bukavu	134,861	146,505
Upper Zaire Province		
Kisangani	229,596	374,000
Equator Province		
Mbandaka	107,910	139,856

*De Saint Moulin, *Atlas des Collectivités* du Zaire (Kinshasa: Presses Universitaire
du Zaire, 1976).
**Unpublished government figures, Kinshasa Bureau, 1975-76.

all indications, the rate of growth in the 1980s will continue. It is therefore imperative that all Communities along with the Missions that cooperate with them should plant churches as fast as possible. The goal is not merely to do the planting we should have done in past years; it is rather to incorporate hundreds of thousands of these multitudes who think of themselves as in some way Christians.

Rural Christians who leave their villages for urban centers do not readily join city congregations. One possible explanation for the large number of marginal and nominal Christians is this phenomenon of misplaced Christians lost from view in the cities. They are not currently counted by any denomination, even as part of its total community. We have discussed this in more detail in chapter 5.

The tragedy is that few Zairian church leaders and missionaries have grasped the enormous size of the task. They still think in terms of the past and are content with what has developed. In one city of 138,000 the one Protestant denomination present contentedly confines its witness to ten congregations! Since the combined geographical areas in which the ten work coincide with the total area covered by the city, this denomination erroneously feels it has adequately churched that city.

Another denomination with *one* church in a city of 93,000 was very troubled when another denomination established one more congregation. The leaders felt this was "unchristian." When it was pointed out that in a city that size in the United States there would be at least 150 congregations, the whole situation was put back into perspective.

In order to help the reader understand how underchurched is the giant metropolis of Kinshasa, we present another table. This one breaks the city down into its zones (similar to burroughs in New York) with their populations. For instance, Mont Ngafula with only four Protestant congregations has one for every 5,000 inhabitants and is much better churched than Ngaliema which has nineteen congregations but only one for every 11,900 inhabitants. Burumbu is even in a worse situation with only one congregation for 65,000 inhabitants. This comparison of the number of known congregations with the huge population of each zone drives home the inadequacy of past church-planting efforts.

At the right of the table some other cities with their populations are given. The reader can compare zones of Kinshasa with whole other cities. The table displays the fact that Kinshasa is a cluster of

TABLE V

COMPARISON BETWEEN THE POPULATION
OF THE ZONES OF KINSHASA
WITH THAT OF OTHER CITIES
1975

Name of Zone	No. of Protestant Congregations*	Population**	Other cities	Population**
Mont Ngafula	4	20,654		
Ngaliema	19	225,973	Mbuji-Mayi	283,219
Kintambo	3	36,311		
Gombe	4	8,162		
Lingwala	1	44,409		
Kinshasa	6	174,664	Bukavu	146,000
Barumbu	1	65,723		
Kasavubu	2	75,000		
Kalamu	6	106,665	Bandundu	84,110
Ngiri-Ngiri	1	68,929		
Bandalungwa	5	68,367		
Makala	7	75,553	Mbanza Ngungu	71,046
Bumbu	4	79,307		
Salembao	4	72,030		
Lemba	9	96,131	Boma	93,933
Matete	6	75,997		
Ngaba	4	47,004		
Kisenso	6	116,192		
Limete	5	64,092		
Ndjili	9	139,932	Matadi	139,084
			Mbandaka	139,956
Kimbanseke	10	171,612	Kolwezi	143,287
Masina	6	77,537		
Nsele	2	20,815		
Maluku	2	23,203		
Total	126	1,944,236		

*Figures obtained from list of churches in Kinshasa Synod, ECZ.
**Population figures from unpublished records, government office.

large cities and towns. In view of these figures any judgment that the Communities already at work in Kinshasa are adequately discipling the city and adequately planting churches is seen to be untenable. Yet we met this attitude often as we visited stations and centers and consulted with Zairian leaders and missionaries.

The story of the Alliance work in Kinshasa merits mention as an example of the growth possible when it is planned. In 1968 the Alliance had not one single congregation in Kinshasa. They had only five home prayer groups. Today, after nine years, they have twenty-two congregations served by five ordained pastors and 112 lay pastors. Half of these congregations came into being after the arrival of a missionary couple in 1974 whose efforts were devoted solely to church planting. Alliance leaders believe they can multiply congregations in Kinshasa. They have set as their minimum goal forty-four congregations by 1980.

At this point, let us recognize that the old doctrine of comity has been thoroughly outmoded. All cities, and Kinshasa in particular, must be regarded as open cities. All Communities should be multiplying congregations there. All Protestants will operate under the overarching umbrella of the ECZ. Mean-spirited competition ought to be avoided. However, the danger is not competition. It is lack of cultivation. Up river in Mbandaka we found communities of the fishing tribes who have become Baptists, but Baptist churches are notable by their absence in Mbandaka. Each Community should follow its own people wherever they go and help them organize and multiply their own kind of churches among their own people. Brotherhood, kindly cooperation, one language for all citizens, the breakdown of tribal unities—all these will come faster when people are Christians and are worshiping God regularly than when they are unshepherded nominals and marginals. The cities urgently require major church-multiplying by all Communities.

The rush to the city is on and will not be stopped. The urban masses who now think of themselves as Christians (*not* Muslims, Marxists, Hindus, or Buddhists, but Christians) call loudly to Christians within the Church in Zaire today. The missionary societies in Eurica, cooperating with the young Churches in Zaire, face huge numbers of winnable people. The cities of Zaire lie wide open, receptive to the gospel. Church multiplication in the cities today will have to be intelligent, meet today's conditions, solve urban problems, and operate in a rapidly changing Africa. It will be a very rewarding process. The miracle God has wrought in the last hundred years is great. The miracle he will work in the churching of the urban populations will be still greater. Only one thing can prevent it. Should denominations in Zaire and Eurica think small, disobey his commands, and glory in a few congregations in the cities when they ought to have hundreds, then God's purposes may be frustrated.

IV. Discipling the Dark Areas

In chapter 6, we pointed out that all across Zaire sections of the land have been seriously neglected. In those areas churches and schools are few. The population is sparse. It is difficult to get there. The people are either practicing animists or marginal Christians.

Just east of Kinshasa lies a strip of land 500 kilometers long, 150 kilometers wide. The map of population density indicates that it is lightly inhabited. When we flew over it (two hundred feet above the ground by courtesy of Missionary Aviation Fellowship), we saw nothing but scrub jungle and anthills. Yet it contains more than 100,000 inhabitants and very few congregations. It is far away from Kinshasa or the Christian concentration around Vanga. The congregations there cannot walk or cycle over and evangelize the strip by near neighbor evangelism. Spontaneous expansion of the Church will not, we believe, bring the peoples of the strip to Christ and firmly establish the Church there. That will take deliberate effort by Zairian Communities or by missionary societies. Possibly some parts of the strip should become Christian in connection with adjacent denominations, while other parts form new ecclesiastical districts.

Since the strip has been bypassed in the era when travel by car was easier and gas was cheap, it may be that its effective evangelization will depend on someone getting a light plane, or helicopter, and establishing a network of stations and schools and congregations. These are details. We do not know the answers to these questions. But we do know that in the strip a hundred thousand persons are yet to be reached.

Similar sections lie on the peripheries of many of the Communities. Between CBZO and CPZ lies a section of land, well-watered and inhabited, which no Mission—Catholic or Protestant—appears to have adequately churched. North of the CPZ field and south of the geographical center of Zaire is another field difficult to reach and only slightly Christianized. North of the Zaire River where it bends to the east lies a huge swamp in which many villages have yet to become Christian. We were told that the population there numbered 200,000. Some were Roman Catholics. Four thousand were members of the Evangelical Covenant, but large numbers remain unshepherded. On the edge of the South Sudan among the Azande in Zaire are many thousands of square kilometers which never see any evangelistic effort.

The discipling of these areas is urgent and constitutes the fourth major task of evangelism in Zaire. These people are highly receptive but will not be won by sporadic forays into their midst. Serious substantial Mission by task forces of Zairians and missionaries, or missionaries and Zairians—depending on whether Church or Mission has the muscle and the will—is demanded. A program sufficiently large and enduring to do the job will take both persons and money. Possibly planes and helicopters will be brought into play. Since such territories are usually occupied by clans or even tribes different from those already Christian, leaders out of new people being discipled will have to be created rapidly. Deacons, elders, catechists, pastors, superintendents, teachers, and moderators must be raised up out of the new segment of society being discipled. Discipling the Dark Areas will often involve a twenty-year program.

Conclusion

Evangelism is the lifeblood of the Church. In Zaire, as in all other countries, the Church is always within one generation of extinction. If the new generation is not evangelized and incorporated in the Body, if the nominals and the marginals are not won to Christ, if the burgeoning cities remain with less than one-seventh of their population church-connected, and if the Dark Areas continue dark, the wonderful progress made by the Churches and Missions during the last hundred years will be reversed as it was in North Africa. We cannot forget that North Africa was substantially Christian at one time. The land of Augustine of Hippo, where assemblages of four hundred bishops convened, is now solidly Muslim.

If Christian leaders now believe that the day of Missions has ended and the principal thrust of missionary societies should be to help young Churches with money but not missionaries, or even to throw young Churches on their own, we see great losses ahead. If, on the contrary, Churches and Missions press forward in partnership in obedience, each giving the other much room to act, both pressing forward under God, each concerned more that the job be done than who gets the credit, *then* the future is bright. Then truly Zaire stands in midday of the Christian Mission.

8

Christian Hospitals and Health Services

The Biblical Base

The healing ministry of Christian Missions and Churches rises inevitably from that of Jesus Christ, the Great Physician.

The Gospel of John tells us that in Capernaum our Lord healed the son of a royal official, that this was the second *sign* He had performed, and that the official believed on Him, together with all his household. In the extensive account of the healing of the lame man at the Gate Beautiful in the third and fourth chapters of Acts we read, "For the man on whom this *sign of healing* was performed was more than forty years old" (italics added). God's mighty power flowed forth to heal the man lame from birth *as a sign* the Risen Jesus was indeed the Messiah, the Redeemer of the world. In the same way, the healing ministry of modern missions proclaims who *Jesus Christ is.* Through this ministry the Lord often says, "Every one who acknowledges me before men, I also will acknowledge before my Father who is in heaven; but whoever denies me before men, I also will deny before my Father who is in heaven" (Matthew 10:32-33).

The Gospels also bear clear witness to the fact that much of the healing done by our Lord arose out of his *compassion.* His healings were humanitarian acts. For instance, when our Lord saw the widow of Nain, he had *compassion* on her, touched the bier, and said, "Young man, I say to you, arise." Matthew records in 14:14 that "As he went ashore, he saw a great throng; and *had compassion on them and healed their sick*" (italics added).

Nowhere does the Bible tell us that the acts of compassion were not intended as signs of his messiahship, or that his signs were not performed out of compassion for men and women. Indeed, the opposite is plainly the case. His ministry of healing proceeded from two intertwined motives: as signs that he was the Messiah, and as acts of compassion and love. These intertwined motives undergird all *truly Christian* health services. The Christian physician rejects the big lie that "only humanitarian service which conceals the Savior is genuine compassion." Instead, he insists that as a Christian, his every healing ministry is intended both as compassion and as a sign announcing that the Savior has come. The two cannot be separated. The Christian physician intends them to be together, and *then leaves the person entirely free under the leading of the Holy Spirit to believe on Jesus or not to believe.* The nine lepers who did not return to thank the Lord (and presumably did not believe on him) were physically healed just as truly as the one who did return.

The Christian physician never offers healing as a bribe to induce patients to believe. He never offers good medicine to those who believe and bad medicine to those who do not. Equally truly he never fails to bear witness that the Great Physician is indeed the Savior of the world—the Messiah.

The Early Years

Animated and guided by these two motives, Christian Missions from the turn of the century have been pouring physicians and nurses into this great land. Eighty years ago Zaire was a trackless wilderness in which lived hundreds of tribes. Warfare between tribes was endemic. Stronger tribes conquered weaker ones, took their women and children, and occupied their territory. The Bantus gradually replaced the Pygmies. Kingdoms arose as strong tribes captured some territory and defended it against all comers for centuries. Infant mortality was high. Yaws, smallpox, and other diseases raged. Aside from the witch doctor there were no doctors. In Zaire, exactly as in the tribal territories of the Saxons and Wends in north Germany in the seventh century, herbal remedies, incantations, and magic concoctions were all the medicine there was.

Perhaps the greatest service, certainly the most dramatic service, which missionaries rendered to the people of Zaire has been compassionate Christian medicine. Most Missions planned to staff each station with a doctor. The doctors opened the hearts of the people to the gospel. They were truly a sign that Christ was beneficent and powerful. They freed thousands from the fear of evil spirits and "bad medicine thrown by powerful sorcerers." The mission hospital not only kept the missionary staff well and ministered to the boys and girls in the boarding schools at the centers, but it also proclaimed Christ in words and deeds which the ordinary tribespeople readily understood.

In the earliest years the great rivers, on which mission steamers plied, brought the missionary physicians, kept them supplied with medicines and equipment, and enabled patients from distant regions to come to the hospital. In later years, the roads driven through by the Belgian Government saw hospital cars and trucks keeping the hospitals functioning. In the last eighteen years planes of the Missionary Aviation Fellowship have enabled Christian physicians to serve the needs of hundreds of tribes and clans.

No sooner were the mission doctors there, than they were training Africans in medical service. First they were called nurses, assistants, or compounders, and they operated under the close supervision of the missionaries. Later on as they learned a great deal about the human body and its treatment, more and more departments of the work were turned over to them. The larger hospitals became training centers, where large numbers of young men and women were trained as nurses, compounders, and technicians. The medical school at Kimpese in Bas-Zaire and similar institutions at Kananga and Nyakunde were organized in the fifties and sixties to produce top-flight African medical men and women. Christian hospitals and health services became more and more African. Splendid men and women were graduated from Kimpese and other institutions of training.

The Christian Hospital at Lotumbe

All this did not happen in a day. At Lotumbe, for example, in 1915 a missionary doctor was located. He was part of a pioneer force, which was learning the Lonkundu language, building residences, constructing the first simple hospital structures, touring among the tribes to minister the gospel and health to them there, and carrying on health services in the midst of enormous difficulties. In 1923, the DCCM built the first buildings of the hospital at Lotumbe. The congregation at the station numbered more than two hundred, and village congregations began to multiply out in the forest. When the doctor went on furlough, the station was left in the charge of some other missionary assisted by the doctor at Bolenge, three to five days' travel away—three by steamer and five by paddled canoe. A succession of missionary physicians ministered at Lotumbe, each adding something to the station hospital. This one built a leprosy ward, that one a maternity ward, and someone else an adequate operating theater.

Then in the fifties, Dr. John Ross came. He had been pastor of a Christian Church in California, had seen the tremendous need for medical missionaries, had gone to medical school for five years, and had then been sent out by the United Christian Missionary Society. He lifted Lotumbe to a new height of effectiveness. When the government of Zaire in 1972 was staffing the great central hospital in Kinshasa (Mama Yemo), it called Dr. Ross to its staff, and for a number of years he was the government medical man operating both in Kinshasa and on a river steamer.

When the UCMS decided to Africanize its medical staff completely, the Lotumbe Hospital lost all missionary connections. The competent persons Dr. Ross had trained became the sole staff. With the tremendous difficulties in transportation which have marked the last ten years, the medicine often did not arrive, and the nationalized hospital began to operate on a rather low level. This condition marks the present Lotumbe Hospital.

We have *very* briefly told the Lotumbe story, because the movement portrayed is what has occurred again and again in mission hospitals all over Zaire. Each hospital has been the scene of a marvelous Christian service carried out over three quarters of a century. Each has seen innumerable acts of skillful compassionate medicine. Each has proclaimed that Jesus Christ is Savior and Lord. Each has had its high moments and triumphs of nationalization. Some have suffered terribly from the withdrawal of missionaries. Where withdrawal has been too rapid, medical and health services have been damaged. Where nationalization went forward with a continued missionary component, there health services have been enhanced.

Tremendous Growth: 1907–1959

Another way of seeing the wonderful service rendered by the hospitals and health services of the Church and Mission to the people of Zaire is to turn to TABLE II "Comparative Statistics," page 71. Here we see that in 1907 all the Protestant Missions together conducted only 27 hospitals and dispensaries. These were simple beginning efforts. In some cases the doctors had nothing but thatch-roofed and earthen-walled rooms, near the station church—or their own residence—where the sick gathered and where they kept their medicines and instruments.

By 1936, however, 72 hospitals and dispensaries were listed. Most of these were permanent structures with corrugated iron roofs and solid brick walls. Many had operating rooms. In addition there were 453 auxiliary medical facilities. Seventeen medical schools were preparing compounders, nurses, and technicians. In these there studied 220 students. Seventeen leprosy hospitals and nine specializing in the treatment of sleeping sickness had been established. Nearly 1,200 lepers were housed in these hospitals and homes. The doctors treated a million and a quarter patients. However, in 1936 prenatal consultations were not entered as a special category.

By 1950 the number of hospitals and dispensaries had risen to 171, and auxiliary medical facilities showed the remarkable figure of 1,097. Medical schools had risen to 29 and African men and women studying there to 432. Leprosy homes had increased to 35 and patients housed there to 6,598. Nearly six million patients had been treated, and a tremendous 67,000 prenatal consultations had been given. Dr. McGavran visited Congo in 1954 and was impressed with the services available. They were in general as good as, and in some cases superior to, those available in India.

By 1959, however, the stupendous rise of effective medical services had plateaued. Only 17 new medical facilities had been built, and auxiliary medical services had declined to 655. The number of leprosy hospitals was not given, though the number of leprosy patients treated had increased sharply to nearly 15,000. In general, one may say that the number of persons treated had increased sharply, while the number of institutions had increased only slightly.

From this general picture across a half century, we turn to detailed pictures of the main medical centers found in Zaire in the late seventies.

Contemporary Health Services

The ministries to the health of Zairians by Missions and Communities have increased greatly in magnitude and in variety since the early days mentioned in the previous section. Of primary importance are the hospitals located on rural stations as well as in cities and centers. Auxiliary services, such as dispensaries and public health programs, radiate from the hospitals. Medical training programs operate under their supervision. We are also concerned with the impact these medical ministries have for the growth of the Churches in Zaire. We will offer a few suggestions on ways of making the hospital and its auxiliary services more of an evangelistic and nurturing agency.

The Role of the Hospital in Zaire

Hospitals are centers of medical work. Here the doctors and other trained staff live and work. Here medicines are ordered and received for distribution. Operations are performed here, and more critical medical problems are treated. Expensive equipment is located at the hospitals rather than in rural dispensaries or public health centers. The direction and planning for the future begins here. Even though planning is reviewed at the headquarters of the Community sponsoring the hospital, the groundwork is laid here by those who are closest to the situation. Their recommendations are nearly always followed, within, of course, the limitations of staff and funds. Unlike American and European hospitals, those in Zaire serve as centers for services radiating many miles in each direction around them.

Location and Description of Some Major Hospitals

For our discussion in this section, we use two categories in order to classify hospitals in Zaire. Some are joint efforts of two or more Communities, whereas others are the sole responsibility of one Community.

We begin with the larger hospitals which are the joint effort of more than one Community. Of these, Kimpese is the pioneer and inspirer of the others. It is located in the Bas-Zaire Province, southwest of Kinshasa about two-thirds of the way toward the port city of Matadi. In numbers of buildings (well over a hundred), as well as in the volume of people treated, it ranks as one of the largest medical centers in Central Africa. Its roots go back to the Sona Bata hospital founded by the ABFMS, which is located some miles to the northeast on the road to Kinshasa. Dr. Glen Tuttle supervised the founding and operation of a school for nurses alongside of the hospital. Along about 1950, plans were made with Dr. Ernest Price of the BMS to open a joint medical center some four kilometers from the union school complex of Kimpese (now CECO). Medical work had been carried on at the school site for some years. In late 1952 construction was begun on the new site, and in early 1953 the first buildings were inaugurated and the Evangelical Medical Institute (Institut Médical Evangélique [IME]) was launched. The twenty-fifth anniversary of its founding was celebrated in May, 1978, and Dr. and Mrs. Tuttle, though retired for several years, were able to return and participate in the ceremonies.

At present ten Communities and Missions cooperate in the program. These are the BMS, the ABFMS, the SMF, the C&MA, the Canadian Baptist Overseas Mission Board, the DCCM, the Methodist Mission (MMCC and MMSC), the United Church of Canada, the Mennonites (Mission Board and Central Committee), and the American Leprosy Mission. Staff from these agencies are present from time to time, though each group does not have a representative on the staff at all times. In addition, the Peace Corps and Protestant Relief Agencies occasionally assign units to IME.

The Kimpese complex has its own board of managers formed by the top administrators plus representatives from each of the cooperating Communities and Missions. Funding comes from many sources. Missionary staff salaries come from cooperating Boards. Locally, fees form a large portion. Then come government subsidies for medicines and salaries of Zairian personnel. Philanthropic organizations and manufacturers of medicines based in England and North America contribute also. Church-related funding organizations give substantially from time to time for special projects. In 1976 forty-two individuals and ten local U.S.A. churches also contributed to the program.

In 1962 some Missions of the Upper Zaire Province decided to enlarge the existing hospital at Nyakunde, far to the northeast near the border with Uganda, and establish a medical school. Very shortly after the rebellion, Dr. Helen Rosevere (Heart of Africa Mission) returned from England in 1965 with supplies of medicines and equipment to operate this notable center. The following Missions were the founding agencies: AIM, WEC, UFM, MBK, and the Brethren.

We were fortunate to be able to tour the buildings and grounds of the Good Shepherd Hospital (134 beds) located about fifteen kilometers outside of the provincial capital of Kananga (West Kasai). Here Presbyterians and Mennonites work together in ministering to the needs of the population. Presbyterians have centralized much of their medical work here. This is the most recently built of the three complexes although the medical work was begun in 1954. Though smaller than Kimpese, it is very compact and well organized. As at Kimpese, the director is a Zairian who works closely with a missionary doctor consultant. Both hospitals operate harmoniously with this arrangement. As we talked with the staff of the Good Shepherd Hospital and watched it in operation, we got the feeling of the enthusiasm and dedication that new enterprises often generate.

We turn now to describe some hospitals sponsored by one Community. In former days nearly every station had a hospital with a doctor in charge or a trained missionary nurse under the supervision of a doctor who regularly visited and operated. Today this picture has changed somewhat. The lack of available doctors has caused Communities to centralize more and more. Of eight hospitals operated by CBZO only three have doctors, and no missionary nurses are in charge of hospitals. We noted that the Methodists of Shaba with fifteen stations and centers have only one hospital—Kapanga. We are not certain about the extent of centralization among other Communities but know it has taken place.

The BMS has operated a large and efficient hospital at Bolobo in Bandundu Province on the Zaire River. From 1973 until 1978 the Bolobo hospital was taken over and operated by the government through the FOMECO program. However, in 1978 the government turned it back to the British Baptist Community (CBFZ).

Since 1920 the DCCM operated hospitals on nearly all its stations. Its more important hospitals in 1960 were: Bolenge, eight kilometers out of Mbandaka in Equator Province, Lotumbe, Monieka, Mondombe, and Wema. Today, without any missionary physicians or nurses, these are in a sad condition.

To the north in the Ubangi-Mongala region, about a half hour's flight due east from Gemena, lies the impressive hospital at Karawa (ECM). There are usually about three doctors here with supporting nurses, all missionaries from overseas. The buildings are in excellent repair and the grounds kept very neat. This hospital serves a very large area around it.

About the same distance to the west of Gemena is the station of Tandala. Here the EFM runs a somewhat smaller operation, also serving a large area. There are two or three missionary doctors here at any time and a supporting staff of missionary nurses and technicians.

The ABFMS has three large hospitals with doctors. Vanga is the largest with two missionary doctors and a teaching nurse in the way of missionary staff. It also has a Zairian doctor and Zairian director and administrator. This hospital is located in Bandundu Province on the Kwilu River and was founded in 1928. It is interesting that one of the doctors is from Germany and the other from Canada. At the time this book was written, the American Baptist doctor usually stationed there was on furlough. However, he returned to Vanga in mid-1978. We mentioned Sona Bata in the Bas-Zaire, an hour's drive from Kinshasa. The doctor there is from Holland. Further southwest at Nsona Mpangu is a hospital with a few more beds supervised by a newly trained Zairian doctor.

In the Manianga area, north of the Zaire River and of Kimpese, lie several stations of the SMF. We are not certain as to which hospitals are open now. As elsewhere in Bas-Zaire Province, critical cases are brought to Kimpese. Since SMF stations have airstrips and a plane and pilot are stationed at Kimpese by MAF, access to Kimpese is easy and rapid.

In the Mayombe district on the Atlantic Coast, the C&MA has a fine hospital at Kinkonzi. This completes our limited survey of the major hospitals in Zaire operated by Missions and Communities.

Description of Medical Programs

With but few exceptions these large hospitals maintain similar programs. Each has an adequate operating theater, wards for various kinds of ailments, X ray and other equipment, well-equipped and well-staffed laboratories, a maternity section which is always active, a pediatrics department, an orthopedic department, a dispensary for outpatients, and a clinic for pre- and postnatal consultations. A few have dental departments. Most operate and supervise rural dispensaries, public health networks, and medical training programs. A new thrust is family planning and attempts at population control.

Kimpese is the only hospital we know that includes a leprosarium in its program. Nyakunde's leprosy program is scattered over nine centers, each with a trained student in charge. Two kilometers from the main hospital at Kimpese is Kivuvu, where a staff of three cares for the lepers unable to return to their villages. The number of inpatients is small, even though Kivuvu serves the entire western portion of Zaire, because new, effective medicine for leprosy was discovered. For this reason a leprosarium at Nsona Mpangu merged with Kivuvu. The American Leprosy Mission has contributed much medicine and technical advice and occasionally has provided staff. Projects like chicken raising, egg production, and raising garden products of fruits and vegetables help in the maintenance of this center.

Scope of Health Ministries

Earlier we described the impact of health services on the population in the beginnings of Missions. Now we will show the growth of the work by giving available statistics from various hospitals.

Kimpese has four hundred beds, making it a large hospital for Central Africa. Its staff includes four missionary doctors and one Zairian doctor. In addition, there are four missionary laboratory technicians, nurses with specialties in X ray, physiotherapy, and nutrition. There is quite a large staff of Zairians, which includes seventy-one units of medical personnel and twenty-two nonmedical people. This does not include the eighty students in the medical program who participate in the hospital routine several hours each day.

In 1977 the number of patients hospitalized were 7,723. Other significant statistics are: 1,264 maternity cases, 52,012 patients treated by the dispensary, 468 private clinic patients, 70,626 laboratory exams, 18,674 physiotherapy treatments, 3,869 X rays, 4,610 dental patients treated, and 1,250 babies born.

The medical center at Nyakunde has two hundred beds and a missionary staff of six doctors, six nurses, and three nonmedical and paramedical units. Its Zairian staff is composed of two doctors, thirty-five nurses, and sixty-nine nonmedical and paramedical units. In 1977 there were 69,636 people hospitalized, 353,261 treated at the dispensary, 4,867 operations performed, 1,609 babies born, 107,004 laboratory exams made, and 1,852 X rays taken.

The Methodist hospital located in Kapanga in Shaba has two resident doctors. It also has a staff of twenty-three Zairian nurses, eighteen nurses' helpers, and twenty-six other helpers trained in varying degrees. It treated 3,124 patients in its wards and 52,103 as outpatients. There were 579 babies born during the year. When compared with the totals from the other stations where only dispensaries are listed, these indicate that the largest part of the medical work is being done at Kapanga. However, there is a significant work being done at the dispensaries located at five other stations and centers, and it may well be that instead of continuing to call these hospitals, they choose to designate them as dispensaries because there is no resident doctor. We have already described the staff of doctors working at three American Baptist hospitals. Vanga has 258 beds, treated 4,849 inpatients and 53,950 outpatients. Sona Bata has 100 beds, treated 3,028 inpatients and 18,784 outpatients. Nsona Mpanga has 120 beds, treated 2,108 inpatients and 39,992 outpatients. Totals for the eight hospitals, including Vanga, Sona Bata, Nsona Mpanga, Kikongo, Moanza, Boko, Kipatra-Katika, and Nselo, are: 770 beds, 14,846 inpatients, and 179,374 outpatients.

From the foregoing it should be fairly clear that all across the vast land of Zaire, thousands upon thousands of people are coming into contact with Christian medical services. There are government-owned and operated hospitals, but these are few and suffer from the same kinds of problems as face the hospitals run by the Communities, though most often to a greater degree.

Some Problems Faced

Some of these problems are as follows: Lack of medicine is often cited as a block to better ministry. Health and even lives depend on a constant supply. We cannot tell how many deaths are due to this lack, but we know that the situation is serious. Linked to this is the high cost of medicines. For example, medicine for intestinal parasites is so expensive that ordinary people cannot afford it. It costs two days' income for one person to be cleared of parasites. It costs one month's income for an entire family to receive this treatment. One solution to the high cost of medicine is for hospitals to buy as many medicines as possible outside the country where prices are lower. Also, some hospitals raise prices charged to those able to afford them in order to lower it for ordinary people.

Another problem is the lack of professional conscience on the part of many Zairian staff members. Some patients have died and others have been held back from earlier recovery because of neglect in their care. This is especially pertinent in connection with the medical training school students. When the medical schools were smaller, the supervising staff could inculcate more positive attitudes and understanding into the trainees. There may be cultural reasons to explain this problem which need to be researched and ways found to counteract them. We suggest that since there are few absolutes in

Zairian culture, it is difficult for a student to comprehend the urgency of following procedures for treatment, laboratory tests, and simple hygiene exactly. However, it has been observed that where students are given opportunity for spiritual growth, these problems are observed less often.

There is a crisis in staffing that prevails in many of these hospitals. Kimpese, already operating with a staff below the number needed, faces the further loss of two doctors and one lab technician with little hope of replacement as of this writing. Missions are finding it increasingly difficult to recruit missionary doctors. Zairian doctors usually are assigned to city or town hospitals, rarely to rural hospitals. The Baptist Council on World Mission has been negotiating with Baptists of South India and the way is clear for two doctors to go to Zaire. We hope that this beginning of exchange of personnel from other Conventions and Churches around the world will become a trend. One other way of helping in this crisis is the upgrading of Zairian nurses with devotion and capability by sending them abroad to study for a year. This has brought satisfactory results in the five CBZO hospitals without doctors and has provided directors at Vanga and Sona Bata.

Church Growth and Medicine

Since these hospitals were established and are run today for the purpose of undergirding the primary task of proclaiming the gospel, founding Churches, and nurturing new Christians, it is imperative that we discuss this subject briefly. In the earlier stages of Mission, health ministries were simple and very basic. Often the doctor and/or nurse doubled as evangelist. Itineration into the district surrounding the station where the hospital was located for purposes of public health programs was combined with the proclamation of the Good News, consultations on the administration and functioning of the churches, and the examining and baptizing of candidates.

Today, specialization, as well as the ever-increasing volume of the work, tends to separate the medical teams from personnel working with the churches. One of two things usually results. Either hospitals become more and more neutral in regard to a Christian witness, or they develop special programs.

The appointment of chaplains uniquely responsible for preaching services in the wards, for personal counseling, for bedside visitation, is one such special answer. The rediscovery by modern medical people in general that body and soul are very closely related has spurred the wide acceptance of this program. IME, Kimpese, has the further challenge of being isolated from a local church and so has formed one (119 members) with a full range of specialized ministries to all the staff, students in the medical school, the patients, and their friends and relatives. Here the pastor of the congregation and the chaplain are one person. Until recently he had a full-time assistant and will probably have one again soon.

Teams composed of medical and agricultural personnel which travel in the district now often have a member devoted to spiritual ministry. At Vanga the self-supporting public health program involves the pilot of the plane and a minister, as teacher and director for the region's Bible Study by Extension program. The team method works well wherever tried in Zaire.

IME, Kimpese, is effectively using choirs, Bibles, portions of Scripture, and tracts to reinforce the ministry of the chaplain. The administration is thinking of piping religious music and sermons throughout the buildings of the complex as another way of reaching people who cannot go to the Church.

There are many acts of mercy which the chaplains and local pastors do for those under their care which demonstrate their love and concern. They have special funds and collect used clothing to help those who cannot afford even the minimal fees charged and who arrive with only ragged, dirty clothes.

The need for evaluation of programs is evident here as elsewhere. The difficulties faced in getting firm data on which to make evaluations were brought out by the director of the Good Shepherd Hospital, who kindly gave us a few minutes of his time. He had the general impression that some patients had made solid decisions to accept and follow Jesus as Lord and Savior, but he had received no reports on how many (IME reported 20 in 1976). A definite system for keeping track of evangelistic visits, their purpose, and results must be set up by the administration and the chaplain, or local pastor where a chaplain is not feasible. This should not be difficult since hospitals are already very efficient in record keeping. The center at Nyakunde has succeeded in this and reports 350 conversions and 362 rededications for the past year.

The need for follow-through on decisions made and incorporating these people into a local church is pressing. Contact with the pastor of the area to which the patient who has received spiritual help is returning is a good way to preserve the decision and to insure further growth. However, as long as the patient is under the care of the chaplain or pastor, he can and should be repeatedly visited and encouraged through prayer and ministry of the Scriptures.

The Missionary Component

Nowhere can the continuing need for partnership in Missions be seen more clearly than in Christian hospitals and health services. These work better when the staff consists of Zairians and Europeans. This is not because Africans cannot manage hospitals. They can. It is rather that the rate of advance in medicine is so great, the tasks so numerous, and the costs of medicine so high, that it helps to have a missionary doctor and/or missionary nurse on the staff.

If someone were to argue that sooner or later the Church in Zaire will have to conduct its hospitals with an entirely national staff, we would at once agree, but maintain that *that* time has not yet come, and does not seem likely to come for several decades. The one world, about which we hear so much in contemporary thought, means that advanced sections of the Church ought to provide help to developing sections.

If one should say that in a sovereign Zaire the honor of the land demands that Zairians occupy all staff positions, we would reply that the argument is faulty. "The honor" of either missionaries or nations is not a major consideration. Christians are concerned that the services be the most effective possible, as many of the sick as possible be healed, and such excellent public health be rendered that the whole nation abounds in energy. In regard to mining copper, for example, the honor of Zaire is better served by employing European technicians in great numbers in Shaba than it would be by Africanizing the mines from top to bottom and getting out a tenth as much copper. In the case of Christian medical men and women, this is even more true. The European mining technicians have to be paid by African money, while the missionary physicians and nurses are loving gifts by sister Churches in Eurica.

Should some Board of Missions, tired of raising money and recruiting missionaries to go to Africa and confident (in the way that people who have never lived in Zaire can be confident) that an immediate moratorium on missionaries should be declared, exclaim, "The dependent stance of Zairian Churches must be corrected. The best way to do this is to send the hospitals and health services no more missionaries," we would reply as follows:

"Eventually fraternal medical workers must, of course, cease to be sent. We have seen excellent Christian hospitals in Japan, India, and Latin America staffed entirely by nationals. However, the evidence we saw in the summer of 1977 makes us sure that in Zaire this is not the time to cut off missionary doctors and nurses. Far from paternalistically insisting that Christian medicine in Zaire should be staffed entirely by Zairians, what you should stress are efficient hospitals and health services. If anyone doubts that missionaries are still needed in Christian medicine in this great land, let him or her visit several hospitals which have maintained a strong missionary component and several which have not. Let him or her ask African pastors and teachers whether they would like to have a Eurican physician on the staff. Let him or her ask the Zairians on the hospital staff, especially the Zairian head of the hospital. Let him or her look at the evidence."

As the population of Zaire doubles in the next twenty-five years, the task of medicine will grow greater and greater. The missionary nurse and doctor—gracious gifts by sister denominations in Eurica—bring not merely medical competence, but also a keen Christian conscience and dedication. They are not looking for jobs. If they were doing that, they would stay in America and work for five times the salary. They are answering God's call.

While the medical gifts are undoubtedly the main reason for sending nurses and doctors to Zaire, their Christian gifts are a very weighty additional reason. They help maintain in Eurica a conscience concerning the evangelization of Zaire. They help build a sense of relatedness of humankind, the new world community, and the reborn humanity freed of all that demeans and debases. Christian medical men and women form an essential part of the mix which Zaire needs for the coming decades. The missionary component in Christian health services? Yes, it must be maintained.

9

Measuring Church Growth

Many Christians have an animus against measuring church growth. They think it smacks of "numerolatry," stresses mere numbers, and exalts big churches just because they are big. As the church growth movement has spread across the world, invariably critics have reminded us that David numbered the people and God rebuked him by sending a great pestilence upon Israel. A more careful reading of the Bible shows that the book of Acts records the numbers of Christians with great care and God commanded the numbering of his people on many occasions. Reflection recalls that all worthwhile enterprises keep track of where they are and where they are going. Physicians record temperatures down to the fraction of a degree. School superintendents know exactly how many boys and girls they have today and are likely to have ten years from now. Owners of coal mines can tell the number of tons mined and sold in any given month. Numbers can be misused, of course, but rightly used they are of inestimable value to the Church, as well as to other enterprises.

What Should Be Measured?

Missions have always kept track of church growth. The number of missionaries on the field, supporting churches at home, dollars of expected income, new churches established, rate of growth of the Church, and many other items have been scrupulously recorded.

It is always important for Missions and Churches to know exactly how many Christians they have and what the ratio between communicants and the total community is. A ratio of one to three, which is what we see in Zaire, is not a good permanent ratio. It means that many more in the community should be brought to communicant status, that is, to confessed and practiced discipleship. We would like to see a ratio of one to two, or even one to 1.6.

It is also important to know the number of baptisms of children of Christians, as compared to the number of people of the world who for the first time are confessing Christ and becoming his followers. We were present at several great baptismal services in Zaire. At all of them, most of those baptized were school children. A missionary remarked, "I often wonder whether we should be baptizing so many who are under ten." Obviously, almost everyone over ten was already a member of the Church in these villages. Only the oncoming generation provided candidates for baptism. A measurement which would show this at a glance for every congregation in the whole Community would immediately reveal the degree to which its villages had been evangelized and its own children brought to Christian decision.

The rate of growth of the Church in all areas where there are many practicing animists or marginal Christians is essential knowledge. If the denomination is growing slowly by biological or transfer increase, it is coming empty-handed out of ripe fields. Sinner-converting evangelism should be stressed. A large part of the income of the Church or Mission should be devoted to finding the lost and returning them to the Father's house. Without accurate and reliable figures year after year and decade after decade, the plain duty of the Church is obscured in fog. Leaders, Zairian and expatriate, continue systems of priorities which no longer are germane.

In the early days, when the average Mission had only a few hundred or a few thousand members per station, the missionaries in charge and their African helpers knew the entire flock as individuals. The need for records may not have been as great then. The right thing could be done because the people were well known. But today, with policies being laid down for whole Communities, and by the ECZ for the whole nation, there is no substitute for accurate figures. The leaders cannot know each Christian. They do not even know each congregation. A responsible system of membership accounting is absolutely essential. When Norman Riddle showed Dr. Bokeleale the Research Instrument, he exclaimed, "This is what the Church needs. It will give us eyes to see where we are going."

As we toured the seven main areas to gather data, again and

again leaders in charge of regions would give us figures with some hesitations. "We think something like this is the fact," one man said frankly. We respected his honesty. Many more could have said just that. It is clear that a more regular and reliable system of accounting will help the Zairian Churches very greatly.

A responsible system means appointing in each large Community one person—a social scientist in the service of the Church—whose main task is to assemble the data month after month and year after year. He would visit many congregations and count houses, families, and individuals. He would check the church rolls against his own count to arrive at some judgment concerning their accuracy. The person would also teach classes in membership accounting in theological training schools for pastors in the making, and in short seminars for pastors in the field. He would prepare and have printed in quantity standardized membership books, baptismal records, and death and marriage records. These enable responsible church membership in any land. Lacking these and lacking training in how to use them, Communities and Missions work in the dark, hoping that what they do is correct.

Gathering Hard Data

As the Riddle-McGavran team prepared for its survey in the summer of 1977, it sent out the five-page Research Instrument which is reproduced on pages 173-179. We print this in full because we want readers to understand what measuring the Church involves. It is not merely counting the number of Christians. There is much more to the task than that. Quality as well as quantity must be measured.

Both quantity and quality ought to be measured in each tribe, each subtribe, each region, each language area, and each ward in the cities. The *particularity* of church growth cannot be stressed too greatly. The denomination never grows "as a whole." It is always in particular segments of the population that the Church grows or stagnates. The "field total" is merely a large number in which defeats on the local scene cancel out victories. To get a useful picture, we must know where defeats are occurring, where there are victories, and the magnitude of each. Then we know what Christ's army ought to be doing.

Observe that we must obtain not merely the membership of one denomination, but of all the denominations at work in a given area. Then, in addition, leaders of the Christian enterprise ought to know how many practicing animists and marginal Christians there are, too. The latter are the most winnable block of people in the world. Church administrators and educators should know how many nominal Christians there are and how many practicing Christians. Responsible statistics give an accurate, meaningful picture of the Christian task.

Our Lord said that the good shepherd knew that ninety-nine were safe and one was lost. How much more urgent would good bookkeeping be if twenty-seven were safe and seventy-three were lost?

The Measurement of Qualities

The *qualitative* aspect of church life is most significant. It can readily be measured. The giving of the Church needs much illumination. Is it being done by the most devout—a small percent of the total members? Is tithing practiced by half of the members or just by a few? What is the average income of the villagers, and how do their offerings to the Church in cash and in kind compare with it?

The degree of devotion also can be measured. What proportion of this congregation attends the worship of God regularly? What proportion reads the Bible daily, weekly, never? After they leave school, do young people keep up their habits of private devotion? How many of them do and how many do not? The improvement of society, the changing of the social structure, the adoption of biblical standards of production, and of the treatment of women—all can be measured. The social scientist in the service of the Church would constantly provide the Church with insights into the degree of excellence obtained in many of these Christian qualities.

Measurement is not done to satisfy curiosity but to enable God's obedient servants to do what He requires. We have stressed the enormous opportunity which God is handing the Church in the return of the parochial schools to its control. However, to extract the greatest degree of Christian living from the parochial school system, educators will have to know accurately a great deal about the quality of life in their Communities. Only then will they be able to judge whether a study of the New Testament book by book is more effective for attaining these ends than, let us say, studying a book which depicts Zairian problems and then takes the high school students to those parts of the Bible which bear on those particular problems.

We are now ready to scan the Research Instrument which was

prepared for the summer of 1977. It was given to leaders in many
Communities. They were asked to assemble information on each of
the topics, looking forward to sharing it with the survey team.

RESEARCH INSTRUMENT
GATHERING HARD DATA
KINSHASA CHURCH GROWTH CONFERENCE 1977

I. **Tribal Analysis of Each Area** (12 Areas)

   A. Map of the area, with the land occupied by each tribe and
subtribe indicated on it. In case of a city, indicate one-tribe
wards or areas and those where many tribes live all mixed up.

   B. Number of villages and approximate size of average village.
In case of cities, omit "B."

   C. Population Facts. If accurate census is available for 1930,
1940, 1950, 1960, 1970, then give facts for each of these years.
Total population . . . of each tribe and subtribe in the area.
Number of men
Number of women
Number of children below the age of 12
Number of adults—above the age of 12
Graph of growth of the population of each tribe 1930–1976.

If census figures are not available after 1950, then give those
for '30, '40 and '50, and estimates for 1960–1970 and 1976.

   D. Relationship of Each Tribe to Surrounding Tribes: friendly,
hostile, cool.
For example:
Tribe 1 to Tribe 2, friendly, intermarriage occurs.
Tribe 1 to Tribe 3, hostile, no intermarriage occurs—serious
linguistic barriers.
Tribe 1 to Tribe 4, friendly, but little intermarriage occurs.

II. **Tribal Analysis of the Church or Churches**

   A. In this area are the following denominations:

      (We all know that there are only three Churches [RC, ECZ,

and Kimbango] and we honor the ECZ . . . but the facts we need are of the building blocks—the denominations—out of which the ECZ was built.

In some cities, where many tribes have flooded in, the building blocks will be obscured and merged. Splendid. *There and there only* enter ECZ meaning "Here new congregations of the ECZ are formed.")

Baptist British, Baptist American, Baptist Australian . . .
Presbyterian Southern, Presbyterian Northern, Presbyterian Canadian . . . Alliance, Mennonite, Evangelical Covenant . . .
Methodist . . . Lutheran . . .
Roman Catholic
Kimbanguist

B. Map showing the tribes (IA), and the portion of each tribe which now belongs to each of the denominations listed under IIA.

C. Growth Tables and Graphs

Each of the denominations in this area has grown as portrayed in the tables and graphs here shown.

(Accurate statistics may not be available but get as good estimates as you can. They are much better than nothing.)

1. For each primary denomination in each tribe. For example, for Denomination X the dates and communicants might be as follows:

At the end of the period Number of Communicants

a) *Exploratory Period 1905-1919* (when the mission was there, but little growth took place.)   315

b) *Considerable growth by conversion of school boys and girls 1919-1930*   2,792

c) *Period of Tribal Inflooding 1930-1940.* Clusters of families and whole villages came in. Revival was on.   30,411

d) *1. Period of Biological Growth 1940-1976* (often decline)   33,988

*2. Period of Biological Growth As-
sisted by "Revivals" here and there
1940-1976*   52,600

2. For secondary denominations in each tribe.

   (Data such as that given in 1 above for *each* secondary
   denomination. The five or six periods listed will vary from
   tribe to tribe. In some, for some denominations, there
   never was any tribal inflooding. That took place into
   another denomination—or has not yet taken place. In
   some, all that *this* denomination got was Conversion of
   School Boys and Girls. In some, emigration to the big city,
   or invasion by the Roman Catholics or Kimbanguists kept
   growth of *this* denomination to slow biological growth, or
   brought decline. *The goal is an accurate picture of what
   has really happened in each tribe shown on the map in
   regard to the denominations there at work.*

   Those gathering hard data please feel free to name their
   own periods their own way. The above names will usually
   fit; but in case they do not, the researcher should give the
   period the name he thinks fits it best. In some cases the
   major denomination in a given tribe will be the Roman
   Catholic. The secondary denomination will be the
   Methodist, or the Disciples, or the Alliance. In other
   tribes, the Methodist will be the major denomination and
   the Catholic will be one of the secondary denominations.)

3. Now draw graphs according to the figures assembled.

   There should be one graph for each denomination in *each
   tribe or subtribe.*

   Please avoid like poison the temptation to regard all
   Christians as one, to insist that tribes really mean nothing.
   The State is against them. Tribalism is the big enemy. We
   want to build up one strong nation in which tribal
   consciousness does not divide the citizens. We want one
   Church, not a series of small Churches each fiercely
   conscious of its tribal rather than its Christian character.

   Of course, the ideal is One Church—neither Jew nor
   Greek, slave nor free, male nor female. But as long as we do

have men and women, we are going to sleep them in separate dormitories. As long as we do have tribes and tribal consciousness, it is the part of wisdom to see the actual situation.

How small units shall we take into consideration in gathering data? Suppose a large tribe has several subtribes; shall we gather data for each of them? The answer to this question depends on circumstances. If the subtribe is a really separate homogeneous unit, has clear consciousness of itself as a separate unit, intermarries largely within its confines, then by all means gather data for it separately. If the subtribe speaks a slightly different language, or dialect, or lives in a clearly demarcated area, then gather data for it separately. If, on the other hand, the subtribe intermarries quite freely with other subtribes and merges into other subtribes, then gather data for this whole tribe.

The graphs of growth will be revealing. When these are brought to the Church Growth Conference July 1-5, 1977, they will give us all a clear vision of what has in fact happened, is happening, and is likely to happen. We shall see where nurture and where evangelism are indicated. We shall see where the Church of Zaire can carry on nurture and evangelism, and where continued missionary effort from abroad—or possibly multiplied missionary effort from abroad—is urgent.

III. **Judgment as to What Particular "Homogeneous Unit Churches" Need by Way of Nurture.**

(The foregoing will—in the several areas we visit—be laid before us to show me the actual face of the Church. Problems which arose in the data gathering will be discussed. We will see not only the data, but also the situation on the ground—the actual Christians and congregations and institutions, and remaining evangelistic task, and the difficulties and problems involved. Possibly out of this, some refinement of the data will come or slight changes in the manner of presentation so that it will harmonize with what is gathered in other areas.

With these accurate pictures of what the Real Churches on the Ground look like, *what the Particular Churches are,* what these

Homogeneous Unit Churches are, we can now ask meaningful questions as to Christian nurture. We can see the perfecting process in regard to particular segments of the Church Universal.

For example, here is a subtribe of 9,000 souls. The major denomination there is the Evangelical Free Church, which now numbers 1,300 communicants. The Kimbanguists have about a thousand in their community. About 3,000 are still animists; and these live in a remote section of the field across a difficult swamp. That is a clear picture and enables us to see what ought to be done there. Observe what a different picture we would have were the 3,000 who are still pagans living a few in every village and constituting those who have steadily rejected Christianity—the drunkards, the liars, the morons, and the cunning—who are part of the total population in all communities.

Under the third and fourth main heads of the Data Gathering Process, we shall be asking, "Given these conditions in this particular segment of the Church, what now needs to be done by way of Christian nurture and by way of church multiplying evangelism?"

The pictures of the situation and the judgments as to what needs to be done will be different *for each segment of the Church, for each homogeneous unit church.* Particularly is this true for rural areas and for urban areas. *The cities present particular problems and opportunities.* The Church Growth Conference of July, 1977, ought to help us see the urban situation clearly and to plan effective strategy for it. I trust that in each of the 12 areas studied, there will be both a rural segment and an urban segment to which particular attention is paid. It is impossible for all Zaire to be studied. So the segments to be studied should be selected with great care. *They must be typical segments.)*

A. At the Level of the Local Congregation

    1. Development of habits of regular and devout worship of God.

    2. Development of habits of regular intelligent study of the Bible and (where necessary) of ability to read the Bible.

    3. Development of stewardship sufficient to nurture and extend the Church.

    4. Development of social action aimed at evils which

oppress Zairians—tribal hatreds, low productivity, drink and gambling, sexual offenses (here fill in what you consider the great evils which oppress Christians and non-Christians in Zaire today and tomorrow).

5. Development of authentic Zairian modes of *Christian* living, evangelizing, and worshiping.

B. Preparation of Pastors of Village Congregations—possibly part-time.

C. Preparation of Pastors of Large Urban Congregations.

D. Preparation of Zairian missionaries to CAR, CHAD, LIBERIA, IVORY COAST, ETHIOPIA, GUINEA, ANGOLA, ETC.,

and as fast as feasible to every other block of unevangelized people in the world. Korea has more than a hundred missionaries to North America actively and effectively discipling Korean non-Christians who have emigrated here. Why should not Zaire send missionaries *to where non-Christians* abound in all six continents?

IV. **Judgment as to What Particular Churches Need to Complete the Evangelistic Task**

A. *Facts Concerning the Pagan Reservoir*

1. In each particular homogeneous unit considered (each particular tribe) how much pagan reservoir is there?

Does this consist in a cluster of solidly pagan villages or as segments of every village?

If as segments of every village, is the pagan segment *organized?* That is, do all its members belong to some animist society, some association of fetish worshipers? Are they followers of given witch doctors or priests?

Or is it *unorganized*—simply those who do not want to walk in the Christian way?

Is the natural linkage of the pagan reservoir with *this* denomination or with *that?*

2. Where are the still unchurched sections of Zaire? (Large map, please)

B. *What Kind of Evangelism Would Reach and Disciple Each Particular Pagan Reservoir?*

(Observe that the answers will differ depending on whether we are speaking about a solidly pagan cluster of villages or a solidly pagan segment of each village or the unorganized individuals who reject Christianity)

C. *What Kind of Resources Would be Needed to Disciple Each Reservoir?*

From the Church (Churches) in Zaire?

Lay effort—Near Neighbor Evangelism E-1
Denominational Effort—E-2
Denominational Effort—E-3

From the World Church?

Resources from the World Church might be missionaries—from Ghana or Nigeria? Or from Korea? Or from North America or Germany?

Resources might be money.

Resources might be Training Schools to prepare the task forces which would develop the particular kinds of evangelism which are required by the particular kinds of pagan reservoirs encountered.

The Outcome

As was to be expected, sending these Research Instruments out to busy missionaries and asking them to put in the weeks of research needed to obtain the answers produced spotty results. A few carried through most of the procedures in their own small fields, villages, or towns.[1] Many missionaries formed estimates in fairly large regions concerning the tribes and the degree of their Christianization. In several places, they prepared maps showing in some detail the tribes in which Roman Catholics, Alliance, Baptists, or Disciples et al. were strong. At Gemena we were given a list of the major tribes of the Ubangi area as well as an estimate as to what percentage of each was Protestant, Roman Catholic, Practicing Animist, or Kimbanguist.

The value of the Research Instrument was repeatedly affirmed, but gathering the data was clearly too big an undertaking for busy missionaries. Using this instrument involved a habit of mind, an ability to see through immediate work to the unevangelized, through those present in church and school to those not present—the marginals and nominals and animists—in the myriad villages. It also required an amount of time which missionaries carrying heavy responsibilities could not give. There was a need for *someone in each major region of this vast country*—as large as the United States east of the Mississippi—*whose major task it would be to compile such data year after year.*

Urgent Need for Social Scientists

Mission executives, on looking at this Research Instrument, have said wistfully, "We need this kind of information at every level— recruiting new missionaries, training missionaries, allocating budgets, raising money, and assisting the Sister Churches in Zaire." Dr. Bokeleale's comment has already been mentioned. Of the desirability of this information there can be no doubt.

We must point out that this new urgent need which Zaire brings before Christian Missions requires more than talk. Action is required. Merely carrying on good church and mission work will not gather adequate data. The light provided by the permanent statistician will not be forthcoming until the permanent statistician is there. The naive policy to avoid like poison is that which says, "In these new days we must give all authority to the young Church. For its own good it must learn to stand on its own feet. If it wants a permanent statistician, it must ask us for one. We shall then give it a small grant toward that end and encourage it to appoint a Zairian to the post." This procedure does not produce responsible membership accounting. Rather, if a Mission sees that the Community with which it works does not yet realize this need, then, as a good partner, it has the duty to sensitize the Community to the need and work with it to obtain competent personnel and an adequate budget.

Keeping accurate records, training pastors to regard them as an essential tool, providing the standardized forms and record books needed, spot checking to make sure that congregational figures are accurate, retraining pastors and district superintendents from year to year, and (hopefully) putting data on computers so that it becomes instantly available, is highly specialized work. Like school work, like hospital work, it will require specialists who devote a major portion of their time to this task.

When a Community has reached 80,000, 150,000, 200,000, 500,000, Missions face a new situation. One of the ordained servants, such as each Community must have, is the social scientist in the service of the Great Commission. We have devoted this entire chapter to drive this point home. Were the Missions and Communities to recruit, train, and keep working a corps of perhaps a dozen men and women—permanent statisticians—they would be making a wise use of their God-given resources. We have a lively conviction of the need for pastors, evangelists, educationists, and physicians, but in addition to these, permanent, well-trained statisticians have come to be an essential part of the team in this large Church of sixteen million Christians now—soon to be thirty million. That is what it means at midday to carry on Mission in a land where "nearly everyone is a Christian."

Should the Statistician Be a Missionary?

Our considered opinion is that at this stage the Churches in Zaire would be well advised to ask their assisting Missions to recruit, train, and maintain in the nation for the foreseeable future a corps of missionary statisticians. We recommend to the Boards that they secure the services of such persons. They should always be career missionaries and often ordained ministers of the gospel. Each should learn both French and the major language of the area to which he or she goes. They should have adequate working budgets and be made available to those Churches which request them.

Furthermore, as fast as any Zairian denomination raises the salary for a Zairian statistician and recruits a suitable man or woman for the post, he or she should be trained and the task made over to him or her. We consider the appointment of a permanent statistician by the missionary societies to be a high priority in staffing their Missions. We do not regard this post as a high priority for the Zairian Churches. Their men and women, for some time to come, should be prepared for schools, hospitals, pastoral posts, the active leadership of the Churches, which can be and will be paid for by the Churches. Let the denominations of this land deliberately accept the free labor which a missionary statistician embodies. He or she will be a very useful servant provided by sister Churches across the seas. The time will come when a wealthy Zairian Church will provide the budget for its own persons to carry on this highly specialized undertaking. That will be normal. All we plead is, "Let the process be natural." Let the post not be regarded as a challenge to national pride. Of course, Zairians can become statisticians, but they are more needed in other places. As long as the missionary societies will provide this free labor, the Churches in this large land should, we think, accept the offering with thanks. The task in countries like Zaire where almost everyone has become Christian is to find segments of the total task, which are urgent, which will greatly benefit the Church, and which can be filled by fraternal workers from sister Churches, without dominating the Church. The small, permanent statistical staff is that kind of assistance.

Having seen the enormous approximations and educated guesses which underlie so much of Church and Mission work in lands of the young Churches, including Zaire, we have a respectful regard for the necessity of hard data. The cause of Christ needs the truth; and while truth can be ascertained, it is a very complex whole. It is made up of many different measurements and judgments and is continually growing and changing. It can be represented by figures, charts, and graphs, but the process is not easy. It requires trained personnel to make it yield the rich rewards which are there.

PART III
Crucial Issues

10

Development and
Christian Mission

Development may be defined as that complex of activities mounted sometimes by governments, sometimes by Eurican nations, sometimes by missionary societies or by individual missionaries or ministers in an attempt to assist a community or a state to a more human existence. As the term is used today, a more human existence is held to mean more to eat, more to wear, less disease, more industrialization, more education, and more harnessing of the resources of the land. Development aims at temporal improvements of all kinds. It does not mean spiritual improvement or the development of congregations and denominations which are more obedient to God's revealed will or more indwelt by the Holy Spirit. Claiming that it also means growth in the Christian life confuses matters. Development does not prepare people for heaven. It attempts to make their earthly life more pleasant and satisfying.

The Tremendous Need and Opportunity for Development

We were struck in every region of Zaire which we visited with the need of the Zairian churches and of our Zairian brothers and sisters in Christ for development. This great land offers tremendous opportunity for development. Missionaries and nationals alike in denomination after denomination spoke of opportunities. These leap out at one. They cry aloud to be done. We mention a few of the many possibilities.

The water power of Zaire is only beginning to be tapped. The

185

Inga-Shaba dam harnesses a very small percentage of the total power. At Karawa in the Ubangi missionaries harnessed the power of one large spring a mile or so from the mission station and provided clean water. Electric lights and power for a very large church and mission establishment are in the planning stage of another project. Both of the streams near Vanga, in which we witnessed baptisms, could be dammed and become permanent sources of electrical power for the surrounding villages. The mountains of the east and of Bas-Zaire are threaded with big streams waiting to be developed.

As we have said in the Introduction, cattle raising offers tremendous scope for development. Abundant grass, land, and water should make Zaire a cattle paradise. The present system of cultivating the land solely by means of hoes wielded by women could so profitably give place to plowing. Abundant water points dramatically toward the making of rice fields and the rearing of water buffalo, which would be a most profitable form of development. With oil playing out in the world, a carting industry would seem to be a natural development. Excellent wood is available for cart wheels and cart bodies. Oxen and water buffalo can do in Zaire what they do all across the advanced countries of Asia—draw hundreds of thousands of carts. These could be a highly needed supplement to whatever cars and trucks are available. Carts do not require nicely paved roads; dirt roads do very well. The discovery of oil off the coast must not deceive us into thinking that internal combustion engines will become as common in Zaire as they are in the United States.

The manufacture of earthen pots on potters' wheels could easily be taught. I watched a woman on the Tschuapa River make a pot by hammering out two big pancakes of clay, forming two half pots laboriously with her hands and then turning one of them over onto the other and joining them into one pot. It was a very skillful performance which I would not have believed possible except that I saw it; but making pottery on wheels is easier, quicker, and better. It should be taught. Earthen pots baked in homemade kilns greatly improve material living. Asian Christian potters could readily be brought in to teach their skills to those people who now make pots in the laborious way.

In Mbandaka and Karawa we saw big healthy teak trees growing along the main streets. They appeared to be forty years old and had no doubt been planted by the Belgians. They prove that teak can be grown in Zaire. Teak is the world's premier wood—lasting, easy to work, termite-proof, not given to warping and distortion. The forests of Zaire have their own good trees, of course, but these can be supplemented by teak and fine Brazilian woods. The native trees and the imports would supply a marvelous base for a skilled woodworking industry. Zaire could manufacture and export fine furniture at a fraction of the cost which other nations can.

Time would fail were I to mention the existing plantations of oil nuts, coffee, and other agricultural products which the world now eagerly buys and which, because of exploding population, the world will all the more eagerly buy thirty years from now.

Huge opportunity for development can be seen in the field of sanitation. At present rural Zairians too often use fields and forests as latrines, although each village has built an adequate number of latrines. As a result, in this land where much rain falls, hookworm is endemic. One public-health worker told us that 70 percent of the population in his villages were infected with hookworm. His effort has been (a) to get the people to dig, build, and use latrines; (b) to cleanse the population of hookworm by medication; and (c) to trust that the use of sanitary latrines will keep the incidence of hookworm down. After a couple of years measurement showed that now only 20 percent of the people were infected. I was reminded of a case in India where public-health workers in a similar fashion taught twenty thousand people to dig and use bore-hole latrines. The plan worked as long as the officials manifested great interest in it. When they turned to other matters, the bore holes were given up and the people went back to the fields. This does not mean that such development is impossible. Rather, it means that one simple demonstration is not enough. It must be built into the educational system and taught, encouraged, and enforced over a twenty-year period.

Cooperatives and credit unions are other development projects needed in Zaire. Both have been tried and some successes have been registered. The CBZO credit union is strong and growing. There has been no hint of mismanagement of funds. Cooperatives outside the Communities have often foundered for lack of integrity on the part of those handling the money and lack of trust on the part of others involved. The Christian Communities offer the best chance for cooperation to succeed.

A team of five Zairian leaders and two missionaries stopped at the town of Kimvula (Bas-Zaire) to discuss with the Commissaire du Zone details of getting an airstrip approved by the local government.

During the course of the conversation the Commissaire pleaded with the team to make his area top priority for evangelism, church planting, and programs of community development since the provincial government had "forgotten" them and the Community represented by the team was their "only hope."

Millard Fuller, of the Disciples of Christ, came to Zaire and built a low-cost housing project at Mbandaka. A loan company was formed so that people buying the houses could pay back by means of low monthly payments. The survey team was very impressed by the appearance of the houses and the reported low incidence of difficulty in collecting the payments. Residents seemed happy and appreciative, some taking the pains to add flowers and plants.

Another large Community is preparing to launch a similar project based on the project described in the book written by Millard Fuller. His inspiration came from the Koinonia Community founded by Clarence Jordan in Americus, Georgia.

The Tremendous Difficulties

The results of the experiments cited above underscore vividly that these great opportunities for development face tremendous · difficulties. Merely describing them is one thing; getting people to do them is quite another. Changing from one system to another is never easy anywhere. It has not been done; therefore, it cannot be done. It is not necessary. It will not work. It does not fit in with the cultural expectations. For example, in one part of India, a huge irrigation system built at great cost by the last Britishers in the 1930s lay totally unused because the villagers believed that irrigation water would rot the rice. Furthermore, one had to pay for irrigation water while sky water was free. Then in 1953 there was a very long dry spell. The entire rice crop was dying. In a sudden rush, the owners of seventy thousand acres signed contracts, saved their crops, and have been singing the praises of controlled irrigation ever since.

We were told in many places in Zaire that improvement of agriculture has met a formidable obstacle in the fact that Zairian men traditionally were the hunters and fighters and the women did the field work. Men are not about to do women's work. In 1954 a Belgian official said to me, "Dr. McGavran, these men just will not do normal field work. It is beneath them." A whole new way of looking at men's work is required; and that will take time.

It is encouraging to see that significant beginnings have been made in reorienting men to cattle raising for beef in the regions surrounding Gemena in the Ubangi-Mongali, Sandoa in Shaba, and Lusekele and Kikwit in Bandundu. Areas like the Kivu which border on cattle-raising cultures in East Africa are much further along in this movement. While these beginnings are cause for hope, the fact remains that the mere introduction of cattle raising is only part of the picture. In the rain forests and in the south of Zaire, far too many people still have the idea that cattle should care for themselves. They do not propose to care for the cattle. Often cattle remain unfed, are not driven out to pasture, get sick and die, or are destroyed by the deadly tsetse fly. They are not housed, harnessed to plows, or treated as members of the family. Dairy cattle have yet to be introduced in most of the country. The complex mass of traditions, customs, and values which have become part of the Maasai, the Hausa, and other tribes in Africa, and are inbred in the Gwalas, Rauts, and other cattle-rearing castes of India, can be taught to and learned by Zairians. But it will not be a simple process done in a few short courses. The cattle and the people must be welded into a symbiotic union, and the profits of such a new form of labor and culture must be shown to be indubitable. Time is required. Once established and proved, the benefits and profits of plowing, carting, milking, and fertilizing will be so great that there will be a rush to cattle culture.

A significant cultural transition can be observed in the field of plantation management. When freedom came, the great plantations were taken over by Zairian managers. Belgians, for the most part, left. The plantations today are proving not nearly as profitable, and Zaire is calling back some Belgians to provide the expert management which alone makes plantations profitable. It would be a disservice to the Zairian people to infer that calling back the Belgians (being done by a powerful Zairian government) is an insult to Zaire. All that it means is that the complex process of management cannot be learned in a few weeks or even a few years. A cadre of Zairian managers, who know the job and pass on to their sons those skills needed, may have to be developed. Development is not merely giving people of one culture tools which they delightedly use. Rather, it is making those cultural changes which will support the use of new tools. Cultural innovations are going on all the time in all populations of the world. They are going on in Zaire, but they take time.

Difficulties can be overcome by a somewhat lengthy period of learning. Development means making available whatever period of learning is necessary to support the new value scale, the new attitudes, the new interpersonal relationships, the new expenditures of time, and the new power distribution which new tools and new skills and new sources of money require.

Development and Theology of Mission

Under the crying need for development which any observant person sees in Zaire and other nations, some Christian leaders have rushed into an uncritical advocacy of development. They have said in effect, "The day of sinner-converting church-multiplying Missions is over. Now the task is to help peóple achieve a fuller temporal life." The following quotation illustrates this kind of advocacy.

> We have lifted up humanization as the goal of mission because we believe that more than others it communicates in our period of history the meaning of the messianic goal. In another time the goal of God's redemptive work might best have been described in terms of man turning towards God. . . . The fundamental question was that of the true God, and the church responded to that question by pointing to him. It was assuming that the purpose of mission was Christianization, bringing man to God through Christ and his church. Today the fundamental question is much more that of true man, and the dominant concern of the missionary congregation must therefore be to point to the humanity in Christ as the goal of mission.[1]

This statement immediately raised serious objection from large sections of the Church. It said clearly that Christianization, bringing persons to God through Christ and his Church, used to be the goal of Mission, but that now humanization was the goal. The Bankok Meeting in 1972 drove home the point. Eternal salvation used to be the goal, but the day for all such "pie-in-the-sky by-and-by" was now over and, in the contemporary world, salvation today (temporal improvement) was what the missionary movement ought to make its sole objective. The issue was declared to be Development *or* Evangelization. Any such overstatement of the issue was bound to divide the Church of Jesus Christ, and that is exactly what happened. Some missionary societies lined up on one side and some on the other. Mission today is properly Development: Mission today is properly Evangelization.

We regret the overstatement. Were we to be faced by it, we would line up on the side of evangelization; but we believe that it does not describe the real situation and must, therefore, be rejected. We set forth our own position in five propositions:

1. Development which is anti-evangelistic, minimizes or ridicules eternal salvation, and loudly proclaims that today humanization is the sole goal or even the chief goal is anti-Christian and must be firmly opposed. Reconciling persons to God in the Church of Jesus Christ is not now outmoded. It is always the chief task of the Church.

2. Development, however, does not need to be proposed in that exaggerated and distorted way. The true way is to say that God wants development. He placed persons on earth and said to them:

> "Be fruitful and multiply, and fill the earth and subdue it; and have dominion over the fish of the sea and over the birds of the air and over every living thing that moves upon the earth. . . . Behold, I have given you every plant yielding seed which is upon the face of all the earth, and every tree with seed in its fruit; and you shall have them for food" (Genesis 1:28-29).

God commands us to secure earth's maximum development. The soul reborn through faith in Christ obeys God in this regard and constantly attempts to create a better world. Born-again Christians are more productive, more just, more industrious, and more humane than they would have been without Christ. The Church which insists that its *first* duty is to lead men and women to love and obey Christ insists that its *second* duty is to teach them to serve other people. We have our Lord's own word that the first command is to love God and the second command is to love our neighbor as ourselves.

3. Sound Christian development, therefore, is rightly a part of Christian Mission. It must never be substituted for evangelism and church growth, and it must never relegate either of these to a minor position.

4. Development must recognize itself as a second priority which must be done. It is not as crucial as conversion. A famine of the Word of God is more serious than a famine of the bread which perishes. Salvation of the soul ranks higher than improvement of agriculture, but God commands Christians to improve agriculture. Both must be done to fulfill the cultural and evangelistic mandates which God has given.

5. Consequently missionary societies ought to devote *a part* of their efforts to development. This is no new doctrine. They always have. When the crying need was for medicine and education, then together with conversion and the multiplication of churches, Missions built hospitals and created vast parochial school systems.

Furthermore, there is abundant biblical support for the care of the physical and social needs of persons. We think at once how readily the early church made provisions for their widows and orphans and note also that the apostles said, "It is not right that we should give up preaching the word of God to serve tables." When Paul was writing to the Thessalonians, he said, "We gave you this command: If anyone will not work, let him not eat" (2 Thessalonians 3:10). Working to get the bread which perishes is part of the Christian life. The Lord Jesus himself fed the multitudes and healed the sick. He did not spend all his life doing this; he turned from healing and feeding to die on the cross for the sins of humankind. However, he did on occasion feed and heal persons.

We do not quote Matthew 25 in support of development because in these passages the Lord may have been speaking not of physical hunger and thirst, but of hunger for the bread of heaven and thirst for the water of life. In John 6:27 we read, "Do not labor for the food which perishes, but for the food which endures to eternal life." Matthew 6:19-20 exhorts us not to lay up for ourselves treasures on earth where moth and rust corrupt and thieves break through and steal. In Matthew 10:28, the Lord says, "Do not fear those who kill the body but cannot kill the soul." In view of these and many other similar passages, we judge that Matthew 25 cannot be taken in a crassly physical sense. Hence, we cite only the passages which give indubitable evidence that God expects Christians to subdue the earth and use the good gifts he has given for their physical and social benefit.

Therefore, we believe missionary societies and missionaries should devote a part of their resources to development because the present Churches, both in Eurica and in Zaire, can do church growth evangelism *and* development simultaneously. It is a false view of the situation which demands that we turn from one in order to do the other.

An illustration of the connection between church growth and economic growth is found in the story of a very poor local church in the Busala region called Muzo. It perennially lacked funds to pay a pastor or catechists. The yearly baptisms never exceeded forty. Then a new resourceful pastor came to the field. He realized that the problem was not lack of will to give nor of products to sell. The problem lay in the lack of a market where agricultural products could be sold. The Belgian local administrator established a market, and soon money and goods were circulating in the area. Zairians are born traders and have no problem generating economic wealth when provided with the opportunities. The very next baptismal day saw 150 enter the water as a sign of the work of the Spirit in their hearts. Salaries were paid regularly to all church workers, and the church grew in maturity and evangelistic zeal.

On the other hand, it needs to be clearly understood that weak congregations or denominations cannot plan and execute effective and enduring development projects. We do not believe that development apart from numerical, qualitative, and organizational church growth will build up weak congregations and denominations. The realization of this fact caused a Baptist agricultural missionary to decide not to return to Zaire after furlough. He felt his efforts at development were not succeeding because the congregations of the area did not understand the purpose and goal of development within the total scope of the gospel and were not strong enough to initiate or to carry out the projects he had developed on the mission station.

A head pastor in the CBZO Community, who formerly worked under the Department of Evangelism in stewardship and development, analyzed the basic cause for success or failure of his Community's development projects as being spiritual in nature. Lack of motivation, vision, determination, and integrity on the part of the congregations doomed projects to failure. Conversely, the presence of spiritual leaders who had these qualities insured proper planning and execution of projects.

The unanimous opinion of all who shared with the survey team on the subject was that the only viable agency in the country capable of insuring the success of development projects is the Church of Jesus Christ. This is true in spite of the fact that not all church-sponsored projects succeed and there are obvious weaknesses of congregations, associations, synods, and communities.

The present high prices in the city for food produced in the country are bringing much hardship to urban populations. In Kinshasa a whole month's wages is required to buy one sack of manioc. Eggs flown in from South Africa are cheaper than local eggs. Many children and elderly people are so weak from malnutrition that they fall prey to disease. It is hard to understand how people can survive with such high prices and so little land for gardens. Even so, church offerings keep coming in and even special offerings are successful. At two special offerings taken in Bas-Zaire, a few hundred

Christians raised $2,350 in a few hours. People in the remote region of Kimbaka gladly paid what would equal several days' wages for hymnbooks. At the annual Minkelo Retreat, those in attendance paid for their own tickets, food costs for a week, many books, and then in addition gave over $294 in special offerings. Motivation is important in giving. Zairians have money and, as development proceeds, will have more. However, intensive and regular stewardship teaching is essential to unlock the resources now available and those greater resources which they soon will have.

The Mennonite Central Committee in its P.A.P. Project has now established a central herd of 750 cattle and has placed on contract nearly that many among members of the churches in the Kikwit area. Arnold Priebe told us of this fine piece of development in which missionaries have played a key part and the pastors have heartily cooperated.

Guidelines to Correct Proportioning of Development and Spiritual Life

1. *Mount maximum joint efforts for the next three decades.*

Maximum effort should be mounted in all major components of the Church/Mission enterprise. To talk of development while rapidly withdrawing missionaries is nonsense. They are the Communities' primary source of technical and spiritual personnel. Neither development nor the perfecting of the Church takes place in an adequate manner in a period of retreat. The formula "Withdraw foreign aid and the Church will leap into life" is a sentimental and romantic deception. If resources are withdrawn by fiat from Eurica, either development will not be done or the spiritual maturing and perfecting of the Church will suffer. The importance placed by ECZ on funds for development is highlighted by the fact that Dr. Bokeleale, along with other staff members of the Secretariat and a few general secretaries of the Communities, spent several weeks in Europe and the United States in May and June, 1977, placing the urgent need of development before Churches and mission boards. Money is one need in development; technically competent and trained personnel is the other. Both are needed in Zaire.

Maximum effort should be mounted by missionary societies. The unfortunate impression which has spread across Eurica that the task of Missions is over and that from now on Mission is only what the Church on the spot does must be corrected. Let missionary

societies tell their congregations and devout supporters that
Christian Mission in Africa will take maximum Eurican effort for the
next several decades.

Maximum effort must also be mounted by the Communities of
Zaire. Nothing will hinder development more than for them to
assume that their founding missionary societies will do the work and
they themselves need not give and live sacrificially. Here much will
depend on the top level leaders of the Communities. Only Zairians
can bring pressure on Zairians. Only they can insist that Zairians give
more. Only they can live sacrificially as pastors and teachers in the
myriad village churches. Only they can tithe and encourage others to
tithe.

A good example of Zairians doing what they can is seen at
Vanga. Rev. M. Pambi is leading his congregations in a project very
similar to the Mennonite P.A.P. project to which we have just
referred. In fact, the Mennonite idea helped the Vanga project get
started. Technicians from Kikwit have been consulted at various
times. Vanga agricultural missionaries have also given counsel.

The Churches should take over all the tasks which they do well
and for which they can pay. This survey team wants it clearly
understood that our strong plea that maximum efforts for Mission
should continue from Eurica into Zaire does not in the least infer that
the Churches in Zaire are poor, cannot do the task, and should be
either pampered or pauperized. The Churches should seek sources of
income within the country and mostly within the congregations for
funding important developmental tasks. Nevertheless, the missionary societies should continue to mount maximum efforts. The need
for Churches to launch out on their own and to assume larger and
larger parts of the work of God in their country must not lead the
missionary societies to do less and less.

Missionary societies from Eurica function in an age in which
Eurica has developed more than Zaire. The gap which separated
America and Congo in 1878 was far smaller than the gap which now
separates both Europe and America from Zaire. The gap widens
every year. Therefore, the responsibility which Christians in Eurica
have for their brothers and sisters in Zaire grows. To whom God has
given much, from him God expects much. A deacon in an American
congregation which had been sending missionaries to Congo/Zaire
for decades said to me, "We have been helping them for nearly a
hundred years. Isn't it about time they stood on their own feet?"

Directors of missionary societies must be prepared to answer such ill-founded objections.

If the Churches of Eurica withdraw missionary resources now, they will badly handicap their efforts to build up their sister Churches and fellow Christians in this great land. On the contrary, if they put in maximum efforts, much good will result. A time of great progress, sprinkled with great difficulties, lies just ahead of us. We live in tumultuous times. However, given maximum efforts of Africans and Euricans, the next half century will see enormous progress.

2. *Maximum efforts must be absolutely clear as to goals and priorities.*

Development must not be *substituted* for medicine, Christian education, the evangelizing of Dark Areas, or the multiplying of congregations in the great cities. The true goal is the achievement of these essentials *and* of much temporal improvement besides.

11

Are Missionaries Needed?
What Others Say

The greatest issue facing Communities and Missions in Zaire, as they enter the Fourth Stage, is the place of the missionary. The subject is complex and occurs in different forms in different Communities of ECZ.

By missionaries we mean specially competent men and women from outside Zaire whom God sends to propagate the faith by word and deed. Missionaries may come from Kenya, Korea, America, Brazil, England, or any other land. For the foreseeable future, however, they will probably come in large part from America and in smaller part from Europe. What is the place of such missionaries? Are they needed? Is there work for them to do? That is the crucial question.

Missionaries are not sent only to "help young Churches." They are not fraternal workers. They are God's special messengers. They are apostles to peoples of other cultures and languages who have yet to hear of and yet to believe in the Savior. However, young Churches, like young children, have great needs and face great dangers. Like young children, the question as to when they ought to leave the parental roof—when the parent should withdraw his or her presence and support—must be asked. Clearly, when the child is two years old, it needs the parent. Equally clear, at age twenty-five, it does not. In between, when does parental help become damaging to the person? In Zaire, despite the fact that 62 percent of the population is Church-connected, do Churches still welcome and need the services of Missions? We say that Mission in Zaire is in the Fourth Stage in which the propagation of the gospel must be completed. In that stage in the Zaire we have described, are missionaries still needed?

In this chapter, five unusually clear thinkers who know Zaire speak to this crucial subject. Sometimes they are talking specifically to the Zairian situation, sometimes to missions in general.

In *The Enterprise,* Dr. John Keith, General Secretary of the Canadian Baptist Board, published an article on "The Employment Crisis in Missions"[1] in which he speaks of the worldwide situation. He gives a clear, true account of the movement of thought and policy concerning the sendings of missionaries. We reproduce it below. CBOMB has nine missionaries in Zaire.

The Employment Crisis in Missions

In former times an employment crisis in missions did not, in fact could not, exist. Mission boards and societies assumed the initiative in missionary recruitment. The board decided where missionaries would go, how many would be required, what work they would do on the field, and so forth. The board sent the missionaries overseas, built them houses, provided them with cars and even supplied them with a work allowance to enable them to carry out their mandate to win converts and establish churches. Besides this the mission board would, from time to time, provide capital grants to build hospitals, schools, and other such institutions. More money would be supplied for the salaries of national workers . . . some evangelists, some compounders and nurses in the hospitals, some teachers in the schools.

Under the old regime everything was marvelously simple and straightforward. Mission secretaries could point with satisfaction to the number of missionaries on the field, the converts made, the churches established, the schools organized, and hospitals administered. The area served overseas was generally divided into "fields," and it was the primary responsibility of the board's General Secretary or Director to see that these fields were properly managed. The sincere dedication of young people in the home churches, together with the romance of service abroad, usually assured a constant supply of recruits for the mission fields.

There is no doubt a tendency today, especially on the part of more senior members in our constituency, to look back upon the good old days of the mission enterprise with considerable nostalgia. And without question they were great days in the history of Christian missions. The strength of the enterprise lay in its efficiency. The work in its totality was mission-inspired and mission-directed. It became in truth "our enterprise" and the people served were known as "our Telugus" or "our Bolivians." The home constituency had a real sense of involvement in the total operation.

There were, however, weaknesses in the old arrangement that were not at first recognized as such. These related to the people overseas to whom the missionaries had been sent. Their role in this mission-dominated enterprise was almost entirely passive. They had little voice or say in the really important decisions that were made. In general they were treated as children, so not unnaturally they came to regard themselves as children in their relationship to the missionaries. This conditioned thinking produced first of all an attitude of almost complete dependence upon the missionaries; but closely associated with it were feelings of inferiority which engendered resentment.

Since the Second World War the rise of nationalism in countries of the Third World has served to change the whole relationship between the Western churches and the mission-founded churches in the developing nations. The so-called "young churches" have come of age. No longer do they regard themselves as the objects of mission; but feel, and rightly so, that they should be participants in mission. They desire, above all else, that their autonomy should be recognized and respected.

The achievement of self-determination by the churches overseas brought about a radical change in the role of the missionary from the West. Where in pioneer days he had been the father of churches, he now found himself in the position of a servant of the churches. Actually this was a very healthy shift in function and most missionaries welcomed it.

But the autonomy of the church overseas also demanded that missionaries should no longer be "sent" by the West. Instead, if they are needed, they should be invited by the receiving church. This stipulation effectively transferred the initiative in missionary recruitment from the home board to the churches abroad. In essence it decreed that unless or until the churches in the Third World sense a need for missionaries, all mission activity by Western churches, as this related to overseas, would cease. In the minds of not a few in the West this precipitated a crisis.

It was generally assumed that since the option to invite or not to invite missionaries from Canada now rested with the churches overseas, they would quite naturally decide not to request further missionary assistance. This pessimistic supposition gave rise to the assumption that the era of overseas missions had come to an end. The employment crisis in missions, as seen from this point of view, would arise through sheer absence of need.

Throughout most of the sixties many church people believed missionary activity overseas would soon come to a halt. As a result young people began seeking alternative avenues of service abroad through organizations such as CUSO (Canadian University Service Overseas) or CIDA (Canadian International Development Agency) or church-sponsored short term programs. It seemed almost certain that the day of the overseas missionary had ended.

With the dawn of the seventies there has been an astonishing turn of events. The churches overseas which, as it had been presumed, were finished with missionaries, surprisingly began to request the Board in Canada to send missionaries for certain specific projects. First, there was the African Christian Church and Schools in Kenya. Then there was the KGPI (Kerapatah Geredja Protestan Indonesia) of Sulawesia, Indonesia, followed by another request from the Brazilian Baptist Convention. All of these immediate needs have been met. Eight Canadian Baptist missionaries are now in Kenya and two families each are under appointment for Indonesia and Brazil respectively.

The employment crisis has been precipitated, however, through the receipt of certain other appeals from Zaire and Bolivia.

Some of the needs existing in Zaire have been formulated by Pastor Mavunguva-Fwita, Evangelist and Chairman of CBZO's (Communaute D'Eglises Baptistes du Zaire Ouest) Board of Home Mission and Evangelism. In brief, the situation there calls for: specialists in evangelism; people to direct centers of extension work; people to prepare materials; people to study feasible projects which might increase church income; and managers for projects.

It is at this point that the employment crisis in mission becomes acute. Because Canadian Baptists have of late been conditioned to think that missionaries, particularly those related to church work, would not be wanted overseas, we now face an actual shortage of theologically trained men prepared to work with the churches abroad.

Always in the past during more than one hundred years of missionary involvement overseas, Canadian Baptists have responded to a challenge. We are therefore confident that the present call to service being issued by our colleagues in Bolivia and Zaire will be received with thoughtfulness, prayer, and determined response.

Dr. George W. Peters, the noted missiologist, writes the following about the "churchman" missionary:

There is no end to assisting the churches, and working with them, to become the Church of Jesus Christ in a local setting, the Servant Church to the community and the Evangelizing Church of the Lord in the country and in the world. Here indeed a great and sacred ministry is to be rendered. We remind ourselves of the pastoral ministry of Paul as expressed in his visits and letters to the churches, the teaching ministry of Apollos in the churches, the shepherding and guiding and counseling ministries of Timothy, Titus, Peter, John, and James.

The churchman missionary is an urgently needed individual of special gifts, aptitudes, relationships, and special training, matured by experience in the church and a steady walk with God. The problems of the churches in a complex world and a sea of paganism are beyond definition and prediction. No church polity, church discipline, or manual of direction will suffice to guide adequately and answer the pressing questions. Only the broadest training in church history, pastoral care, practical counseling, an abundant love for the church as the flock of God and a deep consciousness of being Christ's servant to the churches will suffice in the pressures and tensions of church history.

The next vignette, given below, helps us see the Zairian situation. It is written by Rev. Charles Harvey, a veteran missionary in Angola and Bas Zaire. It might have been written from almost any part of the country. At a time when enormous opportunities and dangers confront the Church, missionaries all over Zaire are uncertain about the future. Are they needed? Will they be allowed to meet the tremendous needs they see? Will they return?

Christian leaders in other parts of the land may find phrases which do not quite represent their situation but will at once know what Mr. Harvey is writing about. Our situation is better, they may say, or worse, but on the whole remarkably like his. While the particular problem he is talking about is training local leaders and the tool he plans to use is theological education by extension, his frustrations and concerns can easily be duplicated as Zairians and missionaries contemplate *many* other tasks.

Note the authenticity of his picture. He does not bewail the lack of well-trained, creative Zairians. Zaire has plenty of supervising ministers of ability and vision; but these are mostly full-time teachers. They get their salaries from the schools. There they put in most of their time. These able leaders of the Church are tied by the schools to the centers. The transport needed to allow them to supervise the far-flung village churches is prohibitively costly. In consequence, the quality of the village churches is rapidly diminishing. Against factual backgrounds such as Mr. Harvey presents—and we could cite many others—Churches and missionary societies must determine the question of what the role of the missionary and the Mission is in the Fourth Stage of Mission.

Village Needs and Frustrated Missionaries

I have recently spent four weeks working in the village churches and a fifth in the city with the supervisory ministers.

I am overwhelmed at the needs in the churches. Everywhere is a *crying need for the training of local leaders.* Relevant Bible teaching is very, very urgent. The Church has well-trained supervising pastors who could do it. However, 90 percent of these are *full-time school teachers.* They do not have rapid transport to get them out to the areas they supervise and back in time for classes Monday. The churches are not ready to pay these men a salary comparable to a teacher's salary, so they supervise chiefly on Sunday!

Where the church has a vehicle at her disposal, it costs two months' salary of a supervising pastor for the vehicle to make one 180-mile return trip. Many of the areas served are wider or longer than that. The churches just cannot pay for such transport. Even a small motorcycle costs about 1,600 dollars. We are stymied. The Church has not found ways to pay for the full time of the supervising pastors or to pay the costs of long-distance travel.

A really alert, committed and thoroughly experienced Christian told me of the drastic changes he has seen over the years. "Our village leaders have no systematic training and their quality is greatly deteriorating. Witchcraft has grown to an intensity that I have never seen during my long life."

In the old days, village pastors were trained at the nearest mission station. The last organized course of the sort ended twenty years ago. In those days missionaries had the *funds* and the *authority* to operate local schools. Village pastors regularly came in for a year of schooling. That approach would not work today.

The logical pattern today, to address one part of the problem, would be Biblical Education by Extension and we have begun to use it, but we face four rough problems.

1. The administrators of such programs will be the supervising pastors (full-time teachers!), but who will pay for their travel on weekends? In many cases they can supervise only lay pastors and laymen who come in to the school centers where they live.

2. Then comes the question of materials. Some decent stuff is available from East Africa in English, and from Ivory Coast in French. But these materials must be put into local languages. This means high cost of production and mimeographed materials. Where does one find an equipped African who has the time and knowledge to adapt materials to meet the specific needs of those village Christians? If you found him, you would need to find foreign money to employ him. Preparing material requires a very good man, not just someone out of a job.

3. The expatriate worker can and should play a key role in training village leaders by extension. His objectivity is a real benefit. He sees certain needs to which he cannot become insensitive. In selecting areas of study he will often be the first to vocalize a felt need.

4. When I glance off to the coming years, I see that virtually all our present missionaries working with the church directly or indirectly will not be in the country six years from now. Yet they are greatly needed. Without exception extension programs and other helpful activities have been initiated by expatriates. They are about the only people with access to money. They alone have the freedom to experiment that permits them to keep trying new ways and means.

Africans who can contribute—and there are many such—are usually up to their necks in administration and are tied to the school five days a week. Some village pastors are creative but have no framework or fellowship in which to function. To help these creative minds express themselves, we might organize a commission on the life of the Church, which would receive enough cash from somewhere to meet and pray, fellowship, and dream. God could bless the churches through such a group. We need each other, in a group which intends to make and keep the Church loyal to her Lord. A creative, imaginative, small fellowship in which church workers pool their gifts and visions will help churches relate their members to the living Christ and to each other. Then our churches will not just exist, but will go where the Spirit of Jesus leads.

If ever there was a priority, it is that of drawing together responsible pastors, missionaries, and other resource people to meet the overwhelming needs of the Church. We need a team which will have as its ten-year objective preparing and imparting biblical education through extension which will correspond to the spiritual and other real needs of ordinary Christians in these villages. These churches have been decreasing in quality. We must reverse that trend. Godly people must unite to feed the sheep.

If we find twelve families of missionaries soon, we can begin to solve the problem. It will take new families about four years before they become fully productive, so recruiting them should begin now. I anticipate that at least six families would come back for a second term and then would be really productive. Believe me, they are greatly needed. They would do the churches a great deal of good.

If no missionaries are available, or perhaps desired by the National Church, employing Zairians to do the job would be a good use of money. Possibly the board would give us a "one shot budget" for a specific period.

Mr. Harvey sees a great need. He believes that the best way to fill it is to get twelve new families of missionaries, but is doubtful that they can be recruited or even that the Church in Zaire will ask for them. He then proposes that the missionary society grant the Zaire Church a "one shot budget" and employ some able Zairian leaders (who are now earning good pay as teachers) and give them a year or two to complete the job, after which presumably they would go back to teaching. All this is good thinking. It is clear that Mr. Harvey believes that training local leaders through theological training by extension and doing many other urgent tasks will be more likely when the roles of the mission and the missionaries are substantially affirmed.

It is of the greatest importance that Christian Mission everywhere reverse the general feeling, of which Dr. Keith and Mr. Harvey speak so clearly, that missionaries are no longer needed. The World Church *cannot* deprecate missionaries, glorify nationals, imply romantically that young Churches can carry on easily without missionaries, publicize chance remarks about a local situation until the word "moratorium" resounds from pole to pole, *and carry on Mission.* It is as simple as that. We must start talking positively about missionaries and Missions. That is one reason why we have titled this book *Midday in Missions.* The unquestioned difficulties in adjustment must not be allowed to convey the false impression that Mission is complete and missionaries are no longer needed. The Church of Jesus Christ has abundant resources to evangelize the three billion who have yet to believe *and* to finish the job of multiplying and maturing churches in countries like Zaire where 62 percent are church-connected Christians and 88 percent want to be known as Christians.

The third vignette, which presents the worldwide crisis in missionary sendings as it appears in Zaire, can be called the slot syndrome. In the following paragraphs, a thoughtful missionary at work in Zaire asks, "When Zairians fill the positions, the slots formerly held by missionaries, should the Boards call the missionaries home, or redeploy them in Zaire to meet new contemporary needs? What share in redeployment do missionaries have?"

The Slot Syndrome

One of the accepted axioms in Mission strategy today is that missionaries must train nationals as leaders for all aspects of life and work in the new congregations and denominations which they found. The value of this procedure is well established. However, does it necessarily follow that to achieve the goal of training capable national leaders, missionaries are to work themselves out of a job and go home? Do only a certain number of slots, or positions, exist on each mission field? When these are filled with nationals, is the Mission's task finished? Would the continued presence of missionaries constitute paternalism or neo-colonialism? Some people answer, "Yes!", but I believe the answer should be "No!", despite the fact that the World Council of Churches publicizes a moratorium on mission personnel and funds in order that young Churches may "find themselves."

Churches want continued relationships with missionary societies so the many needs which surface from time to time can be met. Both Churches and Missions should suggest new ways in which mission personnel can contribute meaningfully to the welfare and growth of the increasingly mature Church. Sharing must be two-directional. Sometimes the Mission may be in a better position to think creatively and objectively, sometimes the Church.

The slot concept is valid in administration and in institutions. These have a limited number of positions to fill. Such is not the case in church-related ministries. Here the kind and number of opportunities are ever expanding as needs are realized and efforts to meet these are launched.

It is doubtful whether missionaries would consent to linger on merely as a "presence" or as fraternal workers without meaningful tasks to perform. Lack of purpose for being on the field has prevented many missionaries from returning after furlough. A major Mission in Zaire keeps only a very few missionaries at work precisely because it did not develop a mutually agreeable plan for their participation in the work of the Church.

We must now ask, "Do Zairian Churches look forward to the day when missionary participation will decline and disappear? Do they equate self-reliance and mature carrying out of responsibilities with total withdrawal of the Mission, or does this idea lurk in the minds of some board strategists only?" My thesis is that creative thinking by national leaders and missionaries on the proper and worthwhile use of mission help of all kinds, and particularly of missionaries, is essential for the welfare of the *Churches*. The Churches continually maintain that denomination-al or congregational-related ministries need the services of missionary personnel. In my judgment, top administrative posts ought to be filled by nationals, but many special services exist which only missionaries can fill. Zairian Churches are as yet only dimly aware of these and cannot yet pay for them.

Looming over all these interior tasks is the huge enterprise of discipling the three billion people of this planet who remain without Christ. Of these, about eleven million live in Zaire. Who will evangelize them? When told by some missionaries that "evangelism and church planting are your job," national leaders often express puzzlement and hurt. They believe missionaries ought to continue to work with them at a task so huge and so persistent.

During my last term in Zaire, the Director of our Department of Evangelism and I met representatives of Mission Boards and Zairian Churches. These wanted us to make concrete proposals for the meaningful use of missionary personnel. The following list is the result of our joint cogitations, born out of experience and observation. We assume that missionaries will train nationals to work in these areas, but do not accept as a necessary corollary that this will remove the need for missionary participation. The task is immense. This list is confined to evangelism, church planting, and nurture. Other lists could be compiled for education, medicine, and agriculture. Our list represents the needs felt by one Community. Other denominations in Zaire would list other needs.

1. Theological Education by Extension
    In Latin America several thousand leaders are being trained by this method. The vast number of trained leaders needed at all levels (Latin America needs 90,000 trained pastors, not to mention catechists and other leaders), the prohibitive cost of constructing seminary campuses, and the obvious lack of qualified professors to staff new schools have given real impetus to this movement. It has now spread to Asia and Africa because the same hard facts face theological educators there, also.
    Other advantages are inherent in education by extension. Leaders remain in their villages and move at their own pace. Biblical training does not require a three- or four-year total investment of time in the artificial atmosphere of a seminary. Learning takes place in real life. In Zaire we ought probably to keep most present residential programs and add extension programs to them. The following staff and travel budget for an extension program will be needed:
    1. People to write programmed texts in several languages for a wide range of subjects.
    2. Professors to teach in extension centers.
    3. Administrators or coordinators for each program.

Extension education based on the following theological training schools will be desirable. These are located at Kikongo, Kinshasa, Kimpese, Kananga, Mbandaka, Karawa, and many other places. The missionary is needed to pioneer and put into effect this new system of theological training so needed by these large, new denominations.

II. Church Planting and Evangelism

A major contribution missionaries can make is in aiding the Communities to evaluate current programs. Too often these go on indefinitely without anyone really knowing if they are reaching the goals for which they were created or if these goals are in themselves worthy of time and money in view of the enormous task of winning people to Christ.

Another important area for missionary participation is in helping Communities to spot responsive unchurched populations. This requires special skills and a warm heart driven by love for people who are without Christ. Criteria which can be used for finding receptive populations in the city will of necessity differ from those needed in rural situations where pockets of tribespeople remain without adequate discipling by the Communities. Once the responsive unchurched populations have been located, a very important task remains —to plan effective strategy in view of present and possible future resources which will enlist the wholehearted support of Zairian leaders, missionaries, and missionary societies. Usually this strategy will of necessity envisage special task forces trained and equipped to plant new churches in complex urban situations. Other task forces are needed to plant churches in the rural "Dark Areas" mentioned elsewhere in this book. These special teams should be composed of missionaries and Zairians in whatever proportion best suits the local situation.

The task of preparing materials for use in the various ministries of the Church is a gigantic one. The subjects to be covered are many and important. Church growth, evangelism, Bible studies, prayer, and preparation for witnessing are among those most needed.

Missionaries are playing an important role in providing transportation to distant places where there is no other mode of travel. Of special note is the work of MAF, without which many programs could not be implemented. Missionaries with Land

Rovers and trucks still carry all told hundreds of teams over the vast regions of Zaire, and they will for some years to come. Zairian chauffeurs are capable but require a salary, which is added to the mileage charged to the evangelism team. This extra expense limits the number of trips the team can make by reducing its already inadequate budget. Another disadvantage to their use is that they take space which a team member needs, thus limiting the effectiveness of the team. Missionaries, on the other hand, are always participating members of the team. And, to be realistic, missionaries raise the money to buy the truck and the gas to run it. It would be an exceptional Zairian chauffeur who could do this.

III. Quality and Organizational Growth

Some special areas of crucial importance to the maturity and growth of Zairian Christians are stewardship, Christian family, and spiritual renewal. Missionaries have already made significant contributions in these areas both in preparation of materials and in teaching and can do so for years to come. We stress again the fact that they do *not* need to be in positions of administrative leadership to be effective. In fact, they may be more effective if not in such positions.

Zairian congregations can still benefit from the special skills involved in the use of audiovisual equipment, in the field of music, and in literature. Each of these requires specialization as well as a vision of how it can be used in evangelizing and discipling Zairians.

Two areas of specialized ministry in which missionary participation is especially needed are youth and men. We have stated elsewhere the enormous challenge that children and young people pose to the congregations. That is especially true in cities and towns where young people form a homogeneous unit with common language, education, values, and goals. Whereas the women of the congregations are well organized into local, regional, denominational, and ECZ organizations, the men remain an untapped source of dedicated service. A brief attempt to organize and mobilize men in Kinshasa in conjunction with the Christ for All campaign vividly demonstrated the desire for this sort of program that men in the congregations have. They need help in creating organizations and programs which will provide outlets for the constructive use of their gifts.

Time for a New Model?

Dr. G. Thompson Brown, Staff Director of the Division of International Mission of the Presbyterian Church in the United States, in the summer of 1977 called for a new model of Missions. In a widely circulated work paper titled "Possible Directions for the International Mission of the Church in the Next Decade,"[2] he reviewed the Church/Mission Relationships seen around the world in all mission fields—the Mission over the church and the Church over the mission—and concluded that in 1977

> the development of a strategy for the international mission of the Church is again at the crossroads. That this point has been reached should be a cause for celebration and thanksgiving for it is a sign that progress has been achieved and solid accomplishments made. As each new stage took the place of what preceded it, a new milestone was reached. Change is in itself a sign of growth, of life and vitality.

He then set forth the shape which the new model of relationship between Churches and Missions might be and proposed steps to benefit the situation. These proposals we consider significant. They form our fourth vignette reproduced below. Dr. Brown clearly sees the impasse which confronts the international mission of the Church and what must be done to blast through it. He writes:

> As changes are contemplated, there is the need for the closest cooperation with overseas partners. And this is, of course, the intent and purpose of the Mission Consultation ordered by the General Assembly of the Presbyterian Church in the United States for early 1978. Prior to that Consultation, serious study and reflection should take place by each of the partners. These should be tested against each other. Different patterns of missionary outreach which are being tried by other communions should be examined. Any changes, to be effective, must have the understanding support of the overseas partners, missionaries, and the constituency of the church here at home.

> The following tentative proposals might serve to initiate this process.

> (1) The church must be the *"base."* Whatever direction is taken in the future, it would seem necessary to affirm the fact that the Church of Jesus Christ must be the base from which mission takes

place. This was the main concern and the major contribution of the "Church Based Approach." And we must be on guard that we do not initiate a new form of colonialism by which the mission board here at home makes all the decisions. There can be no doubt that the primary responsibility for evangelization or Christian social action lies with the church in each land. Other structures are temporary. But the Church is permanent and the gates of hell will not prevail against it.

But what is the Church and how is it to be defined? For us there can be no doubt that the Church in each land is defined in the same terms as we define ourselves. Ours is an institutional church. We represent a denominational mission board and a General Assembly. The Church to which we relate overseas, whether Presbyterian in polity or not, shares this same organizational identity.

(2) *But the "base" cannot be the end of Mission.* Perhaps the weakness of the *"Church-based approach" was that at times it came too close to viewing the overseas national church partner as an end in itself. At times, "Mission" became identified with "Inter-Church Aid."* Resources of personnel and funds should be "shared." This is all well and good, but this use of personnel and funds for the Church's own welfare leads to a preoccupation of the Church with its own well-being. The Church becomes self-serving and self-centered. As personnel and funds from richer churches abroad are used for the welfare of the church in the Third World, new dependencies tend to develop. It was this misunderstanding of mission as inter-church aid that led to a "call for Moratorium" in some quarters. *When "Mission" is reduced to "Aid," then the only way to achieve self-reliance is for the aid to stop.*

(3) *The End of Mission: . . . "that the World might believe."* But all this is to forget that the world is the objective toward which "Mission" must constantly be directed. The Church, whether in this land or any other, must never exist for itself, but exists only that it might be the instrument for the salvation of the world. One of the uneasy feelings some have expressed about "the Church-Based Approach" is that mission as outreach is blunted, the Church becomes ingrown, by its institutions and organizations. Mission, whether understood as evangelism or social action, must always be directed toward the world. And neither emphasis is

possible when mission simply becomes the interchange of people and funds between different members of the Church. The welfare of the "base" may be improved, existing structures and organizations may be supported, perhaps good things are done for the internal life of the church and its members, but mission to the "regions beyond" is blunted and the world is neglected.

(4) *A New Design.* Perhaps a new design may be emerging. Diagrammatically, it might look like this:

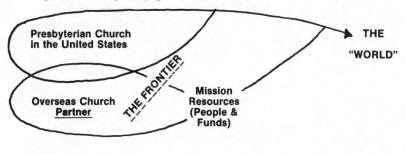

Note the following:

(*a*) *"The Base."* The base of the mission enterprise is still the Church. But it is the Church in this country *with* its overseas partner that together forms the "base"; not one church set up as over against the other. One "base" does not give aid and assistance to another "base," but *both together contribute to a common mission.* Each church has its own sphere of life, which is distinct and separate from the common venture to which each contributes. Neither "receives" from the other: Both are involved in the "sending." Here true partnership and self-reliance are enhanced. Neither is dependent on the other for its own well-being. Both contribute what each can uniquely bring to the joint venture.

(*b*) *"The Frontier."* The "frontier" is that invisible line which separates "Church" from "world." It is the line between faith and non-faith, between love and hatred, between peace and hostility. Sometimes the "frontier" may be geographic, as would be the case when both churches participated in mission in another region, or opening up some new pioneer field. Perhaps *more often it would be a "non-geographical*

*frontier," some area of special need or neglect, some
minority or oppressed group, some underprivileged or
forgotten tribe. To cross this frontier might be to engage in
evangelism or witness, which are basic, or to become engaged in some new thrust into society with some new insights
of the gospel.*

(c) *"The World."* This *"World,"* which is the object of mission,
exists in every land, and in fact, *within every congregation of
every church.* When in the true partnership, each church is
involved in a mission to the world. For example, the
Presbyterian Church of Ghana and the Presbyterian Church
in the United States are together engaged in mission in
sending the Rev. Dora Owusu across the frontier of faith to
the world that exists in the metropolitan area of Atlanta,
Georgia. She is "sent" by both churches. Her field of service
is to bear witness to the love and grace and power of God in
certain situations that exist in Atlanta for which she is
uniquely qualified. She is *not* sent by the Church of Ghana *to
the Presbyterian Church* in the United States. Her purpose
in coming is *not* to bring us aid and comfort, although her
being here among us will no doubt contribute to that end.
She will *not* "serve" the Presbyterian Church in the United
States or Atlanta Presbytery while she is here. Her coming is
to cross this frontier of faith and bear witness to those in the
world (including the world that is present in Presbyterian
Church in the United States congregations) of God's grace.
This world is the object of God's love and both the Church in
Ghana and the Church in the United States are instrumen-
talities for sending Dora Owusu on this joint venture.

(d) *The Missionary Vocation.* A missionary is one who is "sent."
This is the basic meaning of the New Testament concept of
the "apostolate" (the "sent ones") and translated into the
Latin "Missio." This is the distinctive mark of what it means
to be a "missionary"—to be sent by the Church to the
frontier of faith. *If the term comes to mean simply the
sending from one church to another or the "sharing of
personnel," the role of the missionary becomes domesticated
and loses its vitality and prophetic nature.* A missionary is
never to be viewed as a "gift" from one church to another.

"Gifts" of whatever form lead to relationships of dependency. Neither is a missionary one who is "received" by either church partner. *Both* churches participate in the "sending," the commissioning, and the support.

(5) *Implications of this new "model."* This new conceptualization of the international mission of the Church would have widespread implications. Some of these would have to be worked out by the various partners concerned. A few basic ones might be the following:

(*a*) The Priority of "Mission" over "Relationship." One of the characteristics of our present understanding of international mission is our preoccupation with relationships and structural arrangements. As one reads through some of the lengthy, detailed "mutual agreements" which form the basis of our overseas work, one is impressed with the similarity of all this with treaties between sovereign states, or a "status of forces" agreement covering the stationing of troops in a foreign land. Perhaps, initially, the matter of proper relationships between the participating churches was important to safeguard a church's integrity, but with growing confidence, mutual respect, and maturity, maybe some of this is now behind us. Two churches may have a perfectly harmonious relationship between each other, and yet in terms of mission, nothing is accomplished! One is also impressed that in the more recent consultations with overseas partners, there seem to be far fewer "hang-ups" over organization and structure and far more concern about the mission to be accomplished.

(*b*) *All that the Church does is not "Mission."* Each church recognizes that there is a great deal within the life of the other partner in which they need not become involved. Each church has its own life and identity and sphere of activity, apart from the specific joint venture in mission in which both cooperate. The one thing of concern is the availability of a "base" from which mission can be sustained. *Quite frankly, the Presbyterian Church in the United States does not have the wisdom nor the resources, nor the mandate, to support everything good in which our partners around the world are involved.* Neither do we have to pass judgment on everything that is done. To engage in mission means a certain selectivity, certain concentration of effort, a mobilization of existing resources (whether large or small) for specific objectives. Only this limiting factor will save us from charges of "meddling" in the affairs .of another church, of manipulating people and programs or using our resources to form new dependencies.

(c) *Freedom and Flexibility.* One of the complaints of the Church-based approach was that it locked both partners into structural agreements which restricted the freedom and initiative of each. No *church has "territorial rights" to a particular geographical area of the world.* The needs of the world and the opportunities for mission are changing so rapidly that each church needs to have the *opportunity to initiate new programs, seek new partners, and to respond to new opportunities.* It may be more healthy for a church to have "multi-lateral" working agreements with many partners than to have just one partner in a given land. It is interesting to note that the proposed agreement with the National Presbyterian Church of Mexico, which looks beyond the present period of Moratorium, is far less structured and provides for far more flexibility and freedom for all partners than was previously the case. Perhaps this is a sign of the future.

(d) *Resources can be mobilized for new Mission outreach.* Another concern with the present *strategy for international mission* is the tendency to spend our resources to maintain existing structures and organizations. Today we are far more "institutionalized" than we were fifteen years ago, in that a far greater percentage of our missionaries work within institutions. *Fewer of our missionaries and a smaller percentage of our funds are employed at what might be called "the cutting edge."* Part of this is because there is less of an identity crisis for missionaries working within an institution than at "the frontier." Part of the problem is our failure to think of mission except in terms of "inter-church aid." Perhaps this new interpretation of mission would make it easier to free up mission resources (both personnel and funds) for new outreach.

(e) *Mutuality in Mission.* Today, both the "sending" and "receiving" of missionaries is affirmed. And yet one of the disappointments of the past decade has been that in spite of our invitations few overseas churches have taken advantage of the opportunity of sending missionaries to the United States. Most of the activity has been in one direction. As long as the missionary enterprise is thought of as "interchurch aid," the concept of sending missionaries to the United States is hard to explain. Why should an overseas church in the Third World that is weak in leadership and resources send the best that it has to "serve" the wealthier church across the seas? This is how church leaders from abroad have reacted to inquiries that they "send us missionaries." *Once the sending is viewed as a mission not to us but to the world—the world which exists here in the U.S.A., in all its power and seductiveness, just as it does everywhere else—then the concept begins to make sense.*

(f) *An Enlarged Base Means an Enlarged Mission.* If the missionary is viewed as someone who is "received" by the Church overseas and fitted into its structure, then there is a limit to the number of persons who can be "absorbed." There is also a limit to the amount of funds which can be pumped into another church structure without encouraging a new dependency. *This misunderstanding of mission was what the call for moratorium in some cases was all about. But once the overseas Church is viewed not as a recipient of welfare, but a "base" of operations from which a new thrust in mission is to take place, then the whole situation is altered.* The strength and size of the overseas Church, rather than becoming a limiting factor, becomes an opportunity for a *new mobilization of the Church's resources in mission to the world.* This is, in effect, what is happening. As our overseas partner churches have grown, as mutual understanding and confidence have increased, as relationships of dependency have been replaced by relationships of maturity, *opportunities for missionary personnel have* not slacked off, but rather have *multiplied.* The Church here at home has been led to believe that with the growth of our partner churches abroad, the urgency of the missionary enterprise had abated. But the reverse is true. The enlarged "base" means more opportunities for advance and a new challenge to the world-wide Christian community.

We find ourselves in hearty agreement with the main thrust of Dr. Brown's proposals. We believe our times call for clear recognition of the fact that Missions in all lands are not *under* Churches, but are partners in obedience; both are working at Christian Mission. God speaks to each partner. The arrangement ought to allow much freedom to each partner and much flexibility. Some things the Church will do entirely on its own. It believes that under God they are its clear duty. Some things the Mission will do entirely on its own. It believes that under God they are its clear duty. In all things there will be the closest cooperation and consultation. Both are working at the same task. Both are truly partners.

One thing the Church will wish to do on its own is to carry out its own international mission. Every mature Church ought to father a missionary society, either as part of its headquarters organization or as a voluntary society which has its blessing. We want to see Zairian missionary societies sending teams of Zairian missionaries to Mozambique, it may be, or South Sudan, or to Indonesia or the Black Muslims in New York. No Church has arrived until it is sending out its own missionaries.

Among the tasks the Mission may want to do is to evangelize non-Christians in some parts of a nation where its national Church is not working. For instance, why should not the Presbyterian Church in the United States send a strong team of missionaries—half Zairians and half Americans—to disciple the 200,000 Pygmies in the Ituri Forest? It would seek the blessing of the Presbyterian Church in the Kasai, of course; but the enterprise would be funded by PCUS and directed by its Mission in the Ituri Forest, under the general umbrella of ECZ. We believe the Presbyterian Churches in Kasai and Kinshasa would rejoice in such a venture.

We like particularly what Dr. Brown says about the priority of Mission over relationship. Like him, we are amazed at the degree to which preoccupation with relationships and structures has shut out the real task. All who know the situation will agree with Dr. Brown when he writes, "As one reads through some of the lengthy detailed 'mutual agreements' which form the basis of our overseas work, he is impressed with the similarity of all this with treaties between sovereign states, or a 'status of forces' agreement covering the stationing of troops in a foreign land." He goes on, "but with growing confidence, mutual respect, and maturity some of this is now behind us." Some tasks, Missions and Churches will do together; but "each Church has its own life and identity and sphere of activity, apart from the specific joint venture in Mission in which both cooperate."

Truly "no Church has territorial rights to a particular geographical area of the world." This needs to be said loudly and clearly. The problem is not quite so pressing in Zaire where such large proportions of the citizenry have become Christian, but in tremendous stretches of Asia and in many other countries of Africa small denominations of a few thousand have believed that they had the right to forbid their founding Mission and sister Churches from carrying out any kind of mission in their whole nation!

In the coming decades a much more generous and Christian attitude should prevail. Churches should welcome all Christian Missions, whether of evangelism or social action, carried on by anyone. They may not fully agree with it, but they have plenty to do without interfering with it, or attacking it as fracturing the unity of the Church. The needs are tremendous and all allies in the great campaign should be cordially welcomed. The great William Carey in 1800, himself a Baptist at a time that Baptists were scorned by Anglicans as non-Conformists, called for Missions from all the Churches to penetrate India and other lands of Asia with the gospel. This kind of ecumenicity is greatly needed today.

12

Are Missionaries Needed?
What We Say

Many theories concerning the right relationship of Churches and Missions are being tested in Zaire. It is a wonderful nation in which to study how devolution really works. Let us first describe the three main theories. Each has several forms and each is actually the working plan on which the Community and the Mission functions. One form of Theory One, for instance, is held by the Alliance; another by the Africa Inland, and still another by the Evangelical Covenant. Theories Two and Three also have several forms each.

Theory One: Friendly Dichotomy, or Parallel Dualism

Dr. L. L. King, for many years Executive Officer of Alliance Overseas Missions, has long championed the view that as the young Church developed, it would be helped in every way toward full independence, would become, in fact, fully independent and have complete control of all its own affairs, but that simultaneously the Mission would continue.[1] Mission would not merge into the Church. It would continue to manage its own affairs. If the Church wanted it to stay on, it would stay on. It would serve the Church and heartily cooperate with it but would do this as a mature, separate, parallel entity. This, Dr. King called Modified Dichotomy and we call it Friendly Dichotomy. If, for example, the Church wanted to take over some piece of work the Mission was carrying on, the Mission would consider the matter seriously and, if it agreed that the Church could and should take it over, would gladly effect the transfer. If it did not agree, however, it would retain the work gladly.

Modified dichotomy takes partnership in obedience seriously. The Church/Mission relationship is a partnership. Each partner is primarily responsible, not to the other partner, but to God. Both must be obedient to the heavenly vision, and both must be heartily cooperative and loving. Dr. King's careful exposition of this position appears in the *Church Growth Bulletin* for November, 1971, pages 175-185 in *Consolidated Volume Two,* 1969-75 (available from Church Growth Book Club, 1705 N. Sierra Bonita, Pasadena, CA 91104, U.S.A.).

The Alliance Mission came to Zaire in 1884; had a Church of thirty thousand communicants in 1976; and, as we have said, has recently started multiplying congregations among Mayombes who have moved to Kinshasa. Their Community (CEAZ) is strong and vibrant. Its leaders are godly persons of imagination and dedication. Its church-multiplying thrust in the capital city is a going venture of Church and Mission. The Mission maintains a separate parallel existence. In the mind of the missionary society, the Mission has not been fused into the Church. Though legally not existing, the Mission carries on through its missionary staff certain agreed-on activities in which the Community does not participate. One example is the education of missionaries' children. Actually, the Baptists and others do much the same. The Mission reported thirty missionaries in 1972 and nineteen in 1975. Friendly Dichotomy, while maintaining a separate parallel existence, has felt that a smaller number of missionaries adequately meets the needs of its rather mature Church of thirty thousand and carries out its responsibilities in further churching of the nation.

The Africa Inland Mission, which occupies the extreme northeastern corner of the land, similarly has stressed the full independence of the Church, while keeping its Mission strong and reserving its ability to act as God commands. Its Community (CECA) reported total communicants of 250,000. In 1973 it had 115 missionaries, and in 1975, 123. It has evidently judged that the contemporary task in Zaire demanded a slight increase in missionary staff.

The Evangelical Covenant Mission, which works in the northwest corner of Zaire in the lands drained by the Ubangi River, holds the theory of parallel dualism in regard to Mission and Church. Its experienced Executive Secretary of World Mission, Russell A. Cervin, writes as follows in his influential *Mission in Ferment:*

Even though the autonomy of the Church is sought and desired, the Church's needs are so great that it cannot go it alone.... In ... Zaire after independence all mission charters were to disappear and legal charters were to be held by the churches.... If the missionary body held property, such as residences for missionaries, they would be held under the charter of the church with an agreement guaranteeing their use by missionaries.... All of our church studies have shown the greatest spirit of goodwill and appreciation for the presence and contribution of the missionaries so our work continues. This is not true of some other bodies in areas where very few missionaries are left. In Zaire, nationals speak of three categories of Churches: those still assisted by missionaries; others where the missionary staff has been reduced considerably and functions under great limitations; and still others which they call "abandoned churches." Many denominations have virtually abandoned the churches they helped to bring forth.[2]

The Evangelical Covenant Mission reported fifty missionaries in 1972 and forty-seven in 1975. Along with the Evangelical Free Mission, with which it has worked closely in Zaire for many years, it believes that in the Fourth Era of Mission completing evangelization, strengthening the Church, and Christianizing the social order require the continued presence of missionaries. The Riddle-McGavran Team met a fine group of leading Africans and Americans representing both Churches. The picture they gave us of the state of the Church and the task of evangelization was the most complete we received in any Community. Those Churches and their assisting Missions are well aware of the tribal mosaic and of the strength of the Churches—both their own and that of the Roman Catholics in each of the tribes of their area.

Theory Two: Complete Fusion, No Mission Left

The Disciples of Christ Congo Mission (DCCM) has long been one of the strong Missions of this land. It occupied large parts of Equatorial Province. From their headquarters at Bolenge (now Mbandaka) the Disciples missionaries spread east through the Lonkundu-speaking Mongo tribes, along the Tshuapa River and its tributaries. In 1966-1967 the Mission appointed missionaries Galusha and Dargitz to do a careful census of their far-flung congregations. The task took large parts of two years. The team visited every station, every main center, and most of the village churches. It reported that in 1967 the Church fathered by the DCCM numbered 257,000 baptized believers in good standing. This was surprising because the missionary society in 1964 had reported only

139,000. It was also not fully believed because the figure printed in the 1968-69 *Year Book of the Christian Churches* was 229,000. We assume that the DCCM had about 230,000 communicants at the end of the sixties, which made it the largest Protestant Church in Zaire. Under the leadership of Dr. Robert G. Nelson, the United Christian Missionary Society opted for Theory Two: *Complete Fusion, no Mission left* and has systematically put that theory into practice. From eighty-four missionaries in 1961, the society now reports nineteen in 1976.[3] When the team was in Mbandaka in June, 1977, we found one lone missionary family in the vast field of this Mission, a land area as large as Kansas. He and his wife were directed by his home society not to interfere in any way in the work of the Church. The rest of the missionary force of nineteen were in Kinshasa, Kimpese, and other places doing joint tasks assigned to them by the ECZ. A splendid headquarters building for the Church had been built—called The Secretariat—and the Church was in charge.

Theory Two, Dr. Nelson holds, involves encouraging the young Churches to act entirely on their own and sending a few missionaries to the ECZ to be assigned as it directs, but preferably not in the old DCCM territory. To send them there would help build congregations which thought of themselves as Disciples, whereas they should think of themselves as part of the National Church—the Church of Christ in Zaire (ECZ). This dedication to structural Christian unity complicates the Church/Mission relationship and accentuates the impression of domination by the missionary society which we were given by the Zairian leaders in Mbandaka. They begged us to tell their Home Board that they wanted a missionary family in each of the six main stations, and said the missionaries would collaborate closely with Zairians to develop the churches in the area.

We know of no place where Theory Two has been given a more thorough workout than by the DCCM. The deteriorating mission stations and frustration of national leaders raise serious doubts as to whether Theory Two, as operated by the Disciples, was good either for the Mongo churches or for the National Church as a whole'. When we asked at the Secretariat for the communicant membership, they looked up the records for 1976 and told us 92,000. The drop from 229,000 reported by the United Christian Missionary Society in the 1969 *Year Book* apparently tells of a disastrous loss. However, we hazard a guess that it is an apparent loss. The 92,000 is close to the figure which this Mission was reporting back in the late fifties. We surmise it means that the Church, thrown entirely on its own, simply did not have the personnel or the transportation to get the facts in from the far reaches of the field. We were told of no great reversions. However, we were told that in the easternmost areas some communities had gone over to the Roman Catholics who were at hand to serve them better than the missionary-less Disciples.

The high figures of members which the Disciples reported (from 99,747 in 1958 to 229,000 in 1968—for details see chapter 6) indicates that in that decade, very large accessions took place. Possibly in the tremendous instability which freedom brought, the Church seemed the most stable thing around; possibly other factors were at work. However it happened, in the far reaches of the Disciples' field, substantial numbers of new people turned from animism to the Christian faith. The history of Missions clearly indicates that such new peoples need well-planned, thoroughly Christian nurture for *many* years.

Of the 137,000 added to the Church after 1958, some were children of the 99,747; but growth of that magnitude cannot be obtained by baptizing children of existing Christians. There must have been—and there were—large accessions from outside, from new villages, from practicing animists. At this late date, no one can tell how many came from within and how many from without the churches involved. Possibly thirty thousand new children needed to be reared in Christian schools. Thousands of adults needed to learn to read the Bible. Thousands of deacons, elders, and good Christian women needed to be trained. Hundreds of new church and school buildings had to be erected of poles and *endeli* thatch and hence will need repairing every few years. Responsible supervision, regularly carried out, was essential and remains essential. Otherwise, these masses will become Christo-pagans, exactly as did millions of Amerindians in Mexico, Central America, and the Andean Highlands. They will have the name of Christians, but their beliefs, value systems, fears, hopes and worship will be thoroughly sub-Christian.

It seems tragic to the team that at just this time every church headquarters and station is completely denuded of missionaries. The leaders in Mbandaka with whom we conferred expressed grave doubts about the spiritual state of the 137,000, concerning whose existence Mbandaka Secretariat knew little. Zairian pastors in other parts of the nation assured us that unless village pastors are trained and retrained, supervised, provided with biblical materials, encouraged, and fed on the Word, intense belief in witchcraft and evil spirits flood back into the minds of new Christians. Dedication to structural Christian unity in far-off Indianapolis has lessened the amount of Christian nurture available to more than one hundred thousand baptized believers. The old believers living near the mission stations may continue strongly Christian. The new converts across the big swamp, thirty miles down the road, will become Christo-pagans or will turn to other bodies to nurture them.

Theory Three: Friendly Fusion

The Presbyterians in the Kasai and the British and American Baptists have opted for Theory Three. They have maintained a missionary staff of some size. For example, in Kananga we visited a splendid hospital staffed jointly by Zairians and Americans. The prosperity and efficiency in the hospital owed much to the large staff of American missionary doctors and nurses at work there.

The American Baptist Mission (Community CBZO) came on the scene in 1884 and has been one of the strongest and most influential Missions. Location of its headquarters in Kinshasa, the capital (formerly Leopoldville), gave it added prestige. Its great work in Bas-Zaire was eclipsed by its greater work in Bandundu Province, around the notable station of Vanga. It reported to us a total community of 340,000 in 1976.

In the early sixties the American Baptist Mission adopted Theory Three. It should be remembered that these theories were not numbered then. The Revolution was on. From complete subservience to the Belgian rulers, the Zairians were vaulted overnight into the position of complete sovereignty. In the heat of those days, much adjustment had to be done and done fast. Whether it was good for the Church, whether the missionary had been a ruler or a friend was not asked. Whether in order to achieve an autonomous Church it was necessary, or even advisable, to phase the Mission out completely was not asked. The Church strode into power. Missions—Presbyterian, Baptist, and others—made adjustments. Most made decisions which now can be conveniently labeled as Friendly Fusion.

Friendly Fusion holds that the Mission has been merged into the Church. The Mission has disappeared. It is no longer there. But the doctrine is held almost tongue in cheek. The missionary physicians continue to staff the hospitals. The missionary residences are filled with missionaries. The missionary evangelist says emphatically, "I am under such and such a Zairian superior," but feels perfectly free to argue with his superior or to express his convictions about what is good for the Church, confident the missionary society will not call him home for doing so. We found the most cordial relationship between missionaries and nationals. Mr. Harvey's vignette in the preceding chapter shows how free the missionaries are to advocate new and potentially fruitful moves. The nationals are not engaged in putting the missionaries down, nor are the missionaries engaged in putting nationals down. Fusion is there, but it is friendly fusion.

The American Baptists reported that in 1972 they had ninety-seven missionaries, and in 1975, sixty-two. The proportion of decrease is quite similar to that reported by the Alliance which practices Modified Dichotomy. Obviously, both American Baptists (with headquarters at Valley Forge, Pennsylvania) and the sixty-two missionaries on the field intend to stay on helping the existing Church to grow more mature and more Christian, evangelizing the Dark Areas in their areas, and multiplying congregations furiously in Kinshasa. Obviously, the Baptist congregations in Zaire and their forward-looking leaders are delighted that they have this aid.

Does the Theory Make Any Difference?

In the case of Friendly Fusion and Friendly Dichotomy, we are of the opinion that both are working well. Both partners in each case are happy. The Churches are growing in grace and in self-reliance. The Missions are adjusting to the new challenges. The theory is not the critical factor. *The critical factor is the will to mission, the will under God and by his favor to make the Church strong, to evangelize the multitudes who have yet to believe, and to serve each other and the nation in Christian love.* If missionaries are there meeting "those needs the Church cannot or does not meet," if the national leaders focus on the welfare of the Church and not their own status, and if the missionary societies are determined to carry on sinner-converting, church-multiplying, kingdom-building mission until the population has been well-churched, *then* both Modified Dichotomy and Friendly Fusion will work.

We are also of the opinion that two theories will not work. Any Mission which tried to hold a Church under its own power would run into serious difficulties. We know of no Missions which are attempting this, but, if they did, they would cause the Church great loss. Similarly, practicing Complete Fusion—throwing Zairian denominations entirely on their own (to use Cervin's phrase, "abandoning them")—greatly damages them. For one thing, such Churches feel they have been betrayed. They know their founding Missions have tremendous resources and could help them greatly. For the missionary society to withdraw help completely is considered "missionary society paternalism or colonialism." Decisions made in far-off England or America and heavily influenced by the intellectual and religious climate there, though well-intentioned, are likely to miss the mark. Policies laid down by men and women who have not spent long years in Zaire, do not know the languages, and have not lived as brothers with Zairians for long periods are likely to be unwise. Further, the many needs of the Church are not met.

At this point, we must not be misled by the exceptional case in which a Church, whose founding Mission has been driven out, does "flourish." When in 1836 the Mission in Madagascar was driven out by the pagan queen, it feared the young Church would die. When the Mission came back in 1862, it found the Church flourishing. The Sudan Interior Mission was driven out of Ethiopia by the Italians in 1936. When it came back in 1942, it found that a few Christians had grown to thousands. And in Zaire today, the Reformed Church of Shaba, founded by the Belgian Protestants, appears to have grown very substantially, though for eighteen years it has had no missionaries from Belgium.

What shall we say to cases like these? For one thing, if the Mission is *driven* out, the Church feels no sense of betrayal. On the contrary, it is greatly challenged. For another, growth is a very complex phenomenon. Any careful study would reveal that among the many factors *which caused growth,* the absence of missionaries may not be counted. These churches grew despite missionary absence. Furthermore, when missionaries came back and "found the Church flourishing," what they meant was that it was still there and was growing. They did *not* mean that it had no needs, its pastors were all well-trained, its boys and girls had all received thoroughly Christian education, it was eliminating those of its customs which demeaned life and belittled women, and its health care and agricultural development were at a high state of development.

We are now ready to state our three conclusions in regard to the need which Zairian Churches have for missionaries.

Our First Conclusion: National Aspirations Have Been Achieved

The legitimate national aspirations of Zairians vis-à-vis the missionaries have been achieved. We stand in 1978, not 1948. Some of the extreme measures of the last thirty years may have been necessary to put power in the hands of Africans. We assume that they were. But today the task is neither taking power away from missionaries and putting it in the hands of Zairians, nor encouraging Zairians to believe in themselves. Now Zairians are firmly in control of their nation and all its processes. They stand at the head of every Community, every school, every theological seminary, and every diocese, conference, and district. In 1978 the call to Missions is, together with African leaders, to map out tasks of sufficient size and challenge so the elite corps of Christians, who are the missionaries of the Church, will feel that they are not wasting their time and betraying their Lord if they work in Zaire. One missionary told us sadly, "I am doing so little here that I wonder if my Lord is pleased with my staying here. I want to do more. I see much more to do, but I am checked at every point." In 1978 the task is to assure all able missionaries that glorious and needed work lies on every hand waiting to be done, and that Missions and Churches want them to do it. Africans have already achieved their rightful place.

No one but Satan can rejoice in a repetition of the tired, old clichés that "the missionary overshadows the African," that "he wants to control the African," that "the Church cannot thrive in the shadow of the Mission." These slogans never were entirely true and today are more misleading than ever. Christians must abandon them and challenge them whenever they hear them.

Our Second Conclusion: Missionaries Are Still Needed

We believe that missionaries are needed during the Fourth Era of Mission. This is true in Zaire and most other lands. We know we are voicing the convictions of most Zairian and missionary leaders of the Communities. We hope we shall carry our American and European readers with us. We ended our survey with growing certainty that missionaries, as we have defined them and as we have seen them at work, will benefit the cause of Christ in Zaire for many years to come.

Justice demands the presence of missionaries. As we stated in the Introduction, we share the opinion being widely expressed in some circles today that the developed countries of earth (mostly in the Northern Hemisphere) owe much to their developing sister nations. We know of no better way in which that debt can be paid than by the continued sending of the best Christians of Europe and America to work as partners with Zairian leaders to proclaim the gospel and to do God's will in regard to the abundant life he wants all his children to enjoy in Christ.

The myriad needs of both the Church and the nation in Zaire demand a continued stream of missionaries. We disassociate ourselves from those wealthy Euricans who say, "Let the huge populations of Africa and Asia continue to live on a pittance, hampered by false and inadequate beliefs, exploding populations and political tyrannies. They will have to help themselves. We will do nothing." Any such position is irresponsible and unchristian. Missionaries are needed for urgent education and medical and evangelistic tasks. They are urgently needed to train local leaders and candidates for the ministry. Without missionaries, the *rapid* churching of the cities will not be done. Without the power of Christ in multitudes of urbanites, the demonic powers of the modern city will dehumanize millions. Missionaries can do spectacular service in argicultural development, including animal husbandry. A tremendous service, as we indicated in chapter 9, can be rendered in getting and maintaining accurate pictures of the growth and welfare of the Church in each of the three hundred tribes, in all cities, and all other segments of the population. The inroads of secular materialism on the one hand and resurgence of belief in witchcraft and evil spirits on the other are genuine dangers and demand continuous and skillful redress. The Churches are doing much, but more needs to be done.

One of the essential tasks resting on the Churches in Zaire arises from the many major languages spoken and the need to have the Bible in each. In addition to French, Kikongo, Tshiluba, Lonkundu Ngbaka, and the trade languages, Kituba, Swahili and Lingala, there are many languages spoken by a hundred thousand souls or more. Translating the New Testament or the whole Bible into these many tongues is a very large task. The New Testament has not yet been translated into some languages, such as Kimbala. Even when the whole Bible has been translated, changes in the languages and advances in the art of translation make it imperative for new versions to be produced.

Ideally, translators should be those whose mother tongue is the language into which the Bible is being translated. Since, however, the translators ought to be fluent in Greek and Hebrew and thoroughly conversant with the science of communication, highly educated missionary translators working with national informants still do most translations. It seems clear that if the Church is to have meaningful vigorous translations of the Bible into the many languages of the people, missionaries from outside the country are going to be needed for some time to come.

Another task arises from the phenomenal degree to which the mission and church systems depended on motor transport. Missionaries had cars. They toured extensively. They supervised churches in huge districts. When the missionary supervisor was replaced by the African, it was clear that the latter could supervise his district only if he, too, were provided with a car. Some Missions provided African ministerial supervisors with cars; but keeping them running was another matter. With international authorities assuring us that oil will give out in forty years and will be terribly expensive in twenty, and with the price of gas going up annually, the cost of motor transport is becoming prohibitive.

Perhaps what is needed is to redistrict all church areas, so that each of many small districts has a headquarters which members of all congregations in that district can reach by less than five hours' walk. Many more top flight "ministers in charge" will be needed. Let each headquarters be staffed by a top flight Zairian or missionary, all working under the ablest Zairian it is possible to secure, who lives at the old mission station, gives full time to the work, and has motor transport. Let all school and church programs depend mainly on foot work and bicycle.

Our Third Conclusion: Problems Will Remain

Granting all this, sending missionaries to Zaire during the Fourth Era of Mission presents undoubted problems. Let us look at some of them.

Missionaries may damage a Church's will to work. If missionaries are sent to Zaire in large numbers, the Church may sit back and let them do the work. Christians may not do the sacrificial giving which is so desirable. The Church may declare that special needs of all sorts are the Mission's business. It may say, "Let the Mission repair the cars, run the hospitals, pour millions into this country, maintain the mission presses, keep reliable statistics, and evangelize the Dark Areas. Why should we even think about sending Zairian missionaries to Mozambique or Indonesia? That is the business of the Mission. To be a Christian is to receive aid, not give it." In short, as long as the missionaries are there, the churches may demand more and more and fail to become strong and self-reliant.

The danger is real but can be avoided. The able Zairian pastors, headmasters, professors, and laypersons in many walks of life, facing the tremendous tasks of developing the country and solving its many problems, naturally want as much help as they can get from sister Churches in Europe and America. No one can fault them for that. But these persons of good sense are the first to say that such aid must be predicated on Zairian Christians doing all they can. There are two ways—one bad and one good—to encourage Zairian denominations to do more. The bad way is to withdraw all aid in an attempt to *force* them to do more. The good way is to keep a large band of well-trained modern missionaries actively at work among the entire people which has been discipled. No one knows the people better than the missionary who lives among them. It is impossible for chance visitors from America, who drop in for a few days, to form accurate ideas on how much the people ought rightfully to give, whether they are doing their best, and whether their sister Churches ought to help them more.

If the great denominations of Europe and America want to treat Zaire with justice and to follow policies which will carry these new denominations on to more abundant life in Christ, they need the constant input of missionaries working in every tribe and every section of every tribe, in city and country. The Zairian Church has no better and no more intelligent friends than the missionaries who have put in their lives there. The sooner this is recognized by all, the sooner will Christian Mission be able to work single-eyed to the welfare of the Churches of Zaire.

Another problem is that sometimes the Community puts missionaries into situations where they feel they cannot do their best. The Church in all lands of Latfricasia must *learn to use missionaries effectively*. They must be given meaningful tasks. One missionary in the Philippines complained that he was not given enough to do. Another in Brazil declared that he had to ask permission for every small move. He was not given a clearly defined task and told to get on with it. Such difficulties are also met with in Zaire.

Another set of problems arises in the sending countries. If

missionaries are *not* sent, then interest in Missions declines. Young men and women never think of going to Africa as missionaries. Congregations cease writing Africa into their budgets. Missionaries go to other lands and pull their support after them. Theories of Mission which focus on tasks other than discipling the nations multiply. Biblical Mission in Zaire grinds to a halt. It takes *missionaries* to arouse the conscience of the churches of any land to carry out Mission across the chasms of culture, race, and language. They raise the money needed. They plead the cause of the peoples concerned. They leave home and kindred to work in a foreign land and rightfully become special figures in the minds of the millions who pray for them and carry out Mission through them.

It is fatuous to suppose that any body of Christians living in America or England, bombarded every day with the crying needs of their own land and their own neighborhood, will be so bighearted that, without any presentations by missionaries living in Zaire, they will give sacrificially to meet the needs of that faraway land. It is even more fatuous to suppose that Christians in America could form any true idea of what the deepest needs of Zaire and her denominations and congregations are. That takes months of conversation in the tribal language with high and low, leaders and followers, men and women, boys and girls. That takes bearing these peoples on one's heart and enshrining them in his or her dreams. *That takes missionaries.*

If the Churches in Eurica are not to lapse back into substantial indifference to Zaire, they will have to continue to send missionaries. Similarly, if the Churches of Korea or Japan are to flame with missionary concern for Zaire, they will have to send missionaries to that land.

There is no longer any need to add the caution that missionaries must be "of the right kind." We are inclined to doubt that the caution was ever really needed. In the old days of Belgian rule, missionaries (and Zairians) recognized Belgians as rulers, and were well advised to do so. In the new days of Zairian rule, missionaries—being men and women of good judgment—recognize Zairians as rulers. In all our survey we saw nothing but the most cordial relationships between Zairians and missionaries. Missionaries by definition today are people who appreciate other cultures, respect other peoples, know they are guests in the country, and dedicate their lives to serve the peoples and the Church. Consequently, Churches in Eurica should plan to keep their force of missionaries in Zaire at full strength. Zaire welcomes missionaries and is open to the gospel. Christian parents in Europe and America should still ask God to bless them by calling their sons or daughters to be missionaries to Zaire. Prayers for the spread of the gospel in Zaire should still rise from thousands of Eurican churches. Missionary societies should recruit and train and send missionaries there. The need is great.

When there is a Zairian in every post which the Churches in Zaire can pay for, and in many which their sister Churches in Eurica pay for, there will still be many urgent tasks in Zaire which can best be filled by dedicated Christian missionaries. We trust that God will direct Churches in England and America, and Korea and Brazil, too, to maintain strong missionary task forces in this land on which he has poured out such signal measures of his grace. Victories half won are often lost. The Churches of Zaire need further service, and the strong Churches of the rest of the world should send missionaries to help. The Churches in Zaire, we were assured again and again, want this help.

But What Is the Correct Church/Mission Relationship?

After many years of wrestling with the question posed in the heading above, Christian Mission is on the point of clarifying the situation, of going further than it has gone, of laying down guidelines for the coming decades. This is true all over the world and especially in Zaire.

Dr. G. Thompson Brown has thrown significant light on the murky waters. He has opened up the whole field to serious investigation. His proposals look good to us. They fit Zaire well.

As our contribution to the ongoing discussion, we tender this chapter and sum up our thoughts in the following four paragraphs:

1. Mission at no time has been or can be the unquestioned and uncontrolled sending of large sums of money from one Church to another. Those who give sacred funds to the Church for Mission want to know and ought to know for what it is being spent and how it is being spent. In the past they delegated this responsibility to their own sons and daughters who were in constant contact with their families and friends and gave periodic reports in person. Today joint reporting of both partners in the great enterprise seems to be the best policy.

2. A key question is repeatedly asked: In the Fourth Stage of

Mission in Zaire, are there still urgent tasks which the Churches want done, which ought to be done, and which the Churches cannot themselves do or pay for? We reply, "There are, indeed, these urgent tasks and God wants them done. We believe that Churches and Missions ought to work out a system by which they will be done."

3. We believe that system is "Partnership in Mission in Obedience to God." Let the Churches, quite autonomous and in full command of themselves, do all they can. Let the Missions, in cordial cooperation with the Churches, do all they can. Let the Churches in no way hamper the Missions and the Missions in no way hamper the Churches. In all differences of opinion, let cordial cooperation and friendly negotiation as between brothers prevail. The work is tremendous. The center of the stage must cease to be taken by "relationships" between Church and Mission. It must be occupied by the "undone tasks." Training village pastors and top flight ministers, creating a thoroughly Christian parochial school system, maintaining modern hospitals for the relief of suffering, developing the very considerable agricultural resources of the Christians, eliminating the scourge of corruption, churching the great cities, and saturating industrial relationships with Christian principles—all these and many more tasks cry aloud to be done.

4. We like Dr. Brown's analysis of the situation. "The Church is the base of all Mission." *Agreed.* "But the base cannot be the end of Mission." *Well said.* "The Church, whether in this land or any other, must never exist for itself. It exists only that it might be the instrument for the salvation of the world." *Agreed.* "The Church in this country with its overseas partner forms the base . . . and both together contribute to the common Mission." *Splendid.* "No Church has territorial rights to a particular geographical area of the world." *Yes.* "Each Church needs to have the opportunity to initiate new programs, seek new programs, seek new partners, and respond to the opportunities." *Precisely.*

One Remaining Point: Remember the Mosaic

We cannot leave the subject with the impression that all Zaire is in the Fourth Stage of Mission. While most of it is, as we have repeatedly pointed out, some is in the First Stage of Mission, or the early part of Stage Two. We think at once of the Dark Areas and of the hundreds of thousands in the cities yet unchurched. In both cases, the task is establishing multitudes of new congregations.

In the Dark Areas the congregations will have to be established in new tribes or subtribes. In a few cases new languages or new races are involved—as in the case of the Pygmies and the Muslims. In most cases, the people in the Dark Areas constitute different homogeneous units. They will not be discipled into existing clusters of congregations, but into new clusters. A whole new clergy must be built if we are to respect the identity, honor the self-image, and appreciate the culture of the new peoples. We would expect that Stage One and Stage Two will be rapidly superceded and Stage Three will begin soon. People movements to Christ within a very few years should be the goal.

Evangelizing the Dark Areas cannot be done by near-neighbors. Missionaries are required. If these are sent by Zairian denominations, that would be splendid. But if Zairian denominations cannot spare their best sons and daughters to cross lines of culture and language and give their lives to discipling Dark Areas and there multiplying churches led by local sons and daughters, then European and American denominations ought to do the job. Possibly mixed teams funded by Eurican missionary societies will be the best solution. However it is done, rapid completion is the goal.

In the cities, too, both missionary societies and Zairian Churches should pool their resources. Men and money in abundance will be needed. City congregations of several hundred members will be able to finance themselves; but in the beginning, much encouragement and judicious help will be required.

If the administration of new task forces is dropped in the lap of existing Zairian Churches, we anticipate difficulties. But if the Churches and Missions create task forces *which administer themselves,* have great liberty of action, and take all the decisions in their own committees, we anticipate rapid and successful action. Such task forces ought, of course, to be ultimately responsible to either Church or Mission—it does not make too much difference which. On the task force executive committee will sit a representative of the existing Church and of the Mission and the task force will be instructed to operate under God as it deems fit. Let us say again that the goal is not correct Church/Mission relationships. *The goal is the discipling of the tribes.* That will take *missionaries*—both dark-skinned and light-skinned.

Appendix
—The Story of the Survey of 1977

by Norman Riddle

From a simple idea of a retreat for missionaries, there grew over the period of a year much correspondence and research involving as many Protestant Communities working in Zaire as possible. A month before the retreat, we made ten on-the-spot surveys of eight Communities at six locations. Our survey included scores of private conversations, interviews with missionaries and key nationals, much correspondence, visits to government offices for statistics, and comparing of data with those who attended the retreat. This survey provided the basic material for this book. Our hope is that the dynamics set in motion by the survey will inspire Community leaders to focus on the great tasks ahead and to share what they learn about their Communities with others laboring in this fruitful land.

Beginnings and Preparations
How It All Began

The survey and the retreat began without fanfare in March, 1976. The pastor of the International Church in Kinshasa, Rev. John Melton, saw a need for a retreat for all missionaries working in Zaire after visiting a group of missionaries in the interior. He shared his concern with me since I was the chairman of the Commission of Twelve at that time. He suggested the retreat have two emphases to meet the needs effectively: reorientation and inspiration. Rapid changes in role and the upheavals of the past seventeen years had created a climate of uneasiness and confusion among many missionaries. He later asked for a committee to be formed to work on such a retreat, and I was appointed to be chairman with two other members of the Commission of Twelve, Larry Bubek, with MAF, and Doug Crowder, with the Methodist Board.

The twin emphases suggested by Rev. Melton brought to mind two men who would ably handle them: Dr. Donald McGavran, founder of the School of World Mission at Fuller Theological Seminary in Pasadena, California, and now Dean Emeritus, and Bishop Festo Kivengere of Uganda, with whom I had conversed at length on evangelism in African cities and had heard as a conference speaker at the West African Congress on Evangelism at Ibadan, Nigeria. Contact was made with these men and both accepted the invitation. Soon after this, however, Bishop Kivengere was forced by political events to flee his homeland, and he took refuge in the United States. Some thought it unwise for him to return to Africa for the retreat; so it was with deep regret the Commission of Twelve began to make other arrangements. The choice fell on a man deeply involved in Missions (as President of the Baptist Federation of Canada) as well as an inspiring Bible teacher, conference speaker, and pastor—Dr. Roy Bell. When he consented to come, we knew the Lord was indeed blessing in this retreat.

In order to make the reorientation time more valuable, Dr. McGavran conditioned his acceptance by asking that the International Church arrange for him to visit several fields of work during the month prior to the retreat. He asked that I accompany him on the trip in order that we get a more precise idea of what was happening in Church growth in Zaire. The Commission of Twelve generously acceded to this request. My Community, CBZO, agreed to my full participation in the entire project.

Dr. McGavran developed a comprehensive measuring instrument to determine the degree of Christianization of each tribe in the areas studied. He realized that the nation was actually a mosaic of tribes and that this approach would be best suited to the task. Accordingly, twenty-five questionnaires were either mailed to the places we would later visit or given personally to leaders close at hand. Results were discussed in chapters 6 and 9.

We also mailed out letters to the Communities we planned to visit to arrange for our time with them and letters of information about the Retreat. The Retreat planning committee worked closely with the Commission of Twelve in sending out invitations to the Retreat to Communities across the nation. MAF was a tremendous help in making contact with the hard-to-reach areas. Members of the International Church took responsibilities concerned with preparations for special music, nursery and children's activities, transportation, hospitality for special guests and missionaries coming from the interior, mimeographing of program and special reports, and a full-time coordinator for the retreat.

After the project had taken definite shape, I secured an appointment with the General Secretary of the ECZ, Dr. I. Bokeleale. I explained to him the kind of investigation we were encouraging the Communities to make. He expressed his delight at the "eyes" this would give the ECZ. He accepted an invitation of the planning committee to welcome those attending the retreat.

The Contribution of the
Missionary Aviation Fellowship

The Director of MAF's flight program in Africa, Bob Gordon, negotiated with his headquarters about what contribution his organization could make to this nationwide effort to stimulate Church growth in Zaire. MAF generously decided to pay one-fourth of the round-trip fare for Dr. McGavran from Pasadena and to be responsible for his travel in Zaire on the survey. This firm offer gave a significant impetus to the project at a time when the Commission of Twelve needed some clear ideas on financing the Retreat. It also confirmed their belief that the survey and retreat would be of value to the discipling of Zaire.

A further contribution which was absolutely essential to the survey was that MAF placed the trip on high priority so that a plane was available for every leg of the journey. The entire MAF staff was encouraged to attend the retreat along with their families where possible. Bob Gordon contributed hours in preparation of his own fine report on Church growth of the Communities through the sixties. He obtained several maps of provinces in Zaire which greatly aided presentation at the consultations and the Retreat. The MAF short-wave radio network, operated by the pilots' wives, coordinated the flights of the survey as well as those involving missionaries coming to the Retreat. With the services MAF rendered, the preparation time for the survey and retreat was only a year, as compared to two or more it would have taken without their aid, and the extent of the Communities reached and the participation of those groups was greater than it could have been without MAF services.

The Survey
Consultations

Of great value to the survey were the many consultations and seminars. Several were held in Kinshasa and several more at five other locations. Missionaries and Zairian leaders participated in all of them. Some seminars were brief while others lasted for as long as two days. One particular help to our understanding the actual situations was that we were able to visit the actual programs going on in cities and rural areas. We participated in worship services, attended two baptisms of about 150 each in the Vanga field, and saw building programs of sanctuaries in Boma and Kinshasa. We visited hospitals, theological schools, and headquarters of several Communities, which further enlarged our grasp of facts and sharpened details.

One dramatic experience was a visit to a village pastor in the Evangelical Covenant field in the Ubangi who used his gift of healing to help the Community with the blessing of the Community and Mission. The biblical way he carried out his ministry and the tangible results proved to be a definite factor in baptisms and Church growth in the area. Thousands attended and the government officials contributed buildings to house those who came for healing.

The consultations began in Kinshasa with the leaders and missionary representatives of the Assembly of God and the Missionary Alliance Communities. We then flew west to the Alliance headquarters situated on the Zaire River at Boma near the Coast. Returning then to Kinshasa for an overnight stay, we took a long flight north to Mbandaka for two days of interviews and visits with officials and pastors of the Disciples of Christ Community. Afterwards we flew to Gemena where the Evangelical Free and Evangelical Covenant Communities held a joint consultation. It was there we saw the most graphic demonstration of the tribal mosaic. The afternoon of the second day, we flew east to the CEUM station of Karawa. The first interview was with a missionary and a recent graduate of theological school who was interested in evangelizing his own tribe, the Budja, in this field. One evening we spent with missionaries, sharing our findings and answering questions. It was here that we visited the pastor with the gift of healing. Our proposed trip to northeastern Zaire and Kivu Provinces did not materialize; so we returned to Kinshasa for a much-needed rest before flying east to Kananga in the West Kasai Province. On the way there we dropped down at the Mennonite station (CMZ) across the Kasai River from Tshikapa for an hour's interview with a pastor and some missionaries. We spent two busy and informative days at Kananga with key leaders of the Presbyterian Community. The next stop was the Baptist station of Vanga to the west in the Bandundu Province, after dropping down for short consultations at Bulape in the northwest corner of the Presbyterian field and Busala, CBZO's easternmost station. The two days at Vanga were very profitable as the supervising pastor, Rev. Pambi, gave us his personal attention. Each day he drove us to an impressive baptismal service in the district. This was a reminder for me of the years I had spent working in this field and it was a pleasant introduction to the work for Dr. McGavran. The presence of Rev. V. Mavungu, CBZO's Director of Evangelism, further enriched our stay. He was finishing an evangelistic tour of the area. We left Vanga and flew to Kinshasa by way of CBZO's Bible School at Kikongo. We had several informal interviews with the teachers and director before leaving Rev. V. Mavungu to address the Commencement exercises.

Interviews and Conversations

Of a less formal nature were the interviews and conversations which gave us many helpful insights we would otherwise have missed. Sometimes a missionary and a Zairian were present, other times only one or the other. In Kinshasa we met with Rev. N. Kapini, the first General Secretary for CBZO and now the head pastor for their Kinshasa congregations, who told us of the encouraging growth of the CBZO congregations from 12 in 1971 with a membership of 4,000 to 26 in 1977 with a membership of 6,000. In a conversation with a Mennonite missionary and two Zairian pastors we learned of their growth in the city of Kinshasa and in the Bandundu Province. A British Baptist missionary told us the pertinent details of the growth of his Community. We met an African Inland Mission missionary in his hotel room; he also gave us a report on the growth of his Community in the southeast. At Mbandaka, Gemena, and Karawa we had several of these informal sessions. While at Kananga we met with Bishop Onema of the Central Methodist Conference and obtained much helpful information from him. Other valuable meetings took place with missionaries and Zairians of the Presbyterian Community. At Vanga there was ample opportunity for private conversations. We regard these more informal encounters as an important source of facts and impressions about the state of the Church in each place.

Reports to Board Secretaries

Early in the trip around to visit the Communities, the team realized that it would be helpful to share our findings and impressions with the General Secretary of each Board represented. Accordingly, Dr. McGavran prepared a detailed letter to each Board Secretary and mailed it soon after our visits in order that he could be kept abreast of the survey. In addition, Dr. McGavran prepared and sent each Secretary a general letter giving the broader picture of the nation as a whole. A few did not reply, but those who did showed their appreciation. Dr. Brown of the Southern Presbyterian Board incorporated the material into a series of consultations in Zaire between the Board and the Community.

The Retreat
Organization

The retreat took place at the Nganda Retreat Center in Kinshasa for five days. About sixty-five missionaries from the various Communities attended along with members of the International Church, who were freer to attend in the evenings. Several Zairians who knew English attended many of the sessions. One of these, Rev. V. Songo, Director of the Kimpese complex of schools and conference center, submitted a very fine study of the Alliance field in the Mayombe, a region west of Kinshasa on the Coast. At the opening session Dr. M. Masamba welcomed the missionaries in the name of the ECZ as Dr. Bokeleale's representative (who had been called away to America on business). One very prominent visitor and observer was David Fraser of World Vision who was very interested in the results of the Survey and the reports at the retreat. His organization was interested in the possibility of using this retreat as a model for retreats in other countries.

The retreat afforded much insight and inspiration as we heard Dr. McGavran's lectures on "Church Growth" and Dr. Bell's soul-lifting messages on Habakkuk. Other leaders were Rev. Charles Harvey, missionary with the Canadian Baptist Board, who led in a Bible study each morning, and Rev. Ray Downey, missionary with the Christian and Missionary Alliance Board, who headed up the study on Theological Training by Extension and conducted a workshop on the same subject. Other workshops were Church Growth, led by Dr. McGavran; Counseling, led by Dr. Bell; and Witchcraft, led by Charles Harvey. Other missionaries gave special reports covering their areas of work, such as the Alliance in Mayombe, the American Baptists at Vanga, the British Baptists in Bas-Zaire, Equator and Upper Zaire provinces, Disciples of Christ in the Equator Province, the Evangelical Free Church and Evangelical Covenant in Ubangi-Mongala, Presbyterians in Kasai, Africa Inland Mission in the northeast part of Zaire, the Mennonites in West Kasai, and the Christian and Missionary Alliance in Kinshasa. Of special concern are the urban centers. This mutual responsibility led to a special presentation of the challenges of discipling Kinshasa and other cities of Zaire.

Other inspiration came from the special music each morning and evening, the group singing, and the fun and sharing times in between sessions at informal gatherings and at meals.

Results

Judging from the many comments made during the retreat, the twin objectives of reorienting missionaries to the challenge of the seventies and of inspiring them to personal spiritual growth were amply achieved. The precise information given in Dr. McGavran's lectures and in the reports, as well as the comparisons and discussions during the worships, provided the sharpness of detail needed for each one of those present to rethink constructively his or her own task. The blessings of the Bible study and the teaching by Dr. Bell afforded opportunity for spiritual insights and refreshment. Another major benefit was the opportunity for missionaries of various Communities to be able to compare their tasks with others with common goals and concerns. The fellowship which grew out of this common bond of love of Christ and his Church will continue for years to come. Individuals were thus able to relate their personal efforts to the whole and found them to be more meaningful. The immensity of the remaining task, as well as the substantial resources of God's mighty power available in Christ to accomplish them, was realized in new ways.

There was a general recognition that the survey had long-range implications. Each Community was inspired to carry out a more thorough study of its work based on principles discussed at the retreat. It was also apparent that whereas Mission Board executives by necessity must confine their brief visits to the area where the Community with which they are in partnership is working, the team was able to visit consecutively several key areas. This gave a comprehensiveness to the survey not previously possible. Communities working in the same context, such as those in Kinshasa, provided an excellent means for comparison. However, valid comparison was also possible between Communities working in rural areas, even though not among the same tribes and separated geographically. Many people asked that a fuller statement of the findings be issued and distributed among those who attended. It was from these requests and others expressed later that the results of the survey and the retreat in book form were considered both needed and desired.

Subsequent Research

As the idea of writing a book took shape, Dr. McGavran outlined some areas of research which needed to be done before my trip to the States. He suggested renewed contacts with Communities which had not replied to our original letters and questionnaires to encourage them to send us whatever information they could. He also suggested new contacts which should be made, such as the Roman Catholics and Seventh Day Adventists. He outlined areas needing specialized interviews and information, such as the return of the schools to the Communities from the government. I spent many hours gathering this data.

Renewed Contacts

Letters were sent out to all who had been originally contacted. Some who had contributed earlier added new information. Conversations were used to renew contacts and produce additional facts and insights. Especially helpful was Paul Lehman who amplified his report to the Retreat on the city congregations of the Alliance. A special effort was made to reach the Communities in the northeastern part of the country by sending letters and simplified questionnaires in French with an MAF pilot making a special trip there, but we were unable to get any statistics.

New Contacts

Lt. Col. Diakanwa and his colleague, Lt.Col. Mast, were very helpful in providing a good profile of the work of the Salvation Army. My interview with Col. Mast was of special value. Rev. Banga

Mwabo, Legal Representative for the Seventh Day Adventists in Kinshasa and Bas-Zaire, assembled useful statistics and shared his impressions of the work of his Community in Kasai and Shaba, as well as for the congregations under his jurisdiction.

In following up a lead concerning the presence in Kinshasa of Bishop Ngoie of the Shaba Methodist Conference, I was able to meet Pastor Kayumbe of the Protestant Community of Shaba and get a questionnaire filled out by the Legal Representative of the Brethren in Christ of Garanganze Community. Bishop Ngoie graciously gave me more than three hours of his time, even though he was busy getting ready to travel to the United States. He filled out a questionnaire and gave me an interview both of which proved very valuable in getting some idea of the work of Communities in the vast Province of Shaba, recently torn by an invasion. These three contacts helped fill in our understanding of this part of the country.

I was helped in my search for statistics from government and Roman Catholic sources by Rev. V. Mavungu, with whom I work in the Department of Evangelism of CBZO. He guided me to offices which would have remained closed to me had I gone alone. We were able to obtain statistics for the city of Kinshasa and other important cities and towns throughout the country. At the office of statistics for the Roman Catholics, we purchased the *Annuaire for 1974-75,* which is a veritable mine of information on all aspects of this branch of the Christian faith.

Other contacts for information were made. At a meeting of the Kinshasa Pastors' Council I met Rev. Emedi Mwenebanga, who is President of the Kivu Synod of the ECZ, and asked him for some information on the Communities in his Synod. Later I sent him a letter and a questionnaire. Rev. K. Mulukidi of the city Presbyterians promised to help. Lillian Hogan of the Assemblies of God gave information on the work of her Community in the interior, based at Isoro. Conversations and correspondence with Charles Harvey, who works out of Kimpese, were very fruitful.

Two men, Mr. Lala and Mr. Mindana, helped greatly with information on the status of our Protestant schools. They showed the structure, lines of authority, and roles of various officials. Mr. Lala, who is a Baptist, works with the ECZ in the Department of Education. Mr. Mindana is one of the top men in the CBZO headquarters in the educational department. We greatly appreciate their help.

As my wife and I were leaving for the States to begin work on this book, in the Kinshasa airport we met Rev. Bill Washburn, who is field representative for the Presbyterian Mission. He gave some interesting facts about the events which had transpired since our visit to his field in the Kasai in June. The Mission and the Community had completed very fruitful series of evaluation meetings and had also done some planning for the future. He was very optimistic about what lay ahead for his Community.

Sharing Preliminary Findings

As pertinent statistics came to my attention and as I had time to think through some of the implications these had for the task of discipling the nation, I shared them with the ECZ Secretariat, with the pastors of the city through its Council, and with leaders and supervising pastors of my Community. Reactions I received encouraged me to believe that when the full story was known, it would give renewed impetus and direction to the Communities, which in turn would result in greater evangelism and a general strengthening and multiplication of congregations.

Summary

As I close this story, I wish to express the appreciation of the team for the help it was given in conducting the survey and the retreat. The International Protestant Church did a courageous and timely thing in sponsoring such a bold venture. It cheerfully shouldered a large financial and spiritual challenge in spite of transition and change in its constituency. Without this action, the survey and retreat would not have taken place.

We also thank the MAF for its contributions, so essential to the survey, and for its strong support of the retreat. We deeply appreciate the warm reception we received everywhere we visited. We pray that the time and effort invested by the missionaries and Zairian leaders will bring rewards in their work as the Spirit multiplies their investment.

Notes

Chapter 1

[1] Those in a hurry to get to today's problems and solutions may wish to turn at once to Part II, page 107. However, for real understanding we counsel reading straight through.

[2] Georges Deward, *Histoire du Congo: évolution du pays et de ses habitants* (Liège, Belgium: H. Dessain, 1962), p. 9.

[3] E. M. Braekman, *Histoire du Protestantisme au Congo* (Bruxelles IV: Editions de la Libraire des Eclaireurs, Unionistes, 1961), p. 14.

[4] George Peter Murdock, *Africa: Its Peoples and Their Culture History* (New York: McGraw-Hill Book Company, 1959).

[5] The number of tribes in Zaire can be variously estimated. A common estimate is "about 300." Map 3, showing only 93, gives clusters of subtribes and clans *under one name*. Thus, the Mongo cluster is in reality a number of ethnic units. The picture is more complex than Map 3 shows.

[6] David B. Barrett, "Frontier Situations for Evangelization in Africa," A Survey Report, Nairobi, 1972.

[7] Murdock, *op. cit.*, p. 284.

[8] Deward, *op. cit.*, p. 16.

[9] Donald L. Wiedner, *L'Afrique Noire Avant La Colonialisation,* translation from English to French of chapters 1–10 of *A History of Africa South of the Sahara* (New York: Random House, Inc., Vintage Books, 1964), p. 20.

[10] Murdock, *op. cit.*, pp. 290-291.

[11] *Ibid.*, p. 9.

[12] *Ibid.*, p. 333.

[13] *Ibid.*, p. 332.

[14] *Ibid.*, p. 330.

[15] Barrett, *op. cit.*, Map.

[16] Deward, *op. cit.*, p. 33.

[17] Murdock, *op. cit.*, p. 227.
[18] H. Burssens, *Les Peuplades de l'Entre Congo-Ubangi* (London: International African Institute, 1958), p. 25.
[19] Murdock, *op. cit.*, pp. 48-49.
[20] Barrett, *op. cit.*, p. 32.
[21] They surfaced in violence and bloodshed at Independence between the Lulua and the Luba in the Kasai Province. Other intertribal animosities showed themselves in more subtle forms.
[22] Murdock, *op. cit.*, p. 309.
[23] *Ibid.*, pp. 13, 23, 31, 32.

Chapter 2

[1] E. M. Braekman, *Histoire du Protestantisme au Congo* (Bruxelles IV: Editions de la Libraire des Eclaireurs, Unionistes, 1961), p. 18.
[2] *Ibid.*, p. 14.
[3] *Ibid.*, pp. 25, 26.
[4] *Ibid.*, pp. 27, 28.
[5] *Ibid.*, p. 32.
[6] *Ibid.*, pp. 47, 49, 50.
[7] *Ibid.*, pp. 50-53.
[8] *Ibid.*, pp. 53, 54.
[9] Georges Deward, *Histoire du Congo: évolution du pays et de ses habitants* (Liège, Belgium: H. Dessain, 1962), pp. 31-33.
[10] *Ibid.*, pp. 28-30.
[11] *Ibid.*, p. 31.
[12] Interview with Craig Sikes, June 22, 1977.
[13] Deward, *op. cit.*, p. 17.
[14] Braekman, *op. cit.*, pp. 17, 18.
[15] *Ibid.*, p. 20.
[16] *Ibid.*, pp. 18, 19.
[17] *Ibid.*, p. 20.
[18] *Ibid.*, pp. 59-65, 90, 91.
[19] *Ibid.*, p. 67.
[20] *Ibid.*, pp. 65-81.
[21] *Ibid.*, pp. 81-88.
[22] Norman G. Riddle, "Church Growth and the Communication of the Gospel in Kinshasa," Master of Arts thesis in the School of Missions and Institute of Church Growth, Fuller Theological Seminary, Pasadena, California, 1971, pp. 38-66.
[23] Braekman, *op. cit.*, chapters on Provinces.
[24] *Ibid.*, pp. 284-324.
[25] *Ibid.*, pp. 264-284.
[26] *Ibid.*, p. 335.
[27] *Ibid.*
[28] *Ibid.*, p. 337.
[29] *Ibid.*, p. 338.

Chapter 3

[1] As this goes to press, we learn that the Canadian Baptists are helping it and estimate the total community at 70,000. We have not changed the figures in chapter 5, however.

Chapter 4

[1] During the period before 1970, the Communities were known as Churches.

Chapter 5

[1] Leon de St. Moulin, *Atlas des Collectivités du Zaire* (Kinshasa: Presses Universitaires du Zaire, 1976), p. 12.

[2] Howard A. Crowl, "The Bashi: A Church Growth Study," Master of Arts thesis in the School of World Mission and The Institute of Church Growth, Fuller Theological Seminary, Pasadena, California, 1975, pp. 82-84, 110-114.

[3] Organized after the exile of Simon Kimbangu, a Baptist catechist who was impelled by the Spirit to bring renewal to his churches. At first an underground movement, it was officially recognized by the newly independent government of the Republic of Zaire (then Congo) in 1960. Dr. Marie Louise Martin, in *Kimbangu: An African Prophet and His Church,* has described this.

[4] David B. Barrett, *Schism and Renewal in Africa* (New York: Oxford University Press, 1968), p. 292.

[5] *Ibid.*

[6] David B. Barrett, *Kenya Churches Handbook* (Kenya: Evangelical Publishing House, 1973), p. 175.

[7] David B. Barrett, "Frontier Situations for Evangelization in Africa," A Survey Report, Nairobi, 1972, p. 4.

Chapter 9

[1] An Evangelical Free Church missionary, the Reverend Lee Hiegal, gave the team a fine analysis of one small town according to Section I and part of Section II of the Research Instrument.

Chapter 10

[1] Drafts for Sections: Fourth Assembly of the World Council of Churches, Uppsala, Sweden, 1968, p. 34.

Chapter 11

[1] John Keith, "The Employment Crisis in Missions," *The Enterprise,* September, 1973.

[2] Adapted from G. Thompson Brown, "Possible Directions for the International Mission of the Church in the Next Decade," *Church Growth Bulletin,* vol. 14, no. 4 (March, 1978), with his kind permission.

Chapter 12

[1] Please reread our careful statement in the Introduction, pages 19-20. The Mission in Zaire has no legal existence. Yet it is vividly present. (Dr. King is speaking of this vividly present and very helpful Mission.)

[2] Russell A. Cervin, *Mission in Ferment* (Chicago: Covenant Press, 1977), pp. 18, 19.

[3] Edward Dayton, *Mission Handbook: North American Protestant Ministries Overseas* (Monrovia, Calif.: MARC, a Division of World Vision International, 1976), p. 134.

Bibliography

Andersson, Efraim, *Churches at the Grass-Roots.* London: Lutterworth Press, 1968.

Baeta, C. G., *Christianity in Tropical Africa.* London: Oxford University Press, 1968.

Barrett, David B., *Schism and Renewal in Africa.* Nairobi: Oxford University Press, 1968.

_____, "Frontier Situations for Evangelization in Africa," A Survey Report, Nairobi, 1972.

_____, "The Discipling of Africa in This Generation," in Tippett, Alan R., *God, Man, and Church Growth.* Grand Rapids, Mich.: Wm. B. Eerdmans Publishing Company, 1972.

_____, *Kenya Churches Handbook.* Kisumu, Kenya: Evangelical Publishing House, 1973.

Bayly, Joseph T., *Congo Crisis.* Grand Rapids, Mich.: The Zondervan Corp., 1966.

Beaver, R. Pierce, ed., *The Gospel and Frontier Peoples.* South Pasadena, Calif.: William Carey Library, 1973.

Braekman, E. M., *Histoire du Protestantisme au Congo.* Bruxelles IV: Editions de la Libraire des Eclaireurs, Unionistes, 1961.

Brown, G. Thompson, "Possible Directions for the International Mission of the Church in the Next Decade," unpublished study paper. Atlanta: Division of International Mission of the Presbvterian Church in the U.S., 1977.

Burssens, H., *Les Peuplades de l'Entre Congo-Ubangi.* New York: International Pubns. Service, 1958.

Carpenter, George Wayland, *Highways for God in Congo.* Leopoldville: LECO Press, 1952.

Cervin, Russell A., *Mission in Ferment.* Chicago: Covenant Press, 1977.

Christian Churches Year Book. Indianapolis: International Convention of Christian Churches, 1958, 1964, 1968, etc.

Crawford, John R., *Protestant Missions in Congo, 1968-1969.* Printed in the U.S.A. by agreement with LECO Press, Kinshasa, 1969.

Crowl, Howard A., "The Bashi: A Church Growth Study," Master of Arts thesis in the School of World Mission and the Institute of Church Growth, Fuller Theological Seminary, Pasadena, Calif., 1975.

Danker, William J., *Profit for the Lord.* Grand Rapids, Mich.: Wm. B. Eerdmans Publishing Company, 1971.

Dayton, Edward, ed., *Mission Handbook.* Monrovia, Calif.: MARC/DOC, 1976.

Deward, Georges, *Histoire du Congo: évolution du pays et de ses habitants.* Liège, Belgium: H. Dessain, 1962.

Etude Socio-Demographique de Kinshasa. Kinshasa: l'Institut de la statistique, 1969.

l'Etoile, "Recensement de la Population du Congo," August, 1970.

Fuller, Millard, *Bokotola.* New York: Association Press, 1977.

Gayre, R., *Ethnological Elements of Africa.* Edinburgh: The Armorial Limited, 1966.

Gordon, Robert, "Church Growth in Congo," research paper for the School of Missions and the Institute of Church Growth, Fuller Theological Seminary, Pasadena, Calif. 1971.

Keith, Arthur Berriedale, *Belgian Congo and the Berlin Act.* Westport, Conn.: Negro Universities Press, affiliate of Greenwood Press, Inc., 1970.

Keith, John, "The Employment Crisis in Missions, *The Enterprise.* Toronto: Canadian Baptist Overseas Mission Board, September, 1973.

Mabie, Catherine, *Congo Cameos.* Valley Forge: Judson Press, 1952.

Makanzu, Mavumilusa, "L'Eglise du Christ au Zaire, Son Passé, Son Présent, et Son Avenir," unpublished brochure, Kinshasa, E.C.Z.

Martin, Marie Louise, *Kimbangu: An African Prophet and His Church.* Grand Rapids, Mich.: Wm. B. Eerdmans Publishing Company, 1971.

McGavran, Donald A., *Bridges of God.* New York: Friendship Press, 1955.

——————, *Understanding Church Growth.* Grand Rapids, Mich.: Wm. B. Eerdmans Publishing Company, 1970.

——————, *Church Growth and Group Conversion.* Pasadena, Calif.: William Carey Library, 1973.

——————, *The Clash Between Christianity and Cultures.* Washington, D.C.: Canon Press, 1974.

——————, *Ethnicity and Church Growth: Lessons from India.* Grand Rapids, Mich.: Wm. B. Eerdmans Publishing House, 1979.

Murdock, George P., *Africa: Its Peoples and Their Culture History.* New York: McGraw-Hill Book Company, 1959.

Peters, George W., "Focus on the New Missionary for the New Day," *Trinity World Forum,* Fall, 1977.

Riddle, Norman G., "Church Growth and the Communication of the Gospel in Kinshasa," Master of Arts thesis in the School of Missions and Institute of Church Growth, Fuller Theological Seminary, Pasadena, Calif., 1971.

Roman Catholic Church Annuaire de l'Eglise Catholique au Zaire. Kinshasa: Editions du Secretariat General, 1974/75.

Ross, Charles, "The Emergence of the Presbyterian Church of the Kasai, Congo," Master of Arts thesis in the School of Missions and Institute of Church Growth, Fuller Theological Seminary, Pasadena, Calif.

Slade, Ruth, *The Belgian Congo,* second ed. London: Oxford University Press, 1961.

Smith, Viola, *Diatungwa Va Tadi.* Copyright 1966 by the Charles Smith family. Printed in the U.S.A.

St. Moulin, Leon de, *Atlas des Collectivités du Zaire.* Kinshasa: Presses Universitaires du Zaire, 1976.

Wiedner, Donald L., *L'Afrique Noire Avant La Colonialisation,* New Horizons, translation from English to French of Chapters 1-10 of *A History of Africa South of the Sahara.* New York: Random House, Inc., 1962.

World Population Data Sheet. Washington, D.C.: Information Service, 1976.

Zairian Government Bureau of Statistics Unpublished Records, Kinshasa, 1975-76.